HOW TO OWN A S

Naomi Lewis, writing about Joyce Stran¡

" When she writes on animals she shows ⟨
the creatures on their own terms as well ⟨ ... ⌐y ⌐⌐ ⌐⌐servant and
understanding human."

All Joyce's books, fiction as well as non fiction, have a personal background. She lives in the world she writes about, basing her work on her own studies and those of the authorities she has read. Among her friends made over many years are championship Judges of both dogs and horses. Her proudest possession is a book written by a former Obedience winner at Cruft's, which is inscribed to her: 'To Joyce, a lady to whom the dog is more important than the winning and long may it so continue.'

She trained as a scientist, working in industry for four years in research, which has helped her delve deeply into everything she does. She married a scientist and they have recently celebrated their Golden Wedding. Her elder son is an electronics engineer, her second son a veterinary surgeon and her daughter a leading worker in cancer research. She has eight grandchildren, and four step-grandchildren.

Among her more recent animals were Puma, a German Shepherd who gained a championship certificate in Breed, as well as several Obedience awards. She died in 1981. Janus, her deaf Golden Retriever died in 1984, leaving behind many Obedience rosettes. Since then she has had German Shepherds, among them Chita, who competed in Working trials and excelled at agility, tracking, and searching. Josse was bought at two years old after having had six male owners, but proved, sadly, to have haemophilia. He died in 1990 at the age of six. He started off hating men, but Joyce managed to cure him of his phobia and he ended up a very biddable dog.

Her present companion, Troy, was born in 1991.

Joyce has been dog training since 1971. She now spends her mornings writing and her afternoons teaching owners to train up to twenty dogs a week. At a rough tally she has taught well over a thousand dogs in the past twenty five years, of twenty seven different breeds. Many of them are problem dogs. She is a member of the United Kingdom registry of Behaviour Consultants and also of the Association of Pet Dog Trainers.

Front Cover: Chita at six years
Back Cover: The author with her two German Shepherd bitches, Puma and Chita (standing) and her Golden retriever, Janus.

How to Own a Sensible Dog

Joyce Stranger

Cover photographs by Sean Hagerty

HOW TO OWN A SENSIBLE DOG

First published by Corgi   1981
Republished by Joyce Stranger   1988
Republished   1990
Fourth (revised edition) by Joyce Stranger,
  Glanllyn, Dwyran, Isle of Anglesey, LL61 6YU   1996

Copyright © Joyce Stranger 1981
Photographs Copyright Sean Hagerty

ISBN 0 9513357 0 7

Printed by the The Pembrokeshire Press, 4/5 Feidr Castell Business Park,
Pembrokeshire SA65 9BB.

CONTENTS

Dedicated with gratitude to all those whose knowledge has been passed on to me via their courses and their books. Also to the hundreds of dogs who have taught me that book learning is far from being everything needed, as each has been determined to prove every author I ever read wrong. And to all my readers...may you all have sensible dogs.

1
WHY YET ANOTHER BOOK?

A great many books have been written on dog training; on various breeds; on dog showing and many other matters relating to dogs. I must have nearly one hundred on my own shelves.

So why write another?

I am writing this with the first time dog owner in mind. Not for someone who is working with dogs, or breeding dogs, or competing with them, and is already experienced. It is for the owner who wrote and said 'Help. My dog is a headache on four legs.' It is for Mrs Jones with her new puppy; for Mrs Smith with her dog from the rescue centre; for Mr Brown whose uncle died and left his dog to his nephew.

I am in constant contact with first time owners of dogs of many breeds and none, with those who have rescued dogs from various organisations and with those starting out with new puppies.

As well as running classes for both experienced and inexperienced owners, I have a call line, which gives free advice to anyone who rings and asks. As a result, I am never out of touch with those who are just beginning on a new adventure with a little animal that is nothing like us.

Added to that, I have not had easy dogs myself in the past twenty five years, and I do not get rid of a dog just because I can't win prizes with it. One of mine was deaf; he also had bad hips and couldn't digest meat. My vet predicted that he would be dead before two years old. He died when he was thirteen of old age.

Another came to me at two years old. He had had six male owners before me. He hated men and other dogs. He also had haemophilia. I had to devise a whole new way of teaching him, as he was terrified of loud voices and of commands like heel, sit, come and stay. He bolted if off lead; he trembled if on lead. He did learn, as I changed all my commands to Welsh, or hand or whistle signals.

One of my pups was so vicious at ten weeks that even an experienced police dog instructor was startled by her and would not allow any of his children to touch her. By three years old she was coming to schools with me and children were fussing her. It wasn't easy, but it is possible.

The problem I have found is that the majority of books on dogs are written by those concerned professionally with them. They have won championships in Breed, Obedience competition, or Working Trials. Or maybe gundog or sheepdog trials. Or they are veterinary surgeons.

They know an enormous amount, but they have forgotten how it feels to be faced with your first puppy ever; to know nothing about the way it will behave, or even how to feed it. Those first days are long ago and it is difficult for some of them to remember them, so that they may be unsympathetic to someone who finds everything daunting.

I have, in the past, picked up a book which, I hope, will help me with the problem I have with one particular dog. It may be one of my own, or a class dog with an odd problem that can't be cured by simply coming to lessons. It needs much more thought.

I find that the author tells me how to teach the dog, and assumes that it will do exactly as I ask if taught in the way described. It does not tell me what to do if the dog won't behave like that. It simply assumes that all dogs will perform as the writer's very carefully bred and carefully chosen dog did on its way to the top.

I want to write to the author and say 'yes, that worked with your dog. Try it with a two year old rescued Newfoundland that has been cruelly treated in the past; he has come for his first lesson and never been taught anything up to now.' That dog was so delighted to find people who were kind that he stood on his hind legs and put his paws round the neck of anyone who tried to praise him. I did not find the answer to that in any book!

Books written before 1980 are out of date as much more is known today about the way dogs behave, why they behave as they do and how to get the best out of them. The first version of this book is out of date, so that I have had to revise it in the light of the new knowledge, which has only come in the past ten years. Training methods are very different now.

Those who train dogs for the blind, the deaf, and the disabled have added a great deal to this knowledge as that has to be done thoroughly and fast, and owners with major disabilities have to be taught how to cope with their canine companions.

Many of the books are very good, but they are written in technical terms and are heavy going, so that all but the most dedicated give up after a few pages. They are easy enough to understand if you have been dealing with dogs for twenty years, but not if you have never had a dog before and know nothing about them at all.

I have difficulty with some of the books written myself, in spite of having been involved in the canine world for a great many years. I have on my walls rosettes won by my dogs in Obedience and in Working Trials. One gained many first prizes and a Championship Certificate in Breed, so that I have had experience in four different worlds; three of competition and one of pet owning, though I prefer the term 'companion dog'.

Even with that background I find that it is easier to look for a book that is more simply written than to translate all that jargon. My life is too busy to spend time trying to decipher what appears to be a code.

Those hoping for high awards in any of the areas of dog competition have different attitudes to those of us who buy our dogs for companionship and hopefully for fun. This book is for the companion dog owners, as they buy most of the puppies. Only one out of each litter may be kept by the breeder, or be suitable for very rigorous training. The rest are sold to people like you and me.

Sadly, some of us are doomed to disappointment because we do not know that there are many snags to buying a good puppy. The old saying 'he was sold a pup,' can still apply. Twenty five years ago, I bought a puppy and found I had a great deal to learn. Had I known what I known today I would never have taken him home.

Having said that, if I had not, I would not be writing this book. I hope I can help others avoid the mistakes I have made through lack of knowledge and guidance.

One of the difficulties for many people is that they think that dogs think as we do. Unfortunately for us, they don't, but few dog classes ever do tell anyone how the dog does think.

How on earth can any one become a good owner who understands the dog if there is nobody to show them the way? Many classes, I found in the past when I visited, expect too much from newcomers who need far more education than they receive. Who goes to Wimbledon to compete after a few tennis lessons? Yet often people expect to be able to compete with a six month puppy when he is quite incapable of having that skill. Nobody expects a five year old child to start a degree course at university.

The other problem I found when I became the not very proud owner of two very aggressive dogs, (not at the same time), is that all anyone told me was to put the dog to sleep and buy another from better stock.

It was some years before I realised that handlers at the top don't keep this type of dog. They either pass it on, or put it down. They want the perfect dog, chosen from a top litter from a top breeder, with good working ability and brains. They are not going to waste time on an animal that needs hours of dedicated work before he is capable of winning prizes. As a result few of them are ever able to give really useful advice on dealing with aggressive or problem dogs.

I found out how by trial and error. Both my aggressive dogs became much easier. One breeder who saw the bitch's pedigree said, 'I don't see breakers ahead for you. I see coral reefs.' I did not know enough about her ancestors when I bought her.

But she lived to thirteen and no one would believe me, by the time she was three years old, when I said she had once been extremely vicious. I had to spend hours ensuring that she was safe. She became the 1000th P.A.T dog, visiting schools and hospitals until she herself had a stroke.

I had a number of letters about her, referring to her early days. One said:

" I must congratulate you on your progress with her. I find it hard to recognise the hellcat you brought with you last year."

Another, writing a year later, said:

"Instead of the half wild and distinctly schizophrenic dog you brought with you last time, she is now a joy to have around."

I took her, when very young, for lessons and one of the instructors wrote:

"Our introduction to Joyce's dog was so distasteful my partner and I agreed that it was most likely she would have to be put down. Here was a lunging, screaming, snappy bitch which within twenty minutes produced an exhausted handler."

The report ends:

"The dog thoroughly enjoys working now and it is a pleasure to see her off lead at last. Eleven months ago this was just a wild dream."

There were no behaviour consultants then. Many club instructors do become expert in dog behaviour over the years, but I wasn't lucky enough to meet anyone who had lived with a dog like mine. It is easy enough if the dog can be confined to a kennel for most of its life, but we want our dogs as companions, living in the house.

Luck plays a big part in every walk of life. I have often been told I was unlucky with my dogs, but I think I was lucky. I learned through my very imperfect animals things I would never have learned at all had I started with a top quality dog. Though I don't recommend that as a way of life!

I very much object to those who say 'It's the owner, not the dog.' This absolves so many people from responsibility. The breeder, who may have bred an anti-social or sickly dog; the instructor, who may not have asked enough questions. Blaming the owner also absolves a poor quality veterinary surgeon who takes the easy way out and assumes all pet owners are idiots.

That can be a bar to diagnosis as someone is thought to be neurotic who is actually trying to deal with a set of symptoms never before presented in the surgery. I know my dog is unwell long before there is anything to tell the vet.

I am not sure now how much of my latest dog's easy behaviour is due to her breeding and how much is due to what I learned the hard way from the others. Probably something of both as I chose her with great care.

Having said that, 99% of the dogs I have had in my classes over the years, have been easy gentle pets, responding fast to their early training and becoming wonderful dogs.

I do tend to get a number of dogs with behaviour problems because people know that I had difficult dogs myself and cured them. There were three failures, and all, on postmortem, proved to have brain tumours. Sadly, we can do nothing about that.

This book is intended to tell you how to produce a sensible dog, and to tell you the things that the dog classes never have time to tell you. Dogs are not born sensible but have to be taught. The best puppy in the world, without training and guidance, can become a disaster.

I want to show you how to bring up your puppy so that he is a source of maximum pleasure to you, and minimum disturbance to your neighbours. I want people to look at my own dogs and those whose owners I teach and think that they are very well trained and I feel proud when someone says so.

Also, hopefully, this book will help those people who are unlucky enough to live where there is not a dog training club, or to live in an area where there is a club but those who train there repeat the old untruth that it is wrong to train a dog before he is six months old as his brain isn't mature.

The new puppy starts to learn at three weeks old. The pup learns as soon as he comes home and it is up to us whether what he learns is desirable or is going to produce the sort of dog our neighbours would like to shoot.

What we want is a steady sensible dog who will be a marvellous companion and make other people wish that they had one like ours. Believe me, they are made, not born. Good breeding and good rearing help a great deal, but the rest is up to us.

I hope you will now understand why I am adding yet another dog book to what appears to be a very well stocked market. I am not dealing in detail with training to high standards. There are many good books for that. Some will be listed at the end of this.

2
THINKING ABOUT DOG OWNING.

DO WE REALLY WANT A DOG?

So many people don't think about the hazards of owning a dog. They see a well trained dog belonging to a relative, friend, or neighbour, and think how wonderful it would be to own one like that. They do not realise the thought and research that went into the purchase, or the amount of time put into his subsequent training.

Are we sure we want a dog? Can we give him the life he deserves? Do we realise that our dog may live for anything up to twenty years and be there long after the family have grown up and left home?

The dog has his own needs; for food; for exercise; for care; for understanding. So many lead unhappy lives through owners who do not realise that animals have very different perceptions of the world around them to us. And who are also unaware that no dog behaves itself unless taught to do so, and taught very carefully. We can be convinced that we are training our dog to come to us when in fact we are teaching it to run away, as the dog does not think as we do.

WHY ARE SO MANY DOGS RE-HOMED?

Owners have their own needs, and there are many reasons as to why people decide to own a dog. The vast majority feel it would benefit the family, be a good companion and a worthwhile pet, and provided they have considered the matter thoroughly, they will make excellent owners.

Sometimes the timing of buying a puppy is wrong. Few couples, expecting a first baby, realise the time the baby will take. They buy a puppy because the wife has left work and is home all day. This is fine, but often when the baby comes there is no time for the dog, and within a few months yet another unhappy purchase is on its way to dog rescue or another home.

For others, the reasons may be different. This is often where they come to grief, and dogs end up in other hands after purchase.

For some, the dog is a status symbol, probably of a very unusual and spectacular breed. For others, it is merely a living burglar alarm.

It may be a means to gaining high honours in some form of competition, and basking in reflected glory, the owner being on an ego trip, the dog being secondary to that.

The status symbol may prove not to win prizes. The burglar alarm may be afraid of noises in the night. Dogs may fail to qualify in top competition. All will be passed on to someone else and another dog bought in the hope that it will fulfil its owners' expectations. None of these people had a good reason for buying a dog.

What is worse, they may often get rid of each at around a year old, and buy another, so that one person of this type can add twelve dogs in twelve years to those seeking new owners.

There are dogs that are re-homed time and time again, because they need care and thought spent on them due to past mistakes. The dog who had had six homes before I took him suffered from problems caused by past owners. That is not an isolated case by any means.

If the children tease and torment and will never do as they are told, please don't buy a dog. It will lead a miserable life and the children may end up being badly bitten. This is a major cause of death in young dogs.

Those who buy a pup on impulse, without due care, or because the children fell in love with the breed when they saw it on television, often regret their purchase within a few days and sometimes within a few hours.

One of the drawbacks of choosing a breed that has become prominent in film work or in advertising is that cowboy breeders know very well that this will create a demand. They buy a quantity of also ran bitches that are bred to also ran dogs, as these are cheap, and produce numerous pups that nobody knowledgeable would dream of buying.

This is the quickest way to ruin any breed and bring in all the faults that responsible breeders are doing their best to eradicate.

Those re-homed dogs that are lucky end up with owners prepared to put an immense amount of time and trouble into curing these problems, and turn their sad animals into dogs that reward them for the rest of their lives.

Few people realise that those who take these on and reform them really do deserve medals. It takes a knowledgeable person to recognise the dedication and devotion that goes into changing a very difficult animal into a superb dog.

WORKING OWNERS

Dogs are pack animals and need companionship, so that to be left on their own for long hours is very distressing for them.

I am never entirely happy about dogs being left alone all day while owners are working, as this is miserable for the animal. Also it is very hard to housetrain and impossible to feed correctly as pups need four meals a day until they are six months old. No absent owner can housetrain them; it is not something that happens on its own.

There are many owners who do work, or have been forced to work when the dog is a few years old. They have taken great care to make sure the animal does not suffer. They may work shifts, or go home at lunchtime.

Neighbours may exercise it, and go in and feed it, or it has a kennel and run outside, so that it has space and fresh air and does not chew up the home.

There are very acceptable arrangements, some of which are ideal. One family, where all the members work, lives close to the wife's mother. She has the dog during the day, and when the family go on holiday. She very much enjoys her role as part owner, especially as, on a small pension, she could not afford to keep him.

The pup has been used to the arrangement from the time he was bought and adores both his homes. His daytime owner also has the benefit of exercising him, which has improved her health.

It might be possible to find a retired neighbour in the same position who would be only too happy to enter into this kind of arrangement. One dog class member is a part time owner, and the dog's real owners pay her a small sum each week to have him during the day, which also helps her own budget.

She comes to class so that she can learn how to manage him happily, and the dog has made great strides since this arrangement began.

Most people accept that, if out all day, or with a very busy life that entails a lot of time away from home, it is better to wait until retirement before buying a dog. Even then, those who have homes abroad and plan to spend several months a year out of the country, will have to leave the poor animal in kennels for a considerable time and this is not really fair to any dog.

ELDERLY OWNERS

I meet many people who wish they could have a dog but do not because of their age. The dog might outlive them. It might prove too much of a handful.

These are very genuine sensible concerns, but it always seems a pity as it deprives them of a great deal of pleasure and companionship. This is a time of life when many elderly people find that they are on their own and the care of a dog, for those who want it, is most beneficial. There are answers.

Often rescue organisations do have older dogs, whose owners have died. These are usually sensible sober animals who have gone through all the difficult stages of their lives. I have met a number who have settled in very happily, and provided great pleasure to an older owner.

Sometimes a breeder may have a dog retired from stud, or a brood bitch who has done her share of providing puppies. Or an older dog that was perhaps kept for showing, but proved not to have the necessary attributes.

Or a dog or bitch that was to be kept for breeding, but that proves to be unhappy in kennels and would be far better off in a household where she or he is the only pet. Not all dogs like to share their owners.

One very elderly lady has the same system as some of those who work. She has a friend who becomes part time owner if she is ill. She had a spell in hospital and the dog went to her friend.

Ben visits every Sunday, so that if he were left when his owner died, he would not be going to a stranger but to his other home.

Often there may be daughters or sons willing to have the dog. My sister took on my mother's dog when she became incapable of looking after herself, and had to go into a Home.

A friend's dogs have gone to her daughter and settled in very well.

There is the Cinnamon Trust (address at the back of this book) which caters for animals belonging to the elderly who may have to give up caring for them, or may leave them ownerless. This is a very good organisation that guarantees care of the dog for the rest of its life.

There are also a number of Homes that do allow residents to bring their pets with them. The Cinnamon Trust has list of these.

Many owners leave a provision in their wills for their dogs. Some ask for their animals to be put to sleep should the owner die. Others nominate friends who have promised to look after the dog in such an event, but it is wise to get a written statement to this effect to put with the will, or the people concerned may either have forgotten or be in totally different circumstances when needed.

Often a sum of money is left as well, to help provide care, as this is expensive.

CARING OWNERS

For the majority of owners the dog is a valued part of the family. They are devoted to its well being. They make sure that they teach it from the start, or if they have a problem go regularly to training classes and turn it into the type of dog that everyone admires. There is a well known saying from the RAF dog training school that every owner gets the dog he deserves.

Caring owners have good dogs; careless owners have dogs the rest of the world hates. No dog is born trained or sensible. We have to put time into teaching it.

HIDDEN EXPENSES

There are hidden expenses in some breeds, such as the poodle, as they need frequent clipping, trimming, or stripping, which is not cheap. The long coated breeds need daily grooming and this can take up to an hour or more. White dogs need frequent bathing. There is nothing quite so unappealing as a Samoyed puppy covered in mud.

I have judged dogs for best condition at small shows and found some that look wonderful on top are so matted underneath that the lumps need to be cut out. A dog with matted fur is difficult to keep flea free. Often those who have these dogs to groom professionally because the owner no longer can, discover that underneath the mats the skin is infected.

I would never buy a long coated breed as I do not have that amount of spare time. A short coated breed only takes about ten minutes a day to groom thoroughly and remove the loose hair.

Almost all breeds of dogs moult, especially at the beginning of hot weather, and unless time is spent on removing dead fur from the dog, extra time will have to be spent in removing it from carpets and furnishings.

Dead fur also makes the dog scratch to try and remove it as it is not comfortable.

CONSIDERING OUR HOME

Many flat dwellers do become successful dog owners, but there are problems there, as the young pup needs for several weeks to be taken downstairs, or in the lift, and outside, not just twice a day, but at least ten times, if training is to be successful.

Gardens need to be very well fenced. Puppies are very clever at finding the tiniest hole and enlarging it with teeth or paws, and within seconds your valuable new purchase is out on the road and at risk from all kinds of hazards; being run over; attacked by older dogs; being hurt by teasing children; being stolen by someone who finds him and sees a good way to have a dog without paying for it.

In the country, there is a risk of poison from bait laid for rats, and from traps, which though illegal are still set in some places.

Very few people realise that the siting of their home can mean that there may be problems in this alone when owning a dog. Some breeds are natural barkers, and far from ideal on a housing estate. They can be induced to be less noisy, but it is necessary to know how to do this. Basenjis do not bark.

Those who live in busy areas do not have to worry so much about taking the dog out and about, as it sees people passing constantly. Here a dog with a very strong guarding instinct can be a problem, as it will defend its property against everyone who passes.

Those who, like me, live in a very isolated place, with few unknown callers, and no near neighbours, don't have to worry about barking, but we do have to make sure our dog doesn't become so anti-social that if taken anywhere busier, it is either frightened or considers it must protect us from everyone who approaches.

It is necessary to take pups from a home like this into towns and villages and to all kinds of busy places, or they will prove reluctant even to leave the car.

A surprising number of owners, living on a small holding of several acres, do not worry about taking the dog out. It has plenty of space to run.

Then the occasion may arise, and owners discover not only that their dog won't walk on a lead, it won't even tolerate a collar. Veterinary house visits are expensive and a dog that isn't able to walk on a lead without making a scene (and it can be a remarkable scene) poses a considerable problem.

This may sound unlikely, but I have, a number of times, given private lessons to cases like this. It takes a great deal of patience to overcome the fear induced by the sudden feeling of restriction in a dog that, for a year or more, has been able to run free.

One owner moved from a small holding, to a house in a village, with a two year old dog. She was so dismayed by the way he behaved when put on a lead that even after several lessons, she found it impossible to cope with him and he went back to his breeder.

Another, putting her dog on the lead for the first time when he was fourteen months old, was pulled over and broke her arm.

A few puppy lessons and a daily short lead walk would have prevented both problems from starting. There is far more to owning a dog than just opening the door into the garden or paddock and letting it run around like a wild animal.

Taking pups out and about so that they learn to fit into our world is increasingly difficult. Today many people are so divorced from the natural environment that they are terrified of all animals, even those that are gentle sensible companions. The dog senses their fear and reacts to it, frightening them even more. This makes our lives as dog owners more difficult, as we have to re-assure the dog and make sure it is used to all kinds of people, not just those who like dogs.

Twenty five years ago I could take my pups into shops, into pubs, into the forest and parks, and on the beaches. People fussed them and many admired them. Today they are banned in all those places, and it is very difficult indeed to find somewhere safe to take the puppy, and be sure also it is treated with kindness by everyone it meets.

Twice my present dog, when only a pup, was hit by children who passed us. In neither case did the parents intervene, though I did tell them that that was the best way I knew to get bitten. My puppy, chosen for her splendid temperament, had been taught never to bite; an untrained pup would have done so at once.

There are whole estates where dog owning is forbidden. Others where it is extremely difficult to find anywhere to walk the poor animals, as there are 'NO DOGS' notices on every patch of green. Before buying, find out if there are reasonable walks for your dog.

POSSIBLE EARLY PROBLEMS

Pups teethe and when they do so, they chew to relieve the pain. They may chew the bone you have given them, but are just as likely to turn their attention to your new shoes or the legs of the Queen Anne chairs, or the edge of that very expensive carpet.

Some dogs can turn a home into a disaster area. Others, taken for a drive, may damage the car. One of mine, some years ago, excavated the backs of both the front seats. These are not villains. One beautiful and very well trained Guide Dog, left on her own while the owners were at a wedding, ate the middle of one of the seat belts. A police dog neatly bit all the buttons off his handler's uniform coat which he had shed as it was very hot.

A pup can run the owner into unexpected expenses if he has had a bad start in life and either has an inherited problem or is weakly through bad rearing. Among my pupils over twenty five years have been dogs operated on due to road accidents; to problems after whelping; some had lumps removed; several have had to have eye operations due to inherited ingrowing eyelids which cause a lot of discomfort.

Pups explore with their mouths and sample anything that happens to be around, either in house or garden. They need watching, or this can prove expensive. Dogs can swallow the most ridiculous things.

One had to be operated on to remove his mistress's frilly pants, which were recovered intact, much to her embarrassment as she had not known what was causing the dog's pain until after the operation. Another swallowed the valve off a pressure cooker. It is necessary to be extremely tidy with a pup around.

18

Early training and a lot of forethought can prevent many accidents but there are some that astound the owners. A lurcher puppy, chasing a hare, followed it under a caravan but unfortunately did not bend her legs. She was racing at such speed she broke her back and it took several years to recover.

A young terrier hit a rabbit hole at speed, and, trying to insert his head, broke his neck. Amazingly, he did recover.

I live near the sea and every year vets have dogs come to them that chased rabbits or seagulls on the cliffs, and, being unaware of heights, fell on to the rocks below. I never have my dog off lead anywhere that looks as if it might be unsafe.

BOARDING KENNELS

We have to provide for our dogs when we go on holiday. Good kennels are scarce. It is vital to inspect them, and find out from other owners who used them whether or not the dogs came out looking fit and well, or dirty, miserable, and with health problems. I have heard some horror stories from those who did not investigate before trusting their pet to one of these establishments.

I left one of my cats in a cattery for three weeks while we went abroad, a long time ago. He was settled, while I was there, into a big chalet with plenty of room and a run. He was not in that when I returned. It contained another cat.

The owner told me I was not to follow her into her private property, but I was concerned. I found fifty cats in hutches piled on one another in a tiny draughty shed. They had no room to move, they were filthy as the earth boxes had not been cleaned, and neither had their feeding bowls.

Urine from the cages above dripped through rotting floors on to the cats below. It took three days to get my cat free from the stink, and he was seriously depressed, having little interest in life.

A number were ill, including mine, and no vet had been called. It took ten weeks to nurse Kym through a severe case of cat flu. Eleven others who came to my vet and had been there died. Our complaints caused the vet to investigate and the place was closed down but by then much damage had been done.

Insist on seeing around, and visit during reasonable hours (from 10 a.m.- 4 p.m on weekdays) but do so without warning. You can then see if the place is clean, or has only been cleaned up for your inspection. Few house dogs foul their living areas. If clean dogs do it is because attention is not being paid to their needs.

Kennel areas should be roomy, and there should be provision for the giant breeds. Dogs should not share with one another unless they are owned by the same family and that has been asked for. Dogs have been killed in this way by an aggressive animal put in with them to save space, and earn more money. Reductions are unlikely to be made if this is done. Owners won't see those kennels.

There should be space for the dog to move around if there is no run. Floors should be easily cleaned and kept immaculate. Many kennels have dog beds and you can take in your own blankets. Others have a shelf off the floor for the dog to sleep on, out of any draught.

They should be escape proof. Dogs have been lost by carelessness before now.

I would not trust any kennels that allowed young village children to exercise the dogs, or allowed a number of dogs to play together in a compound. Dogs have been injured in this way by fights, and have been lost by the child walking them because the dog was too strong.

The kennels where I take my dogs has big roomy areas for each dog, and each dog is exercised by a short walk, by itself, with a kennel man, three times a day. Each dog also has play periods in a well fenced paddock, again with someone watching. Dogs are not allowed to come out of visitors' cars when any other dog is walking in the parking area, even though it is on lead. Immense attention is paid to safety.

No one needs any qualifications before starting a boarding kennels. All they need is premises that will pass council inspection. I have seen some that have amazed me, as I would never have allowed them a licence.

The cost is from £5 a day upwards for the large breeds, and £3 a day upwards for smaller animals. It is rarely possible to find a place in the holiday season at short notice; bookings have to be made weeks ahead. In a really good establishment, the dog will be booked in for next year when the bill is paid for his keep when he is collected.

Good kennels will also give any medication needed, without extra charge; will make sure that any dog with digestive problems has the correct food: that a vet is called if there is any doubt about health.

One hazard in any kennels, however well run, is kennel cough. Unfortunately all diseases have an incubation period so that a dog that appears perfectly healthy may come into the kennels and develop the cough a few days later, by which time it has infected others. Many kennels insist on inoculation for this.

Mostly it is not a serious illness, but it is serious for any dog with a heart complaint, and for bitches in whelp or with pups, as well as for very old and very young dogs. If neglected it can lead to complications.

A coughing dog should not be taken into the vet's waiting room. Early treatment soon clears it up. I have had my dogs infected by dogs at shows, as some owners are very casual and do not consider other people. I take the animal to the vet the second I hear it cough. but it must be kept away from other dogs.

Kennels can only be blamed if your dog gets it if they have an epidemic and have kept that quiet. Mostly it's very bad luck and they will close and fumigate if it becomes a real problem.

I would be very seriously concerned if my dog came out of kennels with parvovirus or distemper, or with any injuries that appeared to be due to carelessness, such as cuts or bites. The kennels should be insured against accidents, and able to compensate you if there is a serious problem due to their mistakes.

I also expect my dog to come out clean, not covered in muck, and fit. One kennel owner I know spends hours with fretting dogs that won't eat, hand feeding them until they settle happily. There are very few dogs that pine terribly for their owners: those are very difficult boarders.

Most people I know say their dogs go back happily, greeting the kennel staff gleefully and some will even go and look for their usual kennel, which is kept free for them, as a home from home. I have however heard of lost dogs, of injured dogs, of sick dogs, and dogs that look as they have just spent two weeks in a concentration camp when they were collected.

Sadly, a very old dog may die when in kennels, but one does not expect younger dogs to suffer this fate.

As with everything else in this world, it is up to us to make sure we are not trusting our much cherished companion to cowboys in the business. These days I look for holiday places that allow my dog to come with me and only use the kennels in emergencies.

We can't bring dogs straight into our homes when we return from abroad. If we do, they must, at present, go into quarantine for six months as there is fear of rabies. Quarantine is very expensive, costing £1000 or more, so that if we are due to go overseas for a short spell of only a couple of years, and take our dog, it is essential to remember this and budget for it.

DOGS ON HOLIDAY

There are hotels, motels, and caravan and camp sites where dogs are allowed, on the lead, with strict attention to using the proper exercise areas, which is only reasonable.

It is essential to be very responsible indeed if you do take your dog with you. Those who go on courses for various aspects of dog owning often stay in bed and breakfast places. Some of these become anti-dog for various reasons, entirely due to thoughtless owners.

A dog with dirty paws was allowed on a bed: a dog was put in a wonderful new bath and its claws damaged the surface: dogs fouled gardens and no one cleaned up. Others were allowed to chase around, uncontrolled, frightening other people staying who were not used to dogs.

I once stayed, on one course, in a hotel. There were ten of us with dogs. Nine of us received a little present from the owner and thanks for being careful with our animals. The tenth was banned for ever. Sadly that person caused so many complaints that next year the hotel refused all dog owners, as others would not have come had we been there. People remembered the one bad owner: they forgot the nine good ones, each of us with several dogs. I had three on that occasion.

Good owners always clear up after their dogs. There are heavy fines for those who do not if they are caught. It is very easy to keep a polythene bag in a pocket and scoop up if our dog does let us down in a public place. They can be trained to only empty on command, or only in long grass, and never on short grass or on paving.

Dogs can easily panic in a strange place and be unable to find their way back as they are on new territory. One of mine was lost while on holiday, having tried to follow my car, when I went out briefly, to go shopping, leaving the dog with my friend's mother, who she did know well.

As I had gone off in my car the dog probably thought I had deserted her. She jumped the gate and tried to follow us. Luckily she was wearing a disc with our home phone number. My husband was there and able to tell the finders where she ought to be.

The finders notified the police who told us where she was, though in fact I had found her by driving round the streets, stopping every few hundred yards calling her. She heard me and barked. The police told me that they had six dogs reported that day and she was the only one with collar and disc. She was found within the hour: the others were not claimed for some days.

I now take my dog with me even on a short trip rather than leave her in a strange place, and am very careful not to let her off lead anywhere where she might be frightened and take off and fail to find her way back to me.

On one of my courses a husband took three dogs out while his wife worked the fourth. They chased a rabbit and vanished. We spent all day searching. The dogs returned to the space where the car had been parked that evening, having been missing for over eight hours.

Anyone who has lost a dog even for a short time knows how traumatic it is. It is far worse if the dog vanishes and is never found as one's imagination fills in all kinds of horrible fates for the poor animal and you never know what really did happen. So it pays to take a great deal of care.

OUR DOG AND THE LAW.

Today it seems from the number of charters for this and that that are proliferating, everyone has rights. Nobody ever seems to talk about responsibilities.

As I see it, no one makes me buy a dog. It is not forced upon me. I choose to have one, but I do accept that in so doing I must consider other people, and obey the laws that are made.

My neighbours have a right to enjoy their home without noise from my constantly barking dog: they have a right to walk down my lane without stepping in an unpleasant mess created by my dog. Equally I have a right to walk down the same lane without having to avoid piles of muck left by those who consider a private lane can be used as a latrine for their dogs.

Six dogs live on our lane and are never allowed to foul it, but we have people who walk down with their dogs and do not bother at all. This particularly upsets those who live here and don't have dogs.

People have a right to visit me without being bitten, and I do not expect to be bitten by other peoples' dogs. There are those who say it is in the dog's nature to bite. It may be. It is up to us to see that he learns that that is not acceptable.

I must have met thousands of dogs in my life and I have only been badly bitten once. That was in my early days with dogs. I approached a dog of a breed that I had never known give problems without asking about him. He was the exception that proved the rule. He had, it transpired, been brought to class because he bit his owners, but I was not told that.

As, at that time, I had several children and their dogs in that class, he could not come back.

That was over fifteen years ago and though I now deal every week with dogs with quite serious problems, none has ever bitten me, or even attempted to bite.

People driving through the village have the right to expect that they will not have to avoid a dog that suddenly leaps out in front of their car, causing them to brake and have an accident. Those who live in the village have the right to know that my dog is not going to run around, fight their dogs, and leave messes outside their gates.

It is my responsibility to see this does not happen and also my responsibility to ensure that others walking their own dogs are not attacked by my dog.

There are laws which govern undue noise and owners of noisy dogs can be fined. Kennels may be forced to soundproof their premises, because of complaints.

In many areas there are bye laws. Dogs may not be exercised unless on lead, or may only be exercised in certain areas. There are rigid laws about dog fouling in public places, and owners who refuse to carry a poop scoop and clean up after their dogs deserve all that the law can throw at them as it is unacceptable.

Even show goers, who ought to know better, have lost a show because the venue was left in so disgusting a state that the owners would not let it again to that organisation. I have been involved with shows and one of the nastier chores has been to go and clean up the ground after lazy owners have gone home.

Dogs when out must wear a collar and an identification tag. Failure to do so carries a fine of up to £2000.

There are fines for worrying farm stock and killing sheep, and again those who allow dogs to wander in sheep country are irresponsible and deserve what they get. Sadly the dog does not deserve what he may get.

One beautiful two year old dog belonging to one of my class members was shot in a sheep field two miles from home. The blood trail led along the road to his doorstep where the poor fellow collapsed and died. He hadn't let himself out.

The owner had had repeated warnings but as the dog had never been taught not to pull on the lead and taking him out was a nightmare, he was freed every day to go where he chose. That is not responsible dog owning and it does not create a sensible dog, but a wandering villain, likely to chase and bite any animal or person he meets.

The incidents reported in the press some years ago when dogs seemed to be regularly in the news, gave rise to a law that should worry all of us. Many organisations are trying to get it remedied, and made more reasonable,but the Government of today (1996) seems to have no intention of amending its draconian interpretations.

THE DANGEROUS DOGS ACT.

Most dog owners seem to think this only applies to those who own pit bulls. It does affect them more than others, in that their dogs must be registered, identified, neutered, and muzzled in all public places. Within fifteen years this breed will have vanished, as there are no pups born now, or at least, not legally. Dog fighting is illegal too, but it still goes on, under cover.

Under this law many innocent people and their dogs suffer because of a few criminals.

No one denies that a biting dog is a very serious hazard. But there is a section of this law that says that <u>any dog</u> that is out of control in a public place can be seized by the police, removed to a remote and secret kennel, and held until the case against it is heard.

An immense amount of money has been wasted kennelling dogs and prosecuting owners whose animals subsequently proved not to be pit bulls, but were thought to be. Staffordshire Bull Terriers in particular suffer from mis-identification and for some reason those who know the breeds well and judge them are not usually consulted, with the result that there have been mistakes made that have resulted in the death of a dog that most certainly should not have been the subject of a court case.

One dog that died was taken by the police because the owner did not muzzle him in his car, as he thought that was unnecessary. It was declared by law that the car is a public place, and the dog should have been muzzled, a fact I find mystifying.

Since the dog had done no harm, and was not free, the owner should have been given a second chance, as few of us would imagine our cars were not private places.

Unfortunately the law is phrased in such a way that the judges have no option. The dog must be destroyed. So any of us owning a pit bull or a dog that might be mistaken for one, if it is on the list of those that must be registered, micro-chipped, neutered, and muzzled, have to remember the muzzle must be worn in the car.

It took three years to clear an eleven year old partly blind dog that was accused of being a pit bull type...not a pit bull. She was picked up because she was not muzzled, as nobody thought it necessary. She was a cross bred and to an expert eye bore no resemblance whatever to a pit bull.

Her owner was killed by a car before the dog was freed but his widow went on campaigning, and finally did get the right verdict...the dog was not a pit bull type, and so does not need to be muzzled.

Meanwhile the poor animal had been in a kennel for three years, after being used to a happy home with people around her. The cost ran into hundreds of pounds, but her owner did get back her dog and her legal costs in the end. Not all cases have ended so happily.

One dog was destroyed, the day before acquitted, due to a mistake on the part of the authorities.

Dog accidents are reported in detail not because they are commonplace, but because they are rare. There are five line daily reports of terrible murders committed by people, but the very rare death due to a dog receives maximum coverage and more cries for more control.

Death from this cause is unacceptable but few people die from dog bites. We are far more likely to die from being in a car accident.

The dog that bites is destroyed, though a humn who kills may walk free in a few years time. Children may behave outrageously, doing immense harm, yet may not be punished.

The law would be far more acceptable if judges had discretion to consider all circumstances, as there are times when the dog is far from guilty, and should be given another chance.

Another absurdity of the animosity against dogs as a result of the press campaigns has been that many dog clubs have had to close, as the committees in charge of the venues where they were held suddenly decided dogs were dangerous and a health risk.

Those of us who have had, as I have had, to share venues with other organisations such as nursery groups and youth clubs, have found it necessary to wash the floor before putting our dogs on to it, as otherwise they needed bathing when we arrived home. Jam, baby puddles, and chewing gum, as well as drawing pins and small parts of toy cars have all been found when we came in to start a class.

It is as absurd to close down dog schools as it is to ban driving schools on the basis that many people each year are killed or injured by cars. It has meant that hundreds of owners who might have been educated have been left with unacceptable dogs, and matters have got worse, not better.

There should be campaigns for more dog schools, to be run by people who have been taught to teach owners, as this is another area which is neglected. Anyone can start a dog class, without any dog knowledge at all. As in all other areas of dogdom, it pays to make enquiries before becoming involved.

DOGS AND CHILDREN

There are families where the children behave so badly and are so out of control that to bring a dog into that environment is to create an accident waiting to happen. I do not allow my dog to play with children unless I am with them. I don't even allow her in the room with them unsupervised.

A child may distress a dog in a way that nobody has considered. The child does not mean harm; the dog does not understand what is happening.

I once, long ago, left my very soft gentle Golden Retriever with a neighbour's little girl of seven. She came to visit while her mother went to a funeral. I went into the kitchen to fetch her a drink and a biscuit. She knew us well as she lived across the road.

As I went back towards the sitting room I heard a wail from the dog.

I raced in.

'What did you do to him?' I asked.

'I made him sit up and lie down twenty seven times, then he wouldn't do it any more and made that funny noise.'

The child was thrilled with the way the dog would do as she asked. Unfortunately the dog was asked to do it so often he was beginning to feel pain from the constant change of position.

That dog refused, after that, to be anywhere near that child, and if she came into a room, he left it immediately. No dog of mine has ever been alone with a child since.

Another group of children, left with their own dog while their mother went out of the room, began throwing chocolates to one another. The dog snapped at a sweet just as one of the children sat up from lying down on the hearthrug. The dog's teeth met the child's head instead of the titbit, and there was a bad injury.

That wasn't an intentional bite. It was a total accident, but non dog owning people interpreted it differently, as an attack. Often there is a real accident; a dog and a child reach for a ball at the same moment; the child's hand closes over the ball just as the dog thinks it has reached it, and the child is bitten as the dog tries to get the toy.

A child may suddenly think,

'I wonder what would happen if I pull her tail,' and try it. The dog, finding this hurts, will not like it and its only defence is to bite. There are wonderful dogs that put up with daily torture from children, but there are those who do not see why they should.

I do not see why I should, as one writer suggests, pull my dog's tail, and her ears, and hit her, in order to ensure she won't attack anyone who does that to her.

I would rather accept that it is my responsibility to think hard and be very careful with her, ensuring she does not encounter those who might harm her and cause her to retaliate.

It worries me when parents allow young children to take out large dogs. If the dog was attacked by another dog the child could not cope and might be badly bitten. One small girl, some years ago, was pulled under a lorry by her dog, when he saw a cat on the other side of the road.

The child died. The dog was put to sleep the same day. The parents had been repeatedly told by their neighbours and the instructors at the class the dog attended that he was too strong for the little girl.

Children should be taught how to approach a dog; never scream and run away as the dog thinks that is a game and gives chase. The only thing that is safe to do is to stand quite still, hands behind you or in your pockets and behave like a statue. Most dogs are triggered by movement and once it stops they lose interest.

If a dog chases a bike, the cyclist should not pedal faster, as the dog will only run faster. Dismount and stand quite still.

We do have to co-operate in making sure we are safe in a very imperfect world. The dog can't think; he behaves like a dog, we can think and need to be able to foresee what is likely to happen, so that we can take avoiding actions.

Nobody, child or adult, should approach a dog they do not know, and make overtures, especially if it is tied up. Nor should we stare at it.

A tied up dog feels very vulnerable as it can't escape and may bite even a well meaning hand. I warn my owners not to tie their dogs up in public places as there are always people around who treat dogs like teddy bears and expect to be welcomed.

Sometimes, at shows, an owner will tie several dogs to a car or a post and leave them on their own. Even though I am well experienced with dogs, or perhaps because I am well experienced, I never go within range of any group like this. The area where they are tied becomes their territory. They will guard it. Dogs tied up like this have often bitten someone who passed by within range.

Children can do the stupidest things. One of my dogs, many years ago, was lying down a few feet away from me at a combined horse and dog show when a child of about ten years old jumped her pony over him. Fortunately he had been trained to lie down whatever happened and did not move. Another dog might have stood up and either been badly hurt, or have caused the pony to stumble and throw the rider. That was a very stupid child.

At a dog show one hot day my dogs were fastened to a stake by my car and I was sitting beside them, picnicking. Three children came racing by and jumped over the dogs. I told them it was dangerous and got a not very pleasant comment and faces made at me by way of reply.

Five minutes later they jumped over a dog tethered to a small tree. He was between the tree and the car and the owner thought he was absolutely safe. The dog was fast asleep, woke when its side was kicked, and reached up and bit one of the boys badly on the thigh. The dog was blamed! There is something very wrong with the attitude that children are innocent in all circumstances. Some are little monsters.

Burglars, muggers, and murderers are possibly encouraged by being allowed to go scot free when they have harmed an animal. The dog is put down and Junior knows he can get away with being highly unpleasant and it will be blamed on anything but the fact that he is a particularly nasty child. He becomes a nasty adult.

One of my bitches was once badly bitten by a dog I had not noticed, tied up under a table at a show. The dog had been left alone and most probably bit in fright when a strange animal came too near. Had I seen him I would have taken care to pass at a considerable distance, but he was well hidden.

Any one, child or adult, wishing to stroke a dog, should always ask the owner if they may. Some hate being touched. Some, with good reason, hate children. Some are rescues, having been re-homed, and may be afraid of all humans except their owner, again with very good reason. Many dogs are badly abused by both adults and children.

Many children seem to lack all sense, or be so juvenile that they do not achieve adult attitudes. Some never do. They remain babyish in their outlook into old age. Some children may challenge a dog for a dare, or climb into a yard or garden which has been very adequately fenced to protect the safety of those around.

The dog is unaware that the child is not an intruder intent on doing harm. Nobody has ever come on to the property in that way before. The child is attacked, because the dog is doing what it sees as its job...to defend its territory.

Sadly the dog is often put to sleep after an accident due to this and another child grows up thinking the world will adjust to his or her needs, and that children need take no responsibility whatever for their own safety.

A pedigree can tell you if your dog had nervous ancestors; it can't tell you that it may meet with people so stupid that they induce it to behave totally out of character due to its fears of behaviour that it has never met before.

Few of us kick our dogs or throw stones at them or try to tie tin cans to their tails, to get them used to such behaviour without protesting, but there are children who do this. Often when a child is bitten, investigation shows that the child frightened the dog by some uncouth behaviour. This is never reported.

I once stopped a group of children from whirling a kitten round their heads and letting go of it so that it flew through the air. A friend rescued a pup from boys trying to drown it in a public lavatory.

That is another reason for never letting our dogs out of our sight, never mind what the law says. We have to be sensible or we don't have sensible dogs. A dog running free is as much at risk of being harmed as is a child today. In many cases it is children that cause them harm. In both cases humans are the main danger, which is a very sad reflection on society.

I well remember a friend of mine saying to someone who had asked advice about a dog on the phone...

'I see. You want to murder your dog because you can't train your children to behave.' The caller had just confessed that one of her sons had been bitten after driving the point of a pencil through the dog's ear drum.

It was re-homed and proved to be a very friendly happy animal, though it never overcame its very well justified fear of children.

Another dog, brought to be put down for biting, was found, by the vet, to have seventeen staples in its ear. The last one had provoked it beyond endurance of such torture. That dog too was re-homed successfully.

Children, and adults for that matter, should never put their hands into a car to stroke a dog. Even a placid dog may guard his car and consider this an attempt to steal it or him.

It is unwise for adults to separate fighting dogs; children are much more at risk of being injured if they try. A stray dog may well attack a dog on the lead; I have had this happen a number of times in the past thirty years of dog owning. The only safe thing is to drop the lead and stand well back and let the fight take its course.

There are, of course, many sensible children who are able to take part in bringing up the dog and would never dream of harming him.

I have emphasised some of the drawbacks of dog owning, but it is always as well to consider every aspect. It saves so many dogs being bought in a hurry, and then given away after only a few weeks, because nobody has realised the reverse side of the coin.

One of my sons is a veterinary surgeon. One of his friends spent his first year after qualification putting ten dogs a day to sleep. They had all been handed in by owners after a few months, as they were too much of a nuisance to keep.

Those of us in constant contact with owners and with various organisations know that the rescue kennels are full; dogs are brought to be put down all the time because they have become unacceptable.

We live in a throw away society and this sadly, appears also to apply to many children's pets. The child becomes bored after a few weeks, and the animal is passed on. One wildlife sanctuary is over full with rabbits, hamsters, guinea pigs, and even tame rats and ferrets that were bought as birthday presents for children who did not deserve to own them. They cost money to feed but few give a donation with the animal.

BENEFITS OF DOG OWNING

Many of those who come to class with young dogs are in despair as the dog does so many stupid things. Youngsters do. They have to be educated. Most of the dogs that come in for re-homing are between six months and twenty months old as this is a stage of growing up that they all go through, when education is vital.

In human terms they are adolescent, and this is an age when adults are tested to find out their tolerance levels. Dogs mature more quickly so that this stage only lasts about a year with them, whereas with young humans there are several years in which they are sure they know all the answers and put themselves at risk.

I keep meeting owners with lovely steady dogs who I remember well in their adolescence. A number of them went through a stage at which they seriously considered either having the dog put to sleep, or re-homed. I have reached that point myself. I would have missed some wonderful dogs had I succumbed to my feelings.

I persisted as they did, and we have all been rewarded by the kind of dog that other people wish was theirs. It didn't just happen though. It took a great deal of hard work and thought and outlay of time.

We have considered all these aspects. We are sure we want a dog, can find ways to overcome the problems that may arise, and are prepared to give up time to caring for it. We want it to lead a happy life and not suffer through our ignorance.

There is nothing quite like owning a dog for those who are sure they want the experience. They are wonderful companions, rewarding us constantly with their affection. They often make us laugh, which is extremely good for us. Stroking them lowers our blood pressure and those of us who have them have a healthy life style as they need exercise daily.

Many a lonely person has been given a new interest in life by the need to keep active, to care for the animal, and to shop for its needs. Many have found companionship by joining the local dog class, where they make new friends with other dog owners. There is nothing like a dog to promote a sense of well being.

Often people will stop and talk to a dog owner where they would not stop to speak to someone on their own, so that for those who live alone this can be new source of pleasure when they go out. I have had many pleasant conversations through my dog.

Dogs guide the blind, provide ears for the deaf; help the disabled; they are extra eyes and ears and protectors for the police. There are dogs that can detect explosives and there would have been many more terrible incidents if it had not been for that wonderful sense of smell. They find people in bombed buildings, lost in caves or buried in avalanches, or hurt on the mountains.

They find lost property. Many a small child has been prevented from harm by his faithful guardian. There are dogs that can rescue people who are drowning; dogs that can sniff out gas leaks and prevent explosions.

Hundreds of people derive enormous pleasure from teaching their companions to take part in various kinds of competition. Breed Shows; Obedience Shows; Working Trials; Gundog Trials; Sheepdog Trials; Agility; Schutzhund, which is a German form of training. They may never win, but they have fun training and trying.

Even the family pet can be taught to find our lost car keys or gloves, and will enjoy being so employed. A dog is a major asset provided we have thought carefully about our life style and how he will fit into it.

3
ACQUIRING OUR DOG

We realise we are about to take on a considerable responsibility but are quite prepared for that. We have thought about the cost and whether we can afford a giant breed that eats pounds of meat each day, or would be better off with a small breed which will be much less expensive though it will be as big a commitment and need as much exercise and time.

Do we want a pedigree pup of a particular breed? Would we be happier with a cross bred? Or perhaps we would like to visit one of the various rescue organisations and take on a dog that someone else has thrown away as we feel a puppy is too much of a responsibility and we are no longer very energetic.

Much depends also on the type of dog we want. I would not go to a good show kennels with many champions if I wanted a working dog. I would go to someone who breeds that type of dog. They often look quite different from the animals that appear in the show ring, but what we want in this case is brains, not looks.

Before buying a dog, do ask about the breed from as many people as possible. From the local veterinary surgeons; they know which kennels produce dogs that don't try and bite them when they are treated. From the local dog clubs. They know which are a major nuisance if they come to class.

Visit shows. Don't ask the breeders. Ask those who own a dog of the breed you want. What is he like? Is he easy to train? Is he good tempered? Would you buy again from the same breeder? Where did you get him? Does he greet you happily or back away and warn you off? You can find out so much before buying and save so much trouble afterwards.

The best time to buy is in the spring, when we have long light evenings ahead and warm weather in which to house train the pup. There is nothing more miserable than being outside in the dark in a gale in November, with rain pouring down and a puppy that only wants to get back into the warm and refuses to do anything at all.

It is never a good idea to buy one for a birthday or Christmas present, as a puppy that has been used to the quiet of its kennel is going to be very upset by all the noise and bustle. It may well be forgotten.

One owner came to club with the pup that had been bought, aged six weeks, for Christmas for the next door neighbours' children. It was so unhappy and so much in the way and so messy, because no-one remembered to take it outside regularly, that they put it out in the shed.

They then forgot it, and after three days the woman who brought it for lessons realised no one had been near it to either to feed it or let it out. She acquired a free puppy as she threatened to report them unless they gave it to her.

Having considered all the snags of dog owning, we are ready to visit the breeder and choose the puppy, or to hunt round the various rescue organisations to see if a dog is waiting for us there.

It is not as simple as that. There are still pitfalls for the unwary.

THE RESCUED DOG

It is as necessary to be careful of the organisations caring for these as of every other aspect of dogdom, as some may have the wrong reasons for taking on dogs. People have been known to collect money for the dogs they have rescued and put it to their own use. The dogs are an excuse and provide a cover for fraud.

Others may not have the right premises, though they are full of good intentions, and dogs from them may well not be healthy.

An immediate visit to the vet is essential, as if we take home a dog suffering from one of the major illnesses, it will be months before we can have any other dog on our premises. Also we can carry the disease on our shoes and clothes and infect other dogs we meet.

It is not always easy to find out much about the dog's past. Families have taken on older dogs that, within a few days, bit one of them. On returning the dog they find that that has happened before and was the reason for re-homing in the first place.

Good rescue organisations, like good breeders, will want to know as much about you as you do about them. Also the dogs will be healthy before they are re-homed, nursed back to fitness, and some attempt will have been made to cure any major behaviour problems.

The RSPCA insist that re-homed dogs are neutered,so that they can't be bred from, which is a very good practice.

Many questions will be asked of you. Have you the right home? Why do you want the dog? Are you prepared for the expense?

Dogs do not always settle at once; some fret for past owners, even if they were bad owners. Others are bewildered, as they have come into a completely new environment with totally different rules.

Not everyone is a suitable owner for a dog with a difficult past. We can change the dog's behaviour, but it takes months, not hours, and a great deal of patience and commitment.

WHICH BREED?

Mongrel pups are often charming animals that mature into sensible adults. But there is a risk, as if they have been sired by the village Romeo, they are likely to inherit his character, and be possessed by an immense need to escape and find a mate. Also there is no guarantee as to size. Even Great Dane pups start very small.

There is an enormous choice among the pedigree breeds. The types of dog can be, very roughly, divided into groups. There are so many that only a few can be named in each. There are a number of excellent books which will help in the decision. These are listed at the end of this book.

The Gundogs include Retrievers; Labradors; Pointers; Spaniels; and Setters. Each was bred for a different function, but there are some that fulfil all the functions. There are a number of varieties of each.

Dogs of this type bought from a working kennel will be intelligent and extremely active, needing a good deal of training to be biddable, as well as an immense amount of exercise. They are rewarding if you want to shoot, or go for very long walks, or take part in some form of competition. They re-pay teaching.

If you want one as a pet it is important to make sure they are bred for that market, as they are from quite different ancestors. They should then be more biddable and less energetic, and fit happily into homes provided their early teaching is not neglected.

Among the most successful of pets for families and elderly people is the Cavalier King Charles Spaniel, which, well reared and well cared for, makes a wonderful companion.

The hounds include many different types. These are working dogs and the instinct is very strong, as I do not think any are bred specifically for the pet market. They tend to escape and wander, and of course, to hunt. One family with a hound puppy had special dog outfits that were full of holes as the pup worried at clothing, and had not been taught not to do this when they first bought it. It can be taught to respect clothing.

The herding breeds include all the sheepdogs. Many farmers have been told to diversify and now breed puppies. Sadly, few know about the need to make sure the pups meet people and other animals and go into the house before being sold.

Nobody has to take piglets and calves and lambs around, though it is better to take foals out and about to ensure they are used to people. So the pups are left in barn or kennel, see no one but the person who feeds them, and are disasters when sold as they are as wild as any fox cub and have to be tamed.

I love the collie in its proper surroundings and there is nothing like a good dog working sheep, but many of these end up with owners who do not have time to cater for the dog's needs. They become noisy nuisances rushing round the garden, barking at birds and neighbours, trying desperately to work off an amount of energy that needs a good ten mile walk, at least, every day.

Many people now buy them for Obedience competition and some do very well, but as many of them are also rans as are the other breeds. In a big class of thirty or more, there can only be one winner, and that will be the well chosen dog that has a great deal more training than the average animal.

Many of these end up in rescue and when they come to class, they are often very difficult to train as their education has been neglected, and they are not the easy dogs that people imagine.

The guarding breeds can also cause problems to first time owners. They need to be taught from puppyhood what they may and may not guard. Not their beds, or food, or toys, or your bed, or you.

It is flattering to have a dog that prefers you to everyone else but it can be dangerous as the most dedicated will try and keep the family away from their owner. There are also major problems if that one person is ill, on holiday or has to go into hospital.

One police dog refused to eat, and since he was needed while his owner was out of action, his food bowl was taken to the hospital every day for his handler to mix with his hands and to get his own scent on it. It is sensible to have the food prepared by more than one person so that the dog does not react like this.

I have had one owner in class who could not kiss her husband in their dog's presence. He attacked the husband. Another would not allow a child to be chastised, which did not help family discipline; a third slept on her young owner's bed and attacked the father when he tried to wake his daughter one day when she had overslept. Some are so aggressive with visitors that the family ends up friendless.

In every case this is due to lack of early teaching. It is well worth while finding someone to put the owners on the right lines and ensure these faults never develop as they are very hard to overcome. In all these cases the dog was re-homed, and the new owners had no problems as they prevented over attachment, and taught the dog how to greet visitors. These are most wonderful dogs to own when well trained, but disasters if spoiled and allowed their own way.

There are many types of terrier. Some of these can be noisy. Others are great diggers as they were bred for digging out fox and badger cubs. I have not found them so easy to train as other breeds. Some of them can be fighters. It depends so much where you buy and again how much time you put into the early teaching. One Welsh Terrier was among the best dogs I have ever had in class and trained to a high standard.

Terriers are good at killing rats and are triggered by movement. An unwary child wiggling a finger may find it pounced on and bitten as the dog thinks it is a rat's tail. Children have to be especially careful around all dogs, but very aware with these types.

So much depends on us and the way we live, We may want a pet that will guard us well; or perhaps we occasionally go shooting. So we want a dog that is biddable, will train well, but is also prepared to spend hours doing nothing much at all quite happily. This is quite a lot to demand of any young animal. The older ones become more placid and spend more time asleep. A dog is not like a bicycle to be brought out when needed and then put away until next time.

Size is important. I would not buy a giant breed if I lived in a small house or flat without much garden. Also the big breeds tend to be short lived, which means more frequent distress when they die.

Nor would I buy one if I had a small income and could not afford to spend a great deal of money on its food. Vet bills are more expensive for the giant breeds as they need larger quantities of drugs to cure them than a tiny dog like a chihuahua.

Small dogs are as much fun as big dogs and can be terrific characters. They can compete even in Working Trials, where I have seen Pomeranians and Yorkshire terriers holding their own with the police dogs.

A little thought can save so much heartache, as once we have the dog, there are few of us who do not find it has stolen its way into our affections. Circumstances may force us to give it away because we have not thought deeply enough about its needs.

That has happened to several dogs that came to classes for lessons. They proved to be unsuitable for their owners' life style, needing far more money for their keep and care and management than the buyer had realised. This is always upsetting.

WHICH BREEDER?

Breeders, I have found from experience, some of it sad, can be divided into several types.

1) The dedicated breeder who is passionate about improving the breed and is producing excellent stock that anyone would be proud to own. No expense is spared in rearing the bitch and the pups and very little profit is made. This breeder will have a waiting list for puppies and will never breed for the Christmas market. Every buyer is interrogated to make sure the pup is going to the best possible home. This is the breeder we all need.

2) This is often a caring person. Having bred the pups, it is impossible to part with them. There will be a great many dogs and no money at all, but a pup from here will be well cared for, well reared, and a great asset to own. Any buyer will have to pass the most stringent tests before being allowed to take one of those cherished animals.

3) The puppy farmer. These people are not only a menace to the unwary buyer, but are loathed by all those who care deeply about their breeds. Any dog is bred to any bitch, irrespective of age or temperament. Bitches are mated at every season and used as a source of money only.

Often the pups are anti-social, as the mothers have become tired of their lives, having no freedom and no time to rest between litters. They are so exhausted they snap and snarl at the pups, trying to prevent them from feeding from extremely sore teats that have been over used.

The pups will be small, fretful, and puny, as they are weaned on to the cheapest food on the market. Often they are sold at five or six weeks, to save money. This is too young as they have lost the benefit of the extra training from their mother and from interacting with their litter mates, so that they may well be aggressive when they meet other dogs. They have not learned how to behave with them.

They are often very disappointing animals to own. It is best to beware of any place that sells a number of different breeds, and also of dealers and pet shops, though one or two of those do have a reputation for good puppies. These are few and far between. I would never buy any puppy that was not with its mother at the selling point.

Markets are not good places to buy pups either. Nobody knows their background, and market traders don't always tell the absolute truth. They want to sell their stock, and pups are no more than commodities sold this way.

Some places with splendid premises could well be puppy farmers, as money is there to spend. Puppy sales are often cash sales and no one knows exactly how many pups there are in each litter. Six may be reported when there were actually ten. Those who breed in this way may well be hiding profits.

Good breeders rarely have more than two litters a year. These will be from two different bitches who are allowed a long rest before being asked to produce again. As a result, they are never overwhelmed by their duties and enjoy their puppies immensely, making excellent mothers.

We want plump lively pups with bright eyes, clean ears, good strong bone, and plenty of healthy curiosity, who do not startle at the slightest noise, or draw back if we sit on the floor and try to entice them to us.They should come riotously, eager for petting, and to find out more about this new person who has just come into their lives.

I now look for pups that are bred either in the house, or close to it; that are handled by lots of people from three weeks on; that come into the home daily to learn about such things as radio, television, washing machines, vacuum cleaners, lights that switch on and off, sudden noises from intermittent machinery like refrigerators, and curtains that make a noise when drawn. All these can cause terror to a puppy that has only known the quiet of a secluded kennel and no visitors or other environment.

When buying a dog we need to remember the old saying. 'Poor fellow. He was sold a pup!' In other words, he was conned. We need to take care that doesn't happen to us.

BUYER BEWARE

What else do we have to consider when we go to buy our chosen breed? It is a good idea to get good professional advice. There are organisations that recommend the best breeders; many breed societies have lists of those who are taking the greatest care with their stock.

The Kennel Club has a list of good breeders, and in spite of what I am now about to say, those are in the majority, but they do not always advertise, and we do have to watch out for rogues. They crop up in every aspect of life, but if we know the pitfalls, we can avoid them.

There are all sorts of dodges that can catch us out. It is never wise to say you have just lost a valued companion and want to replace him quickly. The wrong type of person knows how to cash in on this. Visit the kennels and you find that no puppies are available. They have all been sold.

Well, they say, seeing your disappointment, there is one puppy left but their own dog has just died, so they do appreciate how you feel. They have the pup to replace their own lost companion, and it is not for sale. They simply couldn't bear to part, but perhaps you would like to see just what kind of stock is produced and return when there are more puppies.

The pup is in a dog bed in the sitting room, if in winter beside the fire, on an immaculate white blanket, looking adorable as all pups do. You ache for it. It trots over and greets you and you pick it up, desperate to possess that little warm body.

But they will not sell. Not for £300; nor £400. '£500? Oh, my dear you must want him badly. I do know he will have a good home. It will break our hearts to let him go, but we do understand. We can bring one of our brood bitches into the house.'

Off you go with the pup in your arms, your bank balance severely decimated. You leave the breeders rubbing their hands in glee, as the pup was only worth £150 anyway. It is immediately replaced by one of the other eight that are still outside in the kennel, ready for the next hopeful buyer.

You don't believe me? Some years ago I had three owners come to class with pups of the same age. On talking to them, I discovered all had been told the same story. They all said that the breeder had been so kind, to replace their lost dog with their own puppy, and how lucky they had been.

I hadn't the heart to disillusion them. I don't know if they ever compared notes.

This is very unpleasant and quite unscrupulous but it is not illegal. The pup is worth exactly as much as the buyer is prepared to pay. I often meet someone who has bought a pup whose parents were both champions and who has paid an astonishing price, well over £500 for it.

The new owner may have bought in a hurry to replace a much loved old dog, or been told that this is champion stock. It is, if one or both parents were champions, but if every litter produced those without fail we would be awash with them. As it is most kennels only produce one or two top dogs in forty years.

I like to have a replacement lined up before I lose my old dog, choosing the breeder carefully. Then I know that I am not likely to fall victim to a scam when I am at my most vulnerable.

There are not many people like this, but I have come across it, and others may. The price of the pup should be given on enquiry and that is the price to pay. Breeds vary.

Your local dog club is a good place to visit, or a local show. You can see who owns dogs of the breed you covet and ask people how much they paid for their pups, which will give you a good guideline.

BUYING A BITCH

I, personally, find bitches are much easier to train, more affectionate and more biddable, though there are always exceptions to every rule. Also they are, mostly, less powerful and easier to manage.

Most, if kept as pets, are spayed, as problems can develop with an unspayed unmated bitch, among them various types of cancer. They will, if not neutered, have seasons which last three weeks, during which they must be kept away from all dogs. This starts between six and twelve months.

Many then have false pregnancies which can cause problems. One of mine specialised in false pregnancies. At around the time pups would have been born, usually in the night, she screamed as if she were in labour and if allowed in the garden promptly dug holes in which to nest. She produced milk and needed to have remedies to stop that.

She had seasons every sixteen weeks, which is unusual as the majority have them every six months. But dogs can't read and there are no hard and fast rules in nature. For twelve weeks of the sixteen she was quite disturbed and anything but a good companion.

She had a litter of pups when she was two, on her fifth season, and complications afterwards so that she had to be spayed. She became much happier and far easier to live with. Probably she had a hormone inbalance which contributed to the frequent seasons and the odd behaviour.

37

Maybe you want a bitch and would like a litter or two and make some money? It isn't that easy. It is never wise to have a litter to steady a nervous bitch; all that usually happens is that she produces more nervous pups and problems for a number of other people.

Another pitfall is to be sold or given a bitch 'on breeding terms.' If this arrangement is made, she should be far less than the normal selling price, as the breeder will want back at least two puppies. One usually makes up the balance on the price and the other is the breeder's profit. Beware of those who offer to sell you the bitch but want all her pups to be their property.

Wouldn't happen? Don't you believe it. I was asked to sign a form, after I had bought the puppy, stating that all her pups would be the property of the breeder. I asked my solicitor to word a form for me, and it ended up with the words, 'if the bitch is mated,' instead of 'when the bitch is mated.'

I had stated I wanted the puppy as a companion and to train for working trials and intended to spay her, but that was ignored. I did have her spayed. It did not form the basis of a beautiful friendship!

Several of the breeders I have bought from have become very good personal friends, who remained interested in their pups and their progress.

I made a mistake in continuing with the purchase of that pup as she was one of the most difficult I, or anyone else, had ever met. I knew several of the dogs in her pedigree. What I, and many other people, did not know, was that if a certain dog in her mother's pedigree was combined with another dog in her father's pedigree, the result was disaster.

After a few such litters had been born knowledgeable breeders took very good care to avoid such matings. Either the dam or the sire with dogs with different pedigrees produced good stock. But until one has seen the results, nobody can foretell what will happen.

If you do want to buy a bitch on breeding terms the Kennel Club has standard forms which set down a useful set of rules. It is essential to make sure everything is in writing, and is signed by both parties to the agreement.

I met one owner who had a bitch given to her on breeding terms, as she could not afford a puppy. They had the understanding that after the pups were born, the bitch would then belong to the family, and all debt would be cleared.

When the time came for her to be mated, the bitch went back to the kennels where she had been born and the stud dog sired her pups, which were born at the kennels, and looked after by the breeder. The owner did not have the right kind of home in which to rear pups.

No transfer of ownership had ever taken place, so that the bitch was still registered as belonging to the kennels where she was born. The only agreements made were verbal.

The unfortunate family who had looked after the bitch and reared her, and paid all the expenses for two years, were sent a bill for the stud fee, for the care of the bitch and of the pups, as well as a large vet bill for aftercare. It came to well over £300, in the late 1970s.

The family were far from well off and it was impossible to find that amount of money. The bitch they had thought was theirs was sold to defray expenses, and their much loved pet never came back to them. I met them some years after and the memory was still bitter. No legal challenge was possible as they had never owned the bitch in the first place. The breeder could have said she had been lent.

Apart from this, which fortunately is a rare case, a written legal agreement is essential as so much can go wrong. Your rights are very clearly stated on the Kennel Club form, as this is a type of partnership.

I consider that the maximum insurance is essential in this case unless you are very wealthy indeed.

Suppose the bitch is killed in an accident before she has had time to have the pups? Who is responsible for her cost? Is compensation to be not only for her but for the loss of the pups which she might have borne?

Suppose half the litter dies during the first weeks of life, or worse, all of them. There is an unpleasant problem known as the fading puppy syndrome and it can happen to the best breeders.

Apparently healthy pups die for no reason that anyone can find. If you are looking after the pups the loss could be blamed on your inexperience. Without an agreement you could be asked for the money they would have fetched, which could come, with a large litter, to over a couple of thousand pounds.

The agreement must be made before you take the bitch home, or you could find a considerable financial penalty.

The majority of breeders are scrupulous, but I have heard of problems, not once, but several times. I had a bitch myself on breeding terms; I bought her at far less than her full price, with the understanding her breeder should have two pups from her first litter and then she was mine.

I paid the stud fee, she had complications and went back to her breeder to be whelped. She had been transferred to me, and she was transferred back for the whelping as the breeder wanted to keep the kennel name for the litter. The re-transfer form was signed at the same time, ready to be sent off as soon as the bitch came home again.

This was a German Shepherd (then known as Alsatian, over twenty years ago). Two pups were long haired which meant that they could only be sold at pet prices and not pedigree prices as they can't be shown. The breeder took one long haired and one short haired, which was not necessary, but was very kind, as it shared the loss on those pups.

The bitch came home as soon as the litter was sold and was then mine for the rest of her life. Her breeder and I are still good friends.

Not every bitch is fertile. Some remain barren all their lives. One, mated every year for five years, never had pups. She was left in a kennel with a dog, luckily one that would have been used on her. Mysteriously, she produced one single puppy when she was about seven years old, amazing everyone, including, as far as we could see, herself and the dog who shared her kennel. She never had another pup.

The normal time for a bitch to be at her most fertile is around ten to fourteen days into her season. Many become skittish and flirty and lift their tail to everything and everyone, including the family cat.

But dogs can't read. I have known of bitches that were only fertile on the fifth or sixth day of their seasons. Others not till the eighteenth. One bitch that was isolated from the family dog for twenty seven days, came out of her kennel quarters on the twenty eighth and mated him. I met the unsellable pups a year later.

Nobody, including the vet, thought her likely to be fertile, but she produced two cross bred extremely ugly puppies that nobody would buy. There are no guarantees in nature.

It is absolutely essential that the bitch is guarded at all times for the whole three weeks of her season. Vets have been told that she can't be in whelp as the other dog is her brother and she wouldn't do that!

Dogs know nothing about incest and matings of mother and son, daughter and father and sister and brother will take place if the dogs are left together.

There are no taboos in the animal world. It is not a good idea as inbreeding done without very great care and knowledge can produce deformities, and doubles the chance of an inherited fault like epilepsy affecting the pups .

During a swine fever epidemic one of my farmer friends mated his sow to her father. She produced fifteen very deformed piglets that all had to be put to sleep. When he rang me he said. 'Father must be turning in his grave. He would never have allowed it. I was stupid.'

Mated next time, when the movements were no longer restricted, to a boar from another farm, she had a very healthy normal litter.

I have had pups in class from a mating of two close relatives and they have had very odd temperaments and been very difficult to teach anything at all, as well as often being over excitable to the point of hysteria.

Dogs are very persistent and can crawl through the most surprising spaces. They have been known to climb in through car windows, through house windows, over apparently unscaleable walls, and even to dig under fences.

One man I met had an unbelievable story. He had been working at a hound kennels. The dogs and bitches were in separate enclosures. Three days running one of the dogs was found in the bitch enclosure. Luckily none was in season.

On the fourth morning the kennelman hid. There was a long water trough that was shared by the hounds. It went through the wall, which was just above the water. This cunning fellow worked out that if he jumped into the trough and crawled along under the water, he could avoid the wall and arrive in the bitch pen.

That ended his adventures as a very strong grid was then put down from the wall to the bottom of the trough and his ambitions were foiled. It is surprising how ingenious they can be when driven by the strongest urge in the animal kingdom.

It is particularly important to ensure the bitch is not mated on her first season when she is far too young and immature to have pups. Her body may not be strong enough to take the stress, so that her future health is affected.

Wild dog packs only allow the strongest and most dominant bitch and dog to mate, so that even in nature precautions are taken to maintain good stock.

So it is vital to take immense care to avoid an accident and pups that nobody wants, and that aren't going to be pleasant for anyone to own. Some vets and some organisations do spay bitches before the first season to ensure there are no accidents. Others prefer them to mature.

It is possible to have an injection to procure an abortion, but it must be done within forty eight hours of the mating. It brings the bitch back into season for another three weeks, so care still has to be taken. The injection itself may cause future problems.

One of my owners had a bitch who was in an insecure garden, yet was allowed out alone, which I never do with an in season bitch. I stand guard over her like a Victorian chaperone.

She had the injection after five dogs had mated her. She was young, terrified, and unwilling. The owner came out too late to do anything about it. Two days after having the injection the dogs got into the garden again.

The injection can't be given twice.

It's quite likely that the resulting litter was of pups which had different fathers. That bitch, ever after, hated dogs so much that she became a major liability as she attacked on sight. Obviously she felt as a woman does when she has been raped.

Some bitches will refuse every dog, but this one was small and overpowered by the big dogs that were lying in wait for her. It is vital to be over cautious, especially if there are children in the house who don't remember about doors. A safe pen avoids disasters if you can't be in constant attendance when she is outside.

Stupid things can happen. Many years ago one owner walked her bitch in season through a small Cheshire town one winter day. A stray dog tried to mate her as they walked along. The woman kicked the dog away. He went up into the air and under my car as I was driving past. I barely had time to see him, let alone stop. My car killed him.

The policeman I reported to discovered the dog was over three miles from home. Two people were to blame in that instant; the woman walking an in season bitch in a public place, which was asking for trouble, and the owners who let their lovely dog wander. I was told the accident was inavoidable, but that did not help me as the last thing I want to do is kill any dog, and I was very unhappy about it.

At the most fertile point many bitches will do her best to escape and find a mate, no matter how young they are. An open door, unguarded for a moment, and she is away, often jumping a gate or fence everyone was sure was too high for her.

It is necessary to make arrangements with the owner of the stud dog well in advance, or he may be booked up when your bitch needs him. Give the expected date of the season and as soon as she starts phone and confirm the booking. Also confirm on the day you are coming and try to give a time of arrival.

I would not take my bitch to a stud owner who did not ask for her to be swabbed beforehand, to ensure she has no infection. One of my bitch's pups was sterilised by a bitch that infected him. She had been in quarantine and nobody thought any infection would last for six months. They were all wrong.

If a dog has unswabbed bitches he may have been infected by the last that came for mating and pass the infection on to your bitch. This could result in either her illness, or no litter.

Take her out to empty herself well before you reach the kennels, as it is unfair to let her do anything there. The smell that remains will drive every male dog crazy. Take her out of the car on the lead, and don't let her run around even if the yard looks secure. She will mark to notify her presence to other dogs if she is free.

Some owners let the dog and bitch run together, and only help when they are actually tied. The dog will mount the bitch from behind, but within a few minutes he turns round so that they are back to back. If the bitch is tight, don't allow anyone to cut her, as has been done on occasion. If things seem to be going wrong, give up. Don't risk your bitch. She may not yet be mature enough; she may do well with a different dog. She may well be very alarmed by the people around her who daunt her instead of re-assuring her.

What comes naturally does not always come naturally. She may be very tight and become aggressive if she is hurt. Any forced mating may well affect her later, and make her difficult in future. There are some horror stories. If you don't like what is going on, take her home. It is so easy to upset her for ever and then there will be no pups at all.

While in whelp she needs careful feeding, and in the last weeks before the pups are born, being very large, she will have to have several small meals a day. She needs supervised exercise in those last days as well. She is enormous, waddling along and very uncomfortable and miserable at this time.

It is never possible to predict exactly the day on which the pups will start to come; some are early; some are late. It is vital to be with her when the pups are born, as they can jam. This means sleeping with her. Most deliveries occur at night, but not all. The breeders I know have a camp bed in the whelping room.

I once helped deliver a litter in which two pups were born the wrong way; the vet was unavailable. With the aid of a book I had to deliver them, as their breeder, who had only had one litter before, was too afraid she might harm them.

They couldn't be left as they were not likely to be born at all. They had to be manipulated very carefully to make sure they were not damaged. Luckily they arrived safely and healthy. Had the bitch been on her own, she would have been in very serious trouble with jammed pups, and probably the litter would have died before birth, as one of these was the second out of nine. The other was the fifth to arrive.

One of my bitches had a pup that we sold to someone we thought both competent and caring. On her first season, at only eight months old, the youngster was mated by a dog that must have got into the garden without the owner's knowledge.

She came down one morning to find eleven dead puppies and a very sick bitch who died a few days later. She was not yet a year old. Nobody had noticed she was in whelp; they thought she had got fat!

There are people who think that the birth ought to be a lesson for the children; this can result in the bitch not being able to deliver as so many people distress her; or in her eating the puppies afterwards as she has been so disturbed. She needs absolute quiet with only one or two people she knows very well, when whelping.

She is not a side show.

When the litter is born, there is very little time for anything but taking care of them, as the kennel must be kept spotless, and nine pups or more produce an amazing amount of mess. Good pups need careful weaning and a lot of socialising so that they meet people, are taken out in the car, and, as I said before, and can't emphasise enough, are taken into the house so that when sold they are not terrified of all that goes on in the home.

It is useful if they can meet other types of animals at this stage as they tend to accept cats and rabbits, hamsters, and sheep, if met before seven and half weeks, and to play with them. At that time the hunting instinct seems to develop and instead of play fellows, the animals, if met for the first time, are prey to be chased. If they are already friendly, they continue to accept them even after eight weeks.

It is as well to think very hard before buying a bitch with a view to breeding. Some of the snags are not obvious, and it is far from being a certain way to earn money.

SHOULD I USE MY DOG AS A STUD DOG?

I have vivid memories of someone, long ago, wanting to use my Golden Retriever as father to her bitch's pups. He had a wonderful temperament. He also had a number of major faults, of which one, and possibly two, were inherited. She was so persistent I told her to ring my vet to ask his opinion.

It was short and to the point.

'Over my dead body.'

It is unfair to anyone to breed from any but a very good dog, and it is essential to be absolutely sure that there are no <u>known</u> faults that he could pass on to his pups. It is impossible to be aware of long ago problems that might crop up unexpectedly many generations later.

Apart from that, stud dogs are not easy to keep. Once they have had a bitch, their minds seem able to focus on nothing else, and if there is the faintest scent of one on the wind, they do their best to escape and find her.

One breeding kennel was very isolated. In spite of that, whenever there was a bitch in season there was a hopeful queue of suitors who had travelled five miles, brought by the news on the wind. Scent carries for a considerable distance as anyone who has lived downwind of a maggot farm knows very well.

The dogs not only queue, but even with no goal in sight, they will fight, resulting often in nasty injuries and expensive vet bills.

NEUTERING

It is far easier to own a dog that is never mated, as what he never has, he never misses. Having said that, while he remains entire, he will do his best to remedy that defect as the instinct is the strongest any dog has. Some will starve for three weeks if a family bitch is in season, and kept kennelled within the grounds.

Stud dogs need management and can be very difficult to live with in the home. Their basic instincts can take over in ways that we would prefer not to have to deal with.

They may become very aggressive with all other male dogs. They may howl all night if there is a bitch in season anywhere near. They can starve themselves if there is a bitch near.

Males are often neutered now, and they only become lazy and fat if overfed and under exercised. It is much easier for a dog that is never to be mated not to be entire. No one keeps entire bulls, rams, or boars if they are not to be used for breeding. Vasectomy is commonplace today among humans.

I live in an area where the RSPCA subsidises every dog and bitch that is sterilised by the amount of £20 which pays for quite a large part of the operation. It is a routine operation and there are very rarely any ill effects afterwards. It is worth finding out if such a scheme exists where you live.

Many owners now accept that neutering is best for males. It can make them less aggressive; it does make them much easier to manage and they no longer have an urge to wander. Any dog from an RSPCA Rescue Kennels will be neutered before it is re-homed, and Guide Dogs for the Blind and those dogs helping people who are deaf or disabled are also always neutered.

It is never easy trying to compete with a male dog as breed shows allow bitches in season in the ring. Obedience competitions may be held alongside and if there is an in season bitch around, those with entire dogs have very little hope of doing well.

One Police Force told a story of a number of dogs on the trail, they thought, of a very dangerous criminal. All converged on one house, so everyone was sure that their quarry was hiding there.

They were embarrassed to discover that all the dogs had one idea in their heads, and the source of their eagerness was a bitch at the height of her season. Neutering does not worry the dog at all, and he is far happier than he would be if left entire yet never allowed to obey his natural instincts.

THE PEDIGREE FORM

I am always surprised to find few owners understand this document. They can't tell me, a year later, the name of the breeder, or the kennel name of their dog, yet with pedigrees this is the most vital information.

This is not a piece of paper to hide in a drawer and forget, or use to prop up the table leg. It is a history. I can look at a pedigree of a breed I know well and pick out the great dogs on it, and also those that have caused problems such as epilepsy or bad hips (hip dysplasia, known as HD), or now, with the German Shepherds. haemophilia. It tells me as much about where not to buy as where to buy.

Champions do not always depict a great dog. There are some that many people wish had never been born and certainly wish had never acquired that status as their pups are disasters. A dog has only to win three championship certificates under three different judges to become a Champion. Ninety seven judges may refuse to give him the accolade; the others may be friends of his breeder. Not common, but it can happen.

All the judges are looking for is a dog that is exactly the picture of an ideal member of his breed. He or she may have a diabolical temperament or any number of hidden inherited faults, but that can't be seen in the showring. If he looks good and moves well he may easily win and probably will, although knowledgeable bystanders are looking on in some horror.

There are pups from dogs that everyone would go miles to find but problems can arise if a stud dog is used so that he has a great many pups in one area. Succeeding litters from various sons and daughters may become inbred, and then the faults do develop. There are lines of dogs and bitches that produce major problems in their offspring if put together, yet with others, unrelated to those, produce wonderful stock. That was the trouble with my difficult pup.

It is not easy to find out what faults are likely to be present as some breeders are very secretive; few are going to admit their stock has problems. Some Breed societies go to great lengths to breed out faults, and have lists of those who are trying their best to do so. It is well worth contacting the secretary of the club of your chosen breed to ask for advice on this.

Dr Malcolm Willis has written a book called 'The Genetics of the German Shepherd.' This can never be up to date, but it does give the names of dogs that have caused problems, as well as those that have been a great influence on the breed for its good. It is very useful indeed for those owning dogs of this breed or proposing to breed from them. He will also give advice to anyone who asks, to ensure that better stock is produced, and can identify problems in a number of breeds from a pedigree form.

A pedigree should be an accurate document, but may not be. I have been asked, a number of times, to act as consultant when one was in doubt. One dog was sired by a famous Champion.The only snag was that that dog had been dead for twenty five years and when he was around no one froze semen. The pedigree was a fake.

It may, at times, be a genuine mistake, writing out the last pedigree form for a litter of eleven. One dog on one of my pedigree forms is stated to have been Best in Show in 1926 and 1963. Some dog! The breeder had simply made a mistake and reversed two numbers, as the correct dates were 1962 and 1963 and yes, they were quite genuine.

Some are just silly, One had the name of a famous kennel on it for every dog and bitch on the form, so that, astoundingly, the mother was 'Funny Kennel', as was the father and all the other ancestors. It would not have been quite so bad if the space said 'Funny Kennel Joe' and 'Funny Kennel Susie' with every name different.

Another pedigree was made of names like 'Joe of Newcastle': 'Polly of Brixton'. This is not a pedigree as there are no kennel names and no dogs that anyone has ever heard of. It is most likely to be invented as no one bothers to keep pedigrees of dogs with names like that. I have been told that there are people who sell pedigrees for fifty pounds. That is fraud, and something no good breeder would ever dream of doing.

What can have happened is that the litter had ten pups, and was registered as having ten. Five are sold without papers, and the other five pedigree forms, which are of registered puppies, are sold elsewhere to someone with a bitch with no background. The new owner has no proof that the pup bought has the correct pedigree, which is why it is useful to have friends who do know the breed well.

You may find a name in your pup's pedigree like Samco Mermaid Cougar of Millrace. Those who know, on seeing it, will understand that he was bred in partnership, the two kennels being Samco and Mermaid. Cougar is his registered name, though you may well want to call him Sam or Ben, which does not matter so long as you put his proper name on any documents, such as the transfer of ownership.

He was bought by a kennels named Millrace who added their name as they wanted to use it on his pups.

I have never understood how some people can be told that a puppy is so much with papers and less without; it doesn't make sense. Either it has a registered pedigree or it hasn't and if it has, I would never dream of buying it without that document. Nobody can sort out which pups will show well and which wont at eight weeks old. They change as they mature.

The only time I would expect it to be withheld is if there was a major fault which had only just become apparent and the pups could not be used for breeding, in which case I would expect to be told why the papers were not given.

Questions should be asked though often at first we do not know which to ask. In many breeds now hips are X-rayed and scored before a mating, and eyes are tested. In the German Shepherds, stud dogs and bitches are tested to be sure they are clear of haemophilia, and lists of dogs that are clear can be obtained from the breed society.

Haemophilia is a problem as it only appears in the males, though the females carry it. If several litters contain bitches only, it may well not become apparent until males are born.

I like to see the pedigrees of dogs that come to my classes, as often one can identify a possible behaviour problem and work to eliminate it before the pup is mature. Or can recognise on sight from past experience that this particular breeder does not socialise the pups and make sure that the owner remedies that at once by taking the pup out and about to as many different places as soon as possible.

Some years ago I made up a pedigree for a talk I was giving on inheritance. One was of an ideal dog and the other of a hound from hell. Neither bears the slightest resemblance to any pedigree I have ever known.

The first pedigree, that of Perfect Sensible Pup, is one of a dog that I would travel miles and spend a fortune to own. I would be reasonably certain he would be a major asset. There are no absolute certainties.

The second, that of Crazy Mixed Up Pup is that of a dog nobody ought ever to buy. Although it was invented many years ago there are still pups like it on the market.

So, do find someone who can interpret that pedigree for you. It can save so much unhappiness, especially if you have a problem like epilepsy in the breed. I have known a number of dogs with this fault and it is not easy to live with.

Those who know their dogs well avoid any lines that might produce it, so again it pays to study that document, and know what to avoid, as others from other parents will be free from the trouble.

The dedicated breeders are doing their best to eliminate it; but the trouble stems from puppy farmers, who don't care at all so long as they get the money for the pups.

If you are offered a document saying ' no responsibility is taken for the puppy once it leaves these premises,' don't buy. Reputable places have no need to make such statements and you might find within a week that the puppy was very ill indeed.

BEFORE YOU BUY THE PUP

It is always advisable to see the parents. The stud dog may be at a distance, but the mother should always be available. If an excuse is made not to show her to you, then be doubtful as she may well have a bad temperament and if so, will have taught her pups that people and other animals are dangers to be barked or snarled at.

The ideal bitch is happy to show off her puppies, and to be petted herself.

Dogs do not always behave in the same way off their own territory as they do at home. There, they are relaxed. Outside, they may well show signs of nervousness, such as a tail tucked hard under the tummy, panting, or lip licking.

My dog that had six male owners before me, seemed a very easy dog in kennels. It was not until he came home and had to stand up to the stresses of everyday life that the problems began to show.

Breed shows are the obvious places to see many of the parents. How do they behave with other dogs? How do they behave in the car park? Are they steady and sensible, or frantically pulling on the lead to get back to the car and out of all the hurly burly? Do they shy off when approached?

Are they happy in the show ring or do they look as if they would rather be anywhere but there? Do they allow the judge to approach, or do they shy away, or growl or much worse, try to bite?

At shows you can see their offspring from six months old upwards. The pups may not behave happily here, as sometimes they are plunged too quickly into big shows. They should start with small shows, and become used to the bustle before they are taken to an enormous show with hundreds of dogs and thousands of people.

Any puppy taken for its first outing to Cruft's (this can't actually happen) would be terrified if it had never been away from home before.

A wall full of red rosettes may not mean that the dog or bitch is a top winner. I had many firsts in both open and championship shows with the bitch I did show in breed, but I also had a number from fun shows for the prettiest bitch, the bitch with

47

the nicest eyes, the bitch with the waggiest tail. She had several Thirds in open show Obedience and a First in a tiny show with a very small number of entries.

Today many shows seem to have very poor entries and a dog or bitch may well be First in a class of one. There is little merit in this.

One of my dogs won many awards from second to sixth at the big shows, but also had a number of Firsts, all won at club progress nights. I could well have pretended these were for much bigger events. Take those rosettes with a large pinch of salt unless they have the names of the shows on them where they were won.

Championship shows only give prize cards as a rule. These do have the name of the show on them.

RECORD KEEPING.

It is very easy to mislay important documents. I buy a big photograph album for each dog I own. The modern album has sticky pages with a cellophane cover over them.

Into this goes the pedigree form, the Kennel Club transfer of ownership document, the insurance cover notes. Also the inoculation booklets which most vets give you, so that the date is clearly shown and you know when to renew.

If I have dogs I compete with, in goes their show records and any interesting snippets about them. My vicious puppy became civilised and was a wonderful companion by the time she was three years old. She had more character than any dog I have ever met and gave me an immense amount of pleasure.

When seven years old, she became the 1000th Pat Dog for Pro Dogs, visiting a hospital and schools until she had a stroke when she was eleven. She came with me to a dinner in London for a presentation.

I have the press cuttings about her, the dinner invitation, and the certificate they gave her, all in her memory book, and enjoy looking back to the days when she was with me. Each book also contains photographs of the dogs. It becomes a wonderful memorial as well as a record that you can't lose, and the documents are easily found when needed.

It is also useful to make notes of any health problems that may arise and file them here, as then you have a record which is useful if you move house, or have to change veterinary surgeons.

IF PURCHASE PROBLEMS ARISE

I have found over the years that one of the most frequent problems is lack of documentation from the breeder when a pup is sold. The pup is taken home, but there is no proof of purchase. There is no receipt for the cash or cheque paid. I once bought a quantity of dog food for one of my puppies but did not think to ask for a receipt. I was billed again, and had no way of proving I had already paid as I paid cash.

Buying a new puppy is exciting. The little animal takes up a great deal of one's attention and it is easy to overlook details like this. I now insist on receipts for everything. It protects both the buyer and the seller.

Occasionally breeders ask for a guarantee that you will buy dog food from them for the rest of the pup's life. This is illegal. It is very inconvenient to travel a distance when there is a pet shop stocking the same food just down the road.

You should be given the pedigree form and a transfer form. Many good breeders also give you enough dog food to tide you over till you can get what you need; they also give a diet sheet, and I have seen exercise sheets which are very useful as young pups should not be taken for long walks. They are too small to be dragged everywhere the owner goes. Many people take these little ones too far too soon and that can help aggravate any leg condition that may be lurking.

The transfer form is a vital document as if not filled in and sent off an unscrupulous breeder could claim that you never owned the pup in the first place. They may say it was on loan, or you haven't yet paid, which is where you need that receipt. I pay by cheque as that is a further proof of purchase.

You may be asked for cash, but few of us want to carry several hundred pounds about with us in notes; and few kennels are likely to operate a credit card system, so that a cheque is the obvious answer for proof of payment.

People have come to classes complaining that the pup is now well over six months old and they still have no pedigree form, though it is promised every time they query. There are various odd reasons given.

The stud dog has gone abroad. No experienced breeder uses a stud dog without having his pedigree first.

The pedigree form has been sent and must have been lost in the post. In this case it must be replaced. That document is your pup's passport, and it is particularly annoying if you want to show him or take up some form of working competition. Especially if the dog is not yet registered in your name as you have had no ownership transfer.

If, after several requests, the pedigree and transfer forms are not sent to you by the breeder, then contact your local Fair Trading officer. This costs nothing and I have never known a query from them fail to produce a rapid result.

If there are unacceptable reasons for the absence of papers (such as that there never were any in the first place, and you were given to understand the opposite) then they will take the matter further and you may find that the purchase price is considerably reduced, as what you have is not a dog with notable ancestors.

The Fair Trading Officers will also check a suspect pedigree form, and ask a reputable local breeder to check it, as this is how one finds out that Champion Goodness Gracious has in fact been dead for so many years that he can't possibly have sired your puppy.

Change of ownership needs to be registered with the Kennel Club if you want to show your dog or take part in any of the working competitions. I would do it as a safeguard even if I did not want to compete, as it gives you proof of ownership should any dispute arise. It is not expensive.

It is worth making enquiries if the registration procedure has gone on for more than a few weeks. Computers seem, if anything, to make such matters take longer than before.

Dogs without pedigrees can be entered for any sort of working competition, but not for Breed shows, as for those all details must be known and the dog must be registered under its pedigree name and its owner's name.

The entry form for any show asks for the name of the sire, (the father), the dam (the mother), the sex of the animal, the breeders' name, the date of birth. If the dog has no pedigree you simply write in the name that you have given the dog (which you must register with the Kennel Club or you can't enter), and then write across the form FURTHER DETAILS UNKNOWN.

You may go to a dog show and see in the schedule against some dogs' names either NAF, or TAF, or both. NAF means Name Applied For, and TAF means Transfer (of ownership) Applied For, and is a sign that the Kennel Club has not completed the documentation, so the dog is not officially yet in its records. So long as the documentation is with the Kennel Club the dog may be shown.

In some countries, among them Australia, a dog like this can't compete in anything, which does seem rather unkind. Here, they may enter so long as they have been duly recorded on the working register at the Kennel Club. Forms are available if you write to them.

INSURANCE

Most good breeders today insure the litter. This covers the puppies up to twelve weeks old and it is useful to extend the insurance yourself and continue with the same firm. There is not a lot of difference between them, so far as I know. The one I use is very reliable, and pays within a few weeks.

They refunded the purchase price of my haemophiliac dog as he died prematurely. I did not even realise that I could have this money back, and had not asked for it.

I have known hundreds of puppies and very few go wrong, but there have been at least twenty cases over the years of pups that died within a week of purchase. Several of them came from the same source, and had contracted distemper or parvovirus before they were sold. These diseases have an incubation period and pups don't develop them overnight.

Insurers will refund the price you paid if the kennels refuses.

You are entitled to expect a healthy well cared for puppy. The one you bought has not come up to standard and as a result the Fair Trading Officer will again help to get your money back. I would never accept a replacement from any kennels that had sold me a puppy that died very soon after buying it.

Puppy farms and big dealers may well have infection present as they buy from so many sources. One of the worst pups I ever met came from such a place. He was both very sickly and very vicious at ten weeks old and grew worse in spite of valiant efforts by his owner to help him.

We discovered, after he was put to sleep at six months, that he had been born on the East Coast of England. He was sold at four weeks to a middleman who drives all over the British Isles in a rickety old van filled from top to bottom with cages, buying in any litter whose breeder wants to get rid of it, because the major expenses start at around that age, when the pups are weaned. The puppies are very noisy after about four weeks old, and also generate an amazing amount of mess.

The breeders I know start their day, once the pups are more than three weeks old, at 5 a.m. and do not finish until midnight, with no time at all for rest as there is so much to do.

Six or more pups can't be left to run around in a mucky kennel. Meals need supervision or one or more pups suffer because theirs is stolen by the stronger litter mates. So there are people only too willing to get rid of a litter at this stage and since they only want the money, they do not care what happens afterwards.

In the case of this particular dealer, the pups are crammed into the cages, without room to turn around. They are travel sick and arrive filthy, to be bathed and put together in large groups in various pens. This one was not sold until he was fourteen weeks old, and by then he was terrified of hands, of feet, and of men in brown coats. I wonder why?

It is very likely that his pedigree form was anything but the truth. He was bought in a hurry as a birthday present for a small boy. In his short life he managed to make a whole family of six people extremely unhappy and frightened of his wild behaviour. I don't think anyone could have transformed that poor animal. He had far too bad a start in life

The owner, not the dog, they say. In this case, and a great many like it, it is the first owner, who actually breeds and rears the pup, who has a major responsibility to produce sensible stock that anyone would be proud to own. Many can take on pups that had a bad start and turn them into good dogs, but never into the kind of dog they would have been if handled correctly from birth.

Researchers have discovered, from observing countless litters of pups, that the age at which they most need to meet kind humans who will treat them well is between three and five weeks of age. Fear seems to begin to develop at about five weeks. This, in a wild dog, is a protective device as the pup that greets every animal it meets with joy is soon going to be a dead pup. Imagine what would happen if a dingo puppy ran up to greet a lioness.

They continue to greet humans happily if met for the first time until they are twelve weeks old, and after that, if they have only had contact with one or two people, and that not close contact, they become very wary.

Unfortunately we cannot yet sue breeders who keep pups in isolation. We can merely try and inform people of the hazards and prevent them from buying from the wrong place.

Taking time and trouble before we buy may make all the difference between having a companion for life, or a dog that is a nightmare to own. He may become a cherished companion but re-modelling him takes years, not days. The two like these I had in the past both changed my life, as so much time had to be devoted to transforming them into the dogs I wanted.

I could have trained a good dog ten times over and probably won at Cruft's had

I been able to devote the time I spent on them on a much more carefully chosen animal. I would not have learned so much had I not owned them. Nor would I be able to write this book!

If we want sensible dogs we must take so many factors into consideration.

4
YOUR NEW DOG

BEFORE YOU BRING THE DOG HOME.

THE OLDER DOG

It is always a good idea to visit the kennels several times, and if allowed, take the dog for a walk, and play with him, before taking him home. It could be an advantage to take him for a short ride in the car, so that a longer journey is not too traumatic.

It is always better to have a companion when you collect him to sit with the dog, as one that is unused to a car could jump around unless there is a crate for him, and could cause an accident. Also, being unused to you, he may try to escape, given an opportunity, as he does not understand what is happening.

When he arrives home, he will, unless he is very frightened, want to explore house and garden, trying to work out all the new smells and memorise them. Hopefully, if allowed in the garden first, with you supervising, he will take the opportunity to relieve himself.

If there has never been a dog on the premises, this may not happen, as he will be worried by the lack of any scent that tells him it is OK to empty here, and will hold on. Some dogs can hold on for as long as forty eight hours. Then they, quite literally, burst, again hopefully out of doors. They need to be told this is fine, this is what you want and they are good dogs.

If it happens indoors there are problems, which, unfortunately, will be aggravated by punishment. It is better to keep the dog, until he has formed a pattern, in a room where the floor is easily cleaned up. If paper is put down, when soiled it can then be taken out and put where he may empty himself, so that it smells right.

There are very likely to be house training mistakes for a few days; he does not know how to tell you when he needs to go out, and you do not know his signals. With patience, and careful watching of him, they rarely last very long.

It is necessary to be very careful not to stare at him until he is very familiar with you. A stare is a threat, to any dog. It may trigger a bold dog to attack. It cows a submissive dog into further fear.

He may need inoculations, unless that has already been done by the kennels. It is a good idea to let the vet check him, to make sure there is no hidden problem.

It will be some time before he really settles in, and it is much better not to overwhelm him with attention. If he had an unhappy past, he will be very wary of all new people that he meets, so it is better to introduce him slowly to those who meet him.

Unless we know dogs very well, we do not always realise when they feel unhappy. A tightly clamped tail means the dog feels very unsafe. A dog that turns his back on you does not want to be approached, and it is better to leave him alone. Few rescued dogs meet our eyes; theirs slide away, and that may also be accompanied by lip licking,which is again a sign of uneasiness.

It takes time for them to recognise that clear loving glance that provokes a return gaze from a happy balanced dog.

Some dogs settle immediately; others need time to adjust, so that it is better not to expect too much from a newcomer of any age.

I would make sure that the dog I had chosen to bring home was happy with children before I took him back. Those that have been tormented may so hate children that they would never settle in any house with a young family.

Children need to be made aware that the newcomer takes time to adjust. Ask them to think how they would feel if they were suddenly taken away from home and put in a completely strange place, with no one who even spoke the same language.

They should not try and interact, entice the dog to play exciting games, wake him when he is asleep, or rush at him and try to cuddle him, for several months. Any one of these actions may well result in a bite, not because the dog is vicious, but because he is frightened. A number of dogs have been taken back to the kennels after only a few hours because this has happened.

If a dog is excitable all rough games must be banned for ever with him, as the dog loses control of himself and again may bite in such circumstances.

It is best to make sure that children and dogs are not left alone together for some considerable time with a dog that is an unknown element in the home. I prefer not to leave children and dogs together alone under any circumstances.

It must also be a very firm rule that no dog, however much you trust it, is never alone with a baby. The baby cries and the dog is curious, and may try to lift it, meaning no harm at all. Bitches carry their pups in their mouths and may try to carry their owner's pup to the owner, knowing the baby needs attention. Unfortunately dogs aren't capable of this as there is no fur to protect the baby and there is a disaster.

Dogs that harm babies rarely intend to do so. Unfortunately they have sharp teeth and babies have no fur. It rarely happens, but it can, so be alert.

If there are other dogs in the household, then let them meet somewhere neutral, not in the car, or at your home. The resident dogs may well feel threatened and defend what they regard as their territory. They will not understand if the newcomer has far more attention than they do and may resent it.

If there is a resident cat, again don't let them meet until you are quite sure no harm will come to either. I put my cats in a cat cage in the same room as the dog, gradually extending the time. Once I am sure the two animals are used to one another, I release the cat, holding the dog.

If nothing goes wrong, then I let go of the dog and let them meet without a barrier. It can take weeks. Some cats refuse to accept a new dog. One of mine simply made it plain that he inhabited the bedrooms, and the garden when the dogs were not outside. As far as the cat was concerned, the dogs could have the rest of the house, and their own time outside.

The other cat, which we had at the same time, had no problems at all and was quite happy to lie beside the dogs.

I have had many rescued dogs in my classes through the years, and only two of them were failures. One should never have been re-homed, as he was dangerous, and bit two people within an hour of arriving home. In both cases the people he bit were sitting still, doing nothing whatever that would have provoked the dog.

Another, a very energetic and large animal, was given by a somewhat idiotic rescue organisation to an elderly man with a paralysed arm. He could not manage the dog at all. He should have been given a small elderly dog that would not need a lot of exercise and strength to control.

It is always a good idea to think hard before taking on any dog. Those with major problems need time and commitment to cure them, but they are curable. It is a tremendous feeling of achievement when a dog that hates mankind suddenly decides that you are, after all, worthy of his trust. The affection such dogs give has to be experienced to be believed.

BRINGING HOME A PUPPY

For a puppy, the first eight weeks in its new home is more important than any other time, except for the first weeks in the nest. If unpleasant things happen to him then they may affect him badly so that even if well bred from steady dogs, he will be a neurotic mess.

Ask questions of the breeder. This will give you a clue to future behaviour and any areas that may cause a problem. Accidents can happen in the best establishments and any caring breeder will tell you if anything odd has happened which might affect the pups.

A single bad experience can remain a cause of fear for all the pup's life. It may affect the more nervous and not bother the others at all. One litter was born in the house and their bed was in a room with a coal fire. A piece of coal exploded. None of the pups was hurt but for the rest of its life one at least would never go into a room where there was any kind of fire, whether coal, gas or electric, and was afraid of matches, lighters and anything that banged.

Where was the puppy born? If in a house with sensible people you have a head start. Just as good is the method used by many of the breeders I know. They have a special whelping area which is next door to the house, so that the pups can see everyone who comes, and are not isolated. The pups come in and meet visitors, have certain times when the family may play with them but still have peace when they need to rest.

The worst litter I ever met was born in a shed right at the end of an enormous garden, as the wife hated dogs. They were gundogs, bred to be sold to shooting people. Unluckily their breeder had a heart attack just after they were born and was not around for some weeks.

I stayed with the family and was asked if I would like to spend time with the puppies and get them used to people. I knew the mother, so had no problem with her. The shed had no windows. The pups, at nine weeks, had never seen daylight except when the door was opened and food put down for them.

It was five days before I could entice them as far as the open door and they had no intention whatever of allowing me to touch them or to come out on to the grass. I spent hours with them and at the end of my holiday they would venture outside but fly in again if anyone else came near.

They were all sold. They all came back within a few weeks. They were afraid of everything that moved and terrified of gunshot. It was a disastrous litter. They did not even make good pets as they were too frightened all the time. Luckily it was a small litter, of only three pups, and they stayed with their breeder for the rest of their lives.

Once I have chosen my puppy, usually at about four weeks old, I give the breeder a number of items. First, a tiny soft cat collar, so that the pup can get used to wearing it round his neck. A piece of blanket that he can sleep on, so that he has something of his own to smell when brought to a new and daunting place. The blanket will be far from spotless, but it will help him to settle and can be removed as soon as he has his own scent on his new bedding. I also give the pup one of my old gloves so that he is used to my scent before he comes home with me.

I contact the vet to find out about his injections, which will protect him from the major killing diseases in dogs, which include parvovirus and distemper, as well as leptospirosis, which is carried by rats.

The cost of these will vary from practice to practice. Town practices with high rates and overheads usually are forced to charge more than rural practices. There are set fees in each practice for such things as inoculations, boosters, and neutering.

The time at which the injections are given can vary, according to your veterinary surgeon. Some give it very young; others won't give it until around twelve weeks, as some people think it possible that the mother's immunity may cover the pups up to this age and prevent inoculations working properly.

Most vets recommend that the pup is isolated from other dogs until it has had the second in~ection, a fortnight after the first. I keep mine off the ground, but carry them about to meet people, dogs, traffic and other things that they are going to encounter when taken out and about. The isolated puppy may well become shy during this period even if well socialised before being sold.

The Guide Dogs for the Blind say that an anti social dog is worse than a dead puppy, and advise their puppy walkers to take the pups out and about from six weeks on. My last pup came to dog classes at her breeder's from the age of eight weeks, in my arms, and saw all kinds of things before she was inoculated. She is quite the most sociable dog I have ever owned.

My first trip is always to the vet the day after I bring the pup home, to have him examined and make sure there is nothing I ought to know about.

WORMING

He will need worming, as this takes several weeks to clear. All puppies are born with worms, which lie dormant in the mother until she is mated. They should not be sold with a large infestation but some are. Your vet will give you a worming programme, to ensure the pup is cleared. They will need several treatments, even if the breeder had already started the sequence.

He may re-infect from other dogs. Fleas carry tapeworms so that it is necessary to keep him free from those. Birds also carry tapeworms, and he may eat grass which has been fouled, so that worming becomes a regular part of his life's routine.

It is very important to clear them as they are a health risk, but a dog that is wormed regularly never poses problems. A great deal of press coverage on the immense risks of blindness from Toxicara appears now and then, but as always they exaggerate for sensationalism.

I have never met any breeder or vet or dog owner who has suffered from this and I have met thousands of owners at dog classes and dog shows over a great many years. Children should be taught to wash their hands always after handling the puppy. Impulse buys may well have fleas or lice.

Vets recommend worming every six months unless there are children in the house, in which case they recommend repeating the process every four months. Worming powders from the vet can be added to their food, and are not noticed. Modern treatments have no ill effects. Worming agents from the pet shops may not be so reliable, and some may be harmful. There are reliable makes, but again ask your vet which can be trusted.

The main worm in the dog is the roundworm, but they can also have tapeworms, which appear in the excreta as ricelike objects. The same treatment works for both, but hookworms, which can come from land where pigs have roamed, or from a place where another dog with hookworms has lain, need a different treatment.

There are also worms which infect sheep and are supposed not to live in dogs, but if worms are suspected, and all the others have been cleared, it is worth having a fecal sample inspected. One of my past dogs had sheepworms living in her, which the vet had never known happen before. But it did and she had to have a special worming agent to clear them. Our footpaths run through sheepfields.

FLEAS

The worst part of these horrible creatures is that they don't breed on the dog, they jump off and breed in the soft furnishings and carpets, so that a home may become infested unless one is absolutely dedicated to ensuring dogs are free. They only climb on to the dog to feed, which they do by sucking blood. Some dogs become allergic to flea bites and have serious skin troubles as a result.

There are all sorts of easy ways of dealing with them. I spray mine routinely every fortnight, after she has been in contact with a lot of other dogs, and if we have had hedgehogs around, as they are covered in them.

If there is a major infestation of household furnishings, fumigation is necessary and the local council will help with this. It is not always possible to avoid fleas, so no shame need be felt if you are unlucky.

I spray my dogs regularly to ensure that any are killed. Re-spraying is needed as unfortunately the wretched creatures lay eggs which hatch and cause another cycle of infestation.

Many dogs hate sprays, but they can be accustomed to them by letting them hear air fresheners used. If there are cats in the house, fleas can be a hazard as they roam and bring them back and they also then infect the dog, so cats must be kept clean too.

Flea collars are obtainable which are very effective though they worry me if they are left on for long periods as they give out a gas which kills the fleas and I always wonder if it might affect the dogs. I use them short term, but not long term.

It is essential to have a reliable make; like most other things there are some on the market that are very little use and others that may cause allergic problems because of the chemicals used. Vets usually know which are the best and the safest, as they see the animals that have been affected by the wrong types.

There are now various methods of having complete freedom for periods of a month or more, by using a special type of flea control which the vets provide.

Many of those used for adult dogs aren't suitable for puppies, so do ask your vet before using any of them. I avoid those sold in pet shops for the same reason, as they may not be right for puppies either.

For bad cases, there are special shampoos.

Careful owners rarely find fleas on their dogs. I have only had them twice in twenty five years of teaching, among club dogs. Once we had a regular Thursday flea, and everyone complained they were taking them home. My dog also suffered and so, once, did I.

I managed to detect the culprit, and brought a flea spray which everyone used on their dogs as part of the lesson to make the dog stand still while being sprayed. This cured the problem without identifying the dog which was causing it to everyone.

They can usually be detected when grooming the dog and show up particularly on white animals. They are more difficult to see on the darker colours. They can jump an amazing distance so are far from easy to catch.

A dog with a major itching problem is a very unhappy dog.

HARVEST MITES

These can affect many rural dogs at harvest time, especially if they are exercised in long grass. These horrid little creatures are also known as jiggers.

They burrow under the skin and feed on blood. They can be seen as little red spots which blister and then scab. The place where they have penetrated is exceptionally itchy and the dog will scratch endlessly and may make itself very sore.

Washing the affected area with a solution of half TCP and half water seems to clear them: the area is dabbed with cotton wool soaked in the liquid. Again, if that fails, veterinary advice is needed as the dog is abominably uncomfortable.

TICKS

These are horrible creatures which may be picked up by our dogs from sheep or deer, mostly. They have a beaked head which digs into the skin and an oval body which bloats as they suck the victim's blood.

It is very easy, when trying to remove them, to take away the body and leave the head behind. This may cause an abscess, and if this does happen it is advisable to go to the vet and have him remove the head completely.

Rather than pull them off, they can be smothered, by covering them with salt, or with TCP on cotton wool, or paraffin, or even whisky, if nothing else is available. Some people remove them by touching with the tip of a lighted cigarette, but you have to be careful not to burn the dog.

Constant infection can lower the dog's state of health as blood is being drained off.

It is also essential to get rid of the tick, not just drop it on the ground, as it may not be completely dead and could re-attach to any passing animal. It should be burned.They are small enough to burn in an ashtray.

OTHER POSSIBLE PROBLEMS

My first pedigree puppy, bought twenty five years ago, when I knew very little about dog breeding, went to the vet on my way home from the kennels where he had been born. He had tonsillitis, ear ulcers, which caused his deafness, a tail that had been broken in two places and never set. He had appalling hips, and was never able to run fast, and he couldn't digest meat. This gave immense problems for two years until we found out that he had a pancreas disorder.

I was told, when I bought him, that he was twelve weeks old, but a very mature puppy. I took him to dog class for the first time when he was, I thought, six months old, and discovered he was the same size as the year old pups. The date on his pedigree was incorrect. I now suspect he had been taken back to the breeder because of his tummy problems, which were severe, and I was his second owner.

I was advised to take him back. My heart ruled my head, He was a charming little animal and I couldn't bear to give him back to someone who had so neglected him.

My vet rang the breeder to suggest the price was reduced and was told I had owned him for six weeks and all his problems were my fault. He knew this was untrue as he had been paying house visits to my dying cat for some days, but there was nothing we could do without more aggravation than either of us wished.

I now ask all kinds of questions, but it needed a vet to show me all that was wrong with him. It would not have occurred to me to look down his throat or into his ears. The vet was sure he would die, and offered to put him out of his pain. This was not an option for me. We very quickly become fond of the tiny animal we have just bought and unscrupulous breeders rely on this.

He had health problems, due to that pancreas trouble, all his life, but of all the dogs I have ever owned, he was the one who found living an absolute delight when he was well. Possibly because he knew what it felt like not to be well. He was so full of joy that he gave us immense pleasure for nearly fourteen years and though he died many years ago, we have never forgotten him.

PUPPY NEEDS

What does your puppy require? His own space is important. There is no need for an expensive bed at first. He will only chew it. A strong cardboard box that he can get in and out of, lined with a warm rug or blanket, is ideal. It is best if it is in a safe corner where people won't fall over it, and it needs to be out of draughts. The smaller and cosier it is the better, as he has been used to sleeping cuddled up against a mass of warm little bodies and his mother. The first nights alone can be frightening.

Many people put the box beside their bed at first, and remove it later when he is used to the house. I have a camp bed downstairs and sleep in that for the pup's first week. He is then in the room in which he will sleep later, and seems to settle happily after a few nights, when I do leave him, as he is now used to the room and aware that we all wake up and keep him company next morning.

A ticking clock or a radio turned low can help. I don't use a hot water bottle; that can be chewed and may harm him. This does not apply to stone or aluminium but the pup could well chew the wrapping and burn himself.

Puppies can do surprising things with their bedding. One of mine tore it regularly until she was two and then stopped overnight and has never done so since. Another only tore it when he was left alone in the car while I shopped. He was a rescue and he felt unsafe. Destructiveness is often an anxiety reaction. I found I could stop it by giving him one of my old jerseys to lie on.

It is necessary to think about the site of his bed. One extremely lethargic puppy that came to club proved to have his bed placed in between the Aga, which was on summer and winter, and the electric cooker. I suggested they moved his bed to the hall and put it under the stairs away from the heat. Within days they had a normal lively puppy.

The pup needs an easily cleaned feeding bowl. I find stainless steel better than china as dogs can push them around vigorously while eating. I have had two broken by being slammed into the wall by an over enthusiastic dog while eating. A bowl is also necessary for clean water so that the dog can drink whenever he feels the need.

My last pup was a remarkably messy drinker when she was small, either splashing with her paws or lapping so vigorously that she flooded the floor, so I found a large cat litter box useful. If the bowl is in that the splashing is confined. They usually learn to be tidier as they mature and manage better.

Some breeders will identify pups by putting on different coloured collars, as many of them are sold before they are ready to go home. This ensures that you get the right puppy. It is a useful habit as then by the time the puppy comes home he is used to wearing it. If you do as I do and offer a cat collar, then a pup that would not be so identified will soon ignore its presence.

I never put my dog's names on their tags. That gives a handle for a thief. That is another reason for a pup never being left alone outside. They are very easy to steal, and take away and sell 100 miles away. It only takes a second to lift one from a garden.

A number of dogs are stolen countrywide. Thieves often target bitches for their breeding capacity, and take pups because they are easier to steal than adults. With easy travel by car, it is simple enough for a crook to be a hundred miles away in three hours and to sell the pup in a pub for as much as he can get. My dog is tattooed on her ear, with a number given her by the National Tattoo Register, and this is an additional safeguard.

The dogs can have microchips inserted, but there is controversy over this as there is some evidence that these travel through the body. Also there may be areas which do not have the necessary equipment to scan the dog and detect that is micro chipped.

The pup needs a lead. Some people get a length of chain with a handle, but this is very hard on the hands. The pup can be easily taught not to chew his lead. He should start with a very light one, but heavier equipment is needed with the larger dogs as they grow. It is surprising how much pulling power a dog the size of a Springer Spaniel can have.

At first everything he wears needs to be light in weight, but the big guarding breeds need police dog type collars and leads when full grown.

TOYS

Toys are easily made at home. A toilet roll inside a sock will provide good games; or a ball in a sock, as balls can be chewed and small ones may be swallowed. Golf balls are lethal for any dog, as, if chewed, the dog reaches an endless string of very peculiar stuff which if swallowed, can do immense harm.

Thick climbing rope can be tied in a knot and used as tug toy.

There are a great many toys on the market. Most dogs enjoy kongs and balls on a rope, which are safer than an ordinary ball.

Sticks are best avoided, though many dogs adore them. Our next door neighbour, some years ago, threw one for his dog, which stuck in the ground. The dog ran on to it. It pierced his soft palate and he bled to death before they could reach a vet. Others I have known have had their cheeks pierced as they turned their heads to try and catch and one was blinded.

Small balls, if thrown, may be swallowed as the dog tries to catch them and they slip down his throat, because he has not gripped them with his teeth. Dogs move so much faster than we realise, and have no built in sense of self preservation.

Pups need watching as they chew their toys and those made of rubber or plastic can cause problems if pieces are swallowed. Squeaky toys can be a nuisance and if chewed the squeak may be swallowed. Squeaky toys also bring out the killing instinct as that is the sort of noise a dying animal makes.

Dogs addicted to squeaky toys may well develop a very undesirable game. Usually the squeak breaks without being eaten, and the toy is then safe, as long as not chewed up.

One of my dogs chewed a baby's rubber duck and swallowed the pieces. We had a great deal of trouble as a result as they did not pass through her.

It is useful to have training sessions with the puppy, with family property on the floor as well as his. Every time he picks up something of yours he is called and given his own property. Dogs taught properly learn very fast what they may or may not touch. Food can also be put down to teach them not to steal.

This can be done. One class member has a three year old daughter, and the dog has been taught that even if a sandwich or biscuit is left on the floor or a chair or table, he must never touch it. Although he lives in a hotel they make very sure nobody is ever given the opportunity to offer him human food.

He has learned from eight weeks old that this is forbidden and now will lie with food on the floor beside him which the little girl has dropped, and not even attempt to lick it. It is a matter of making firm rules and ensuring that everyone obeys them. When I first met him this had already been trained into him and he was only seven months old.

If there are people staying who may think it funny to try and tempt the dog, his owners make sure he is never left alone with anyone who won't co-operate.

It is necessary to sit on the floor with the pup when playing this game and keep the area small, so that you deal quickly with anything he may not have.

My training area will contain my purse, books, letters, gloves, shoes, slippers, saucers of food and anything else in common household use, as well as his toys.

I praise him lavishly when he picks up one of his own toys, and call him to me if he has something of mine. I don't shout at him as that will startle him and make him run off and may drop it or chew it in panic. This paid dividends with one dog taught this way. He picked up a full milk bottle and, called to his owner, brought it safely. Had he dropped it he could well have cut himself very badly.

A bitch who developed the habit of jumping into the hen run and stealing eggs was taught to bring them back to the house and hand them over to her owner. She could carry an egg a hundred yards without either dropping it or breaking it, and constituted herself as family egg collector.

I don't give my pups shoes or slippers as playthings, as they can't distinguish between the old one you were about to throw away and your brand new handmade shoes that cost a fortune.

I don't leave the toys around all day either, as apart from anything else, the dogs become bored and you have nothing with which to reward them when you want to play with them. The kong is my present dog's favourite toy. She has been taught to take it out of its storage place for our game and then when that is finished to put it away again. Now she does that without being told. She is very proud of herself as a result.

If your pup is a chewer do inspect all toys that friends give as not all on the market are safe, any more than all childrens' toys are safe. If you have children it is essential to teach the dog the difference between its own toys and theirs, or life will be very expensive and unhappy.

I watch that paint does not come off. I am wary of paint as it can have harmful constituents. One of my bitches suffered from lead poisoning before she came home, due to the white paint on her kennel wall. No one realised that lead paint was still available.

A lonely puppy can be comforted with a large sterilised marrow bone from the pet shop, filled with tiny cat biscuits or dog treats, scaled at each end with cream cheese. He will spend hours trying to get the goodies out of it.

INTRODUCING THE PUP TO OTHER ANIMALS IN THE FAMILY

It is best, with a new pup, to introduce it to the other animals in the family in the same way as with the rescued dog.

If there are older dogs it is very necessary to make sure that their routine is not interrupted so that they go without play periods and walks because of the puppy's needs. If puppy is taken out and they are left at home, they will resent it and may hurt it if they get the chance.

Bitches often adopt a new puppy as if it were their own, but not all do so. One of my dogs appeared, all his life, to be afraid of pups, possibly because he had a very sensitive skin and they chewed him if they had the chance. He never harmed one, but he always warned them off with a very threatening growl. Once I knew that I kept him away from them as I did not want new pups to learn that old dogs were unpleasant.

Most older dogs accept new pups in time, but one recent pupil of mine became so depressed and so protective of her owners with the new puppy, which she kept away from them, that they took it back to the breeder. They hope to try again when this one is older, as she is young herself, but she may prove not to wish to share her home.

It often takes time for the newcomer to be accepted by other animals in the house. They usually come round in the end, but I never expect any animal to welcome my new acquisition without reservations and am very careful indeed when introducing them. When I introduced my difficult pup, the older dogs took nearly a year to accept her, mainly because she tormented them if I did not stop her. The last survivor of my four most recent dogs would not tolerate puppies, and though she met my new acquisition, I did not bring the little one home, as she would have been attacked and I knew that very well. I kept her with her breeder until the old dog died. I walked her and took her to classes almost daily for some months, as the old dog was unable to go far.

She came home the day the old one went and slipped into her new role so easily it was hard to believe I had not had her in the home from puppyhood. She was then seven months old, but knew me very well.

FIRST DAYS.

Your new puppy is a baby, around eight weeks old. If he is too young he may turn anti-social with other dogs as he hasn't had enough mothering, and has left the litter before he learned dog language.

Too old, and he will never be entirely yours as he will have formed a pack allegiance with the dogs he has lived with. He will always want to play with other dogs rather than come when you call him, unless you do a great deal of work to

63

make sure you are far more interesting than anyone else or any other dog, to him.

If he is brought into a house with one or more older dogs, he may bond to them and not his owner, so again it is necessary to try and make sure this doesn't happen. A dog that is always with other dogs in a household pack may well lack all confidence if he ever has to be taken out on his own. So he needs plenty of contact with the family, rather than with the other dogs, and to have play periods, by himself, with the humans in the home, as well as being taken out and about on his own.

BUYING TWO LITTER MATES

On the call line, among the queries I have come to dread, are those from people who have bought two litter mates, thinking they will be company for one another. In a great many cases, at about ten months old, the two begin to fight. These fights can be so serious that one of the dogs has to be re-homed, which always causes unhappiness.

It is much better to buy one puppy and then, when he is about a year old, to get another, preferably from a different place. If the first is a dog, it is better to have a bitch and vice versa. It is possible to have several bitches or several dogs without trouble. I know of households where there are three or more of one sex, but they are all with experienced owners, not first time buyers.

EARLY TRAINING

It is not fair to start off with a puppy, fail to teach him anything, find at eight months he is a much detested hooligan and give him away, dump him, or sell him. I well remember one owner who arrived in class with an eighteen month old Rottweiler.

I looked at her in dismay as the dog careered into the room and set upon another dog.

'I never knew it would be like this,' she said, almost in tears.

She had only had him a week. He had been free to a good home and it was easy to see why. She had taken him on police advice after a burglary. It took a year of private and class lessons before he was anything approaching a sensible dog, as he had so many faults through having been left to his own devices for so long. Within two years he was everything a dog should be, but it was very hard work.

Dogs may learn all kinds of strange things in their first home. One would only drink from a dripping tap. On questioning the owners it was discovered nobody had ever put water down for him. The only way he could get it was to jump in the bath and take it when he could.

Another used to leap up and break light bulbs wherever he could reach them, as in reading lamps. The new owners discovered that in his previous home the children had tormented him with torches, flashing them constantly in his eyes and trying to persuade him to catch the beams. He was determined to get rid of any light source before it could be shone at him.

That is not a good idea.

HOUSEHOLD RULES

The puppy you buy, if he is to prove sensible, has to be treated sensibly from the start. Silly pups turn into silly dogs, and if they are spoiled, babied and fussed, they turn into remarkably silly adults and can be a great nuisance to everyone who meets them. Also they cause a great deal of unnecessary work.

If your puppy is taught not to jump on the furniture and not to leap at you, there is no need for constant washing of household fabrics and your clothes because he had muddy paws. Even puppy claws can cause an amazing increase of expenditure on tights. All he needs to be taught to avoid this is to sit when told, so that he sits in front of you instead of leaping up, and to come when called and sit again, so that if you see him trying to climb on the settee you can discourage him at once.

My dog is allowed on certain chairs, but only when her rug is on them. She will come and ask me to put it there for her, as our floors are remarkably draughty. That is fine in the summer, and she appreciates it then, but it is not pleasant on a cold windy day.

You can't teach the dog anything in one or two attempts. The commands have to be repeated and rewarded at least thirty times a day, for several weeks before they even begin to sink in. Pups, like small children, have short memories.

When he comes to you, he gets rewarded with a cuddle and words of praise, an enthusiastic 'Good dog! Clever dog!' as well as a tiny piece of food. Titbits, carefully given, when he does right, teach him far faster than any amount of yelling 'NO'! When my pup is small treats are reserved for rewarding good behaviour.

Once the pup has learned that, then they can be given at other times, if you want, but it must always earn them by obeying a command first, even if it is just told to sit and does so.

I don't give human chocolates as the theobromine in them is poisonous to dogs in quantity. I use tiny dog treats or liver cake. The recipe for that is at the back of this book. It is guaranteed to excite almost any dog.

Doggy chocolate drops are fine in winter; in summer they melt, as does cheese, so titbits need to be chosen carefully. Some of the dogs that come for training are rewarded with small slices of garlic sausage and one worked her heart out for pieces of cooked black pudding. The dog must really want the reward, or it has no effect.

Tiny puppies jump up. They want petting and cuddling and attention and to lick your face, because that is how they greeted their mother. If the puppy is taught, from the very first, to sit instead of jumping up, you have taught him one of the most important lessons he will ever learn. Every single time he does try and jump up, just put him quietly into a sitting position and then kneel down and pet him.

He soon learns provided it is done every single time without fail.

I say 'OFF' when a dog jumps on me. If dogs come to class that have heard the word DOWN constantly for 'DON'T JUMP UP' then they have to have another word for lie down; and we use 'FLAT'. Again it is essential for all family members to use the same word, or the dog is confused.

Often a dog that won't come has been taught by different members of the family.

Mum says 'Come'; Dad says 'Here'; Junior just uses the dog's name when he wants him. The result is the dog doesn't go to anyone as he has no idea what they really want. Everyone seems to assume the dog knows without being taught.

It is amazingly easy to confuse our poor puppy. That odd look you see in a dog's eyes when given some command is rarely rebellion. It's 'Help. What DO you mean?' It is as difficult for him as it would be for us if we were suddenly flown to China, with only Chinese speaking companions and taken to a place where no-one spoke our tongue at all. Sit, but we haven't understood the word, so we do nothing. We aren't being naughty or disobedient; we are very confused. We have to be shown what is meant. I am very aware of this as I live among Welsh speakers, and am often unable to understand a word of what is being said. I know just how dogs feel!

'O.K. I'd like to do as you ask but please make it clear to me as I can't do it unless you explain properly.'

BONDING WITH OUR PUPPY.

Someone once wrote, 'if your dog wont come when called, you don't have a dog.' We have to be so important to our dogs that they prefer our company to anything else in the world, and certainly to all those dogs romping on the beach when we want to go home.

Dogs do not bond automatically. They do not give their affection automatically and sometimes outside events can prevent the right relationship between owner and dog.

The little pup that was so charming and seemed so loving turns into a monster, and nobody knows how or why. There is always a reason. Dogs are telepathic. It is all very well after hours of calling him to remember that when he comes he must be greeted as if he had come first time.

You smile (after a fashion) and say 'Come. Good little dog.' But your eyes and tension are saying 'you little monster. I hate you.' So he is, not very surprisingly, very reluctant to come. We can't hide our feelings from our dogs. They knew very well whether we really are pleased or only putting on an act.

So, if a training session is causing frustration, the best thing to do is forget it. Have a game, and make friends with the dog again, and try next day. I don't try to teach my dog if I am feeling ill, or am frantically busy, or have major problems through a family member being very ill indeed. We have to concentrate if we expect the dog to concentrate too and forget everything else while teaching. I play with her instead, which relaxes both of us.

Often people ring or come to class or courses and say 'I don't know what's wrong with him. He's suddenly changed.'

On questioning them you discover that a partner, or another dog in the family, has recently died, or they are nursing someone who is terminally ill, or looking after a family member with Alzheimer's.

All the things that affect us, including a new baby, divorce, death, moving house, will affect the dog as well as the family. Once everyone has settled down again the dog will revert to his former happy self.

A child growing up and going away from home can upset the dog. We can't communicate with them and tell them what is about to happen, or has happened.

A DEATH IN THE FAMILY

It is very sad when our dogs have to go, but the end is easy for them; it is over so soon that they have no idea what is happening and when a dog has come to the end of his life, or is suffering extreme pain which can't be cured, then it is kinder to say goodbye. There is no pain, and they simply go to sleep. We suffer; they don't.

If someone dies in the family, at home, or a dog or cat is put to sleep, it is better to let the survivors see the dead dog or person. I have always done this, except with the haemophiliac dog. They sniff the body and recognise that he has gone. They may grieve for a day or two, but do not suffer as much as the bitch I had who survived her companion.

As my poor dog was bleeding from the mouth and the nose I rushed him over to the vet who had to put him to sleep at the surgery to save further suffering. There was no way of stopping the bleeding. Usually my dogs are put to sleep at home, and always in my arms. He did die in my arms but his companion only knew that I took him out and did not bring him back. I left her at home, as the situation could have upset her had I taken her too.

She searched the car, the house and the garden for days, looking for him, unable to understand why he had suddenly vanished. I should have taken her with me and let her see him after his death. She had seen the other dogs and cats when they died and would have known what had happened.

It was almost a year before she began to play again. Those who had seen their dead companions recovered within a week. In the same way they will grieve for a dead owner, but not fret waiting for them to come home.

The saddest creature I ever saw was a bitch who had given birth. The pups were unwanted and removed at once and put to sleep, away from her, by the vet. She spent days searching everywhere in the house and in the garden, crying for them. She would not have hunted like that if she had seen them after they were dead, though she would still have grieved.

If there is a big litter and a pup or two dies, the bitch does not seem to worry. One of mine had eight puppies, of which two were very undersized. One was enormous. She refused to have anything to do with the two tiny animals and every time they were put back with her, she very firmly put them outside the whelping box again.

Finally she was so irritated by the persistence of these people who thought she should rear them that she managed to pull up a floorboard in the kennel and dropped them both down into the hole. At that point they were removed, but in spite of care both died within the next few hours. Meanwhile she busied herself very happily with the survivors.

We know now that management of the dog in the home is as important as training, if not more so. Once we have a very good relationship with the dog, he will be eager to please and very easy to teach.

It is usually wise to take the dog to training classes, but the wrong kind of class can do far more harm than good. A good class is quiet, the dogs progress, there is no barking, no shouting,and everyone is relaxed and happy. All dogs are leashed all the time, unless working under instruction for an advanced exercise. There are not many dogs on the floor at a time. If I have more than ten people, I split the class and have two separate lessons.

There is no free for all off lead when the class is over, or before it begins, as this may produce fights, which will do a great deal of harm. Previously placid dogs may well become aggressive; the aggressive ones do not become placid; they get worse as they are being rewarded by their success in scaring other dogs.

Sadly just one encounter can so affect a dog that it attacks every dog it meets afterwards on sight. One very nice little collie, set on three times by other dogs, is now so aggressive that her owner can never take her to class, to shows, or to places where she meets other dogs. It is vital to avoid a fight, and her owner is well aware that if her little bitch, in her turn, attacks a previously safe dog, another fighter will be produced.

In any class, a ten minute session with five dogs is worth far more than an hour's session with thirty. Classes where handlers walk endlessly round and round the hall, supposedly doing 'heelwork' for an hour or more are teaching nothing.

It is no use going to class and expecting that that one lesson once a week will produce a sensible dog. It wont. Work has to be done on the dog all the time, to check his bad behaviour and replace it with good behaviour.

With daily practice, the dog soon becomes biddable, but without it, there is no change in him at all. Those who come each week get on fast; those who come occasionally do not progress unless they are practising what they are taught at home.

Many people come full of enthusiasm and have one lesson. When they realise that no one is going to wave a magic wand and produce a well trained dog in an hour, they never come back. Often they ring up a year later with a major problem that is very hard to cure and could have been prevented had they persisted.

Sadly, the dog does not learn as fast as that. Nor do we.

Did you have one lesson and then drive from Manchester to London on the motorway alone next day? Yet that is what many people expect of their poor dogs.

A bad dog class can do an immense amount of damage. One of my owners came to class with Hardy, a dog that had been attacked on his first six evenings at another dog class, and had been taken by the instructor and jerked off his feet. He bit the instructor (not very surprisingly) and was expelled.

Our meeting was horrific, but he was muzzled. He tried to attack me and every dog there at first. He was a large powerful dog, just a year old.

His owner was tearful, having been told she had caused the dog to have a bad temperament. He had been an adorable puppy but had changed overnight after that first evening in the dog class.

A trusting little animal that had met only kindness had suddenly been plunged into an enormous room filled with large dogs, with people who weren't careful to see that their animals did not scare the puppy, but allowed them to attack him, and then to crown it all he met a person who took him and treated him abominably.

This method of controlling a dog, by a jerk, was in use everywhere until a few years ago. I used it myself twenty years ago, and still do if it is necessary, though I use it correctly and would never jerk a dog off its feet. I only use it on the type of dog that is able to benefit by such treatment, as it is not a method I like. It is not taught now. There are far better methods of getting a dog to walk quietly at heel that do not stress him.

It is also very difficult indeed to teach first time owners, and if applied wrongly does far more harm than good, as dogs have been injured. One dog that came recently from a class that does still teach such methods had no fur round his neck and the beginning of a sore area. The constant jerking, that did not work as it was done wrongly, had worn away the fur and the hard chain had begun to wear away the skin.

Slip chains are not used today either for normal dogs. There may be exceptional circumstances which indicate their use, but owners must be very thoroughly trained or the dog will suffer. Private lessons are best for this.

When Hardy first came he was unsafe with people and dogs and his owner was scared of an accident. The result was that he went out on a lead that was held tightly, keeping him close to her, and was not allowed contact with either people or animals. This made him feel that they weren't safe, and he was being restrained because he would be hurt, so he grew worse.

This in turn meant that he was never praised, even when he did right. That was ignored. If he did wrong he was constantly scolded and shouted at, which made him even more uneasy and less able to learn. I don't learn from people who yell at me or belittle me. I need encouragement, and so do dogs.

It was not surprising that he trusted neither human nor canines that he met. We muzzled him for twelve weeks. By then he had learned that nobody was going to hurt him, that I was not going to take him from his owner and jerk him off his paws, and that the other dogs were not going to harm him.

I told his owner that his behaviour was most certainly not her fault, but due to the poorly controlled environment of her first dog class, which helped her confidence, and made her determined to cure him. He had lots of games, which relaxed him, and she was told to praise him and tell him he was a good dog every single time he did anything she liked him doing.

By the twelfth lesson he was relaxed with other dogs and did not shy away from people and he was unmuzzled. A few weeks later, I greeted him by stroking him, as I do every dog in the class. I suddenly thought 'I couldn't have done that six months ago.'

I had a card from his owner that Christmas which said 'Thank you for your help with my dog. I hated him. He's wonderful now.' He was never nasty; merely very frightened, having met the wrong kind of dogs and people when he was only a few months old.

As a result of his changed behaviour, the relationship between the two deteriorated and the owner/dog bond weakened. It is so easy to turn a nice pup into a nasty one by wrong treatment. I would never go back if my dog were attacked by another dog when I had gone to learn. I would also spend the next few weeks looking for nice dogs so that he learned that not all are villains.

There can be an odd accident, often due to new and careless owners, but constant fighting is not part of any good dog training class. It shows lack of knowledge and control on the part of the instructors. I know only too well what can result as four of my dogs were spoiled in this way, each of them by just one unhappy incident. They were all attacked by off lead dogs in the park. The classes I went to were well run, and nothing like that happened there.

Though I did manage to convince my dogs that they did not need to attack every dog we met, it took more than a year of daily carefully controlled encounters to do so, not just a few days.

Before risking your puppy go by yourself and watch what goes on. Is there progress? Do people appear to enjoy the class? Is there sufficient explanation or is everyone left baffled? I do not like being told 'Do this because I say so.' I want to know just why I should. Do people pay attention or keep talking while being taught? Are the dogs quiet and sensible or does it appear as if a riot is going on?

Any one can set up a dog class and there are different reasons for doing so. In some areas the clubs are run by breeders who help train the dogs they have produced, which is sensible, especially with the guarding breeds.

There may be a few people who compete and want a hall to train in, so they start classes. The pet owners, who make up the bulk of the classes, then pay for the venue, which the few who compete could not afford. This can be a benefit, if those who run the classes teach well and give value, but it can be a form of con. Pet owners have a brief lesson and then the hall is reserved for the top people to practice what they failed in last week at the show.

They can be run by someone who sees it as a good way of making easy money.

The best classes are run by people passionate about dogs who are anxious to ensure that as many people as possible know how to teach them, and to avoid having dogs in the community that will make the anti dog factions worse.

PUPPY CLASSES

Puppy classes, run correctly, are a good idea. Those where pups are off lead playing together constantly are not, as all the puppy learns is that every time he sees another dog, he can go and play. That is the quickest way to have a dog that never comes when he is called.

They need to be very well managed, or big pups will bully smaller pups; a dominant puppy in a group can be a major headache as he will upset all the other dogs and may well alarm them, especially if he is of a big breed and the rest are smaller.

70

Some puppy classes are a recipe for disaster.

I have run puppy classes, and still do if I have enough pups, but they rarely all appear at the same time. I find that to introduce the puppy carefully into a group of pleasant part trained older dogs does quite as much good, and the puppy learns quickly that when he is there, it is to learn and not to play with other dogs.

He does parts of the lesson, walks among the other dogs, meets them, is greeted by other owners, but does not do the full lesson. Merely being there, watching the older dogs, is good for his confidence. No pups are ever in a class where there are difficult older dogs.

One of the most useful parts of the lesson is to lead two pups, or a puppy and an older dog, towards each other, and then, after an initial greeting the two owners separate, calling to their pups, making a big fuss and having a little game, to ensure that the owner is always more interesting than anything else the pup may meet. It is essential to know every dog in the class extremely well as only the well behaved can do this.

Owners meet, shake hands, and have a short conversation, the dogs being encouraged to sit quietly and not jump up or fuss.

Dogs pass one another, being encouraged to look at their owners and not at the other dog, to ensure that when out walking in the street it is possible to meet and pass other dogs without a puppy bounding to greet a dog that may not wish to be treated like that, or attacking the other dog, or trying to bolt in fear of it.

It is useful to introduce objects into class for people to carry; like shopping bags or holdalls, or a cardboard box. Dogs seeing something new for the first time can panic. Often we meet a dog that barks at any one carrying something of an unusual shape.

The pups need too to meet people wearing hats; or carrying unfurled umbrellas. And to be shown what happens when an umbrella is opened, as one meeting this for the first time may be scared and bolt. The dog sees a mushroom on legs and may not be able to see the person under the deep shadow.

It is useful to teach them in a car park, at a bus station, or near a railway station; or somewhere where a lot of people may come, such as a tourist attraction car park. Just walking round such a place is actually training, though most people might not realise this.

EARLY DAYS

All dogs benefit from being taught the moment they enter a new home, even if straight from the nest. The breeders I know well have already begun that training. The pups are taught to empty on paper away from their beds. When it is feeding time the breeder calls 'puppies, puppies, puppies' and they come running, learning to come when called.

People who study animal behaviour have learned in the last few years that the dog's brain is _fully mature at twenty two weeks old_. All he lacks is experience.

All he learns in these first few weeks is with him for life. What comes after is harder for him. If he has learned that he may play the fool, growl and be laughed at, bite and not be reprimanded, and riot as much as he chooses, chasing the children and the cat, then no amount of re-training in future months will make him reliable.

One class member once rang me and asked when her dog would learn a sense of proportion! Dogs don't. They understand that they may never do a certain action, or that they must always do it. They never learn that sometimes they may and sometimes they may not.

Teaching dogs is made more difficult because, like some of us, they have a gambler's instinct. Nine times out of ten they are stopped from chasing another animal; the tenth time the owner can't be bothered, or doesn't notice. That is the time they remember. Just as the punter forgets all the times he lost at the races, but remembers the time he won.

Teaching is a step by step process, which needs to be taken very slowly. Many people see an older dog doing something and try to make their pup do it. Unless he is taught properly, he never will. Most dogs need at least twenty lessons before they even begin to show signs of understanding, yet many people come once or twice, then drop out and are convinced they have exceptionally awkward dogs. They don't. They simply haven't bothered to do the necessary work to get a good dog.

HELPING OUR DOGS BECOME ADULT

Many people complain that the dog they own behaves sensibly with them but not with other family members. On enquiry I always find that those who cause the dog to riot greet it with as much enthusiasm as it greets them. It is extremely selfish, if the dog is being trained to behave, for others for their own gratification to spoil all that teaching by encouraging the dog in its baby behaviour.

The person who announces the dog is spoiled rotten because she loves it to bits makes my heart sink, as that is the dog with problems brought on by wrong handling.

The dog, like the child, needs to have its behaviour monitored and limits set. The dog is not allowed to pester us to pet it, to feed it, to play with it. It has to learn that it waits until we choose to play, or pet, or feed, or take it out. Otherwise we have the family that says 'we can't do so and so, because of the dog. It wouldn't like it.'

It is very flattering indeed to be met as if you were the only person on earth that the dog loves. However, dogs that are greeted wildly think that this is the way they should behave and they never learn to be sensible. Fine at eight weeks. Lethal at eight months.

It is fun to be met by a wild little puppy full of the desire to lick you, leap at your face, and generally make his presence known. It is not nearly such fun to be thumped on the chest or in the stomach by eighty pounds of full grown powerful dog, still intent on licking your face and generally smashing up everything around him as he riots. Especially if he is wet or muddy has just rolled in the pig field.

By this time even those who formerly enjoyed this behaviour are usually tired of it, and the dog is met with yells of 'Down', 'Get off, you beast,' and the owner is desperately asking the experts how to stop him from behaving in the way he, quite unconsciously, has been taught.

Maybe no one meant to, but as far as the dog is concerned, this is what he has been trained to do. Our dogs are trained whether we train them or not. If we don't they train themselves and what they then do may be entirely unacceptable in a civilised household.

Pups need to be taught from the day they come home that people will only greet them if they are sitting quietly, waiting for attention. Sit the pup, kneel down and cuddle him. Stroke his chest, not his head and shoulders and make sure he enjoys your presence.

If he won't sit, then ignore him. Pretend you haven't seen him. If he is still at the house training stage, simply pick him up without saying anything, put on his lead and take him outside. The only words he hears now are those that praise him for relieving himself.

The minute he starts rioting to greet you, he is again ignored. If you have had great scenes when you came home, then stop them. Walk in, pretend you haven't seen the dog, remove your hat and coat and hang them up, go into the kitchen and put on the kettle, Sit down at the table and read the paper.

Pack leaders ignore the lower pack members until they choose to greet them. If you respond when your dog chooses to greet you, you are indicating to him that he is your boss, and not vice versa.

When the dog has calmed down, then call him and greet him, but sensibly. When he is behaving like a whirling dervish he is completely out of control, and nothing you can say or do will go into his silly head. Out of control dogs can be dangerous. If we want them to be sensible we ourselves must also be sensible.

Anyone who has taught dogs and their owners for any period of time can watch a dog for ten minutes and tell you exactly what sort of home he comes from, and whether anyone has ever made any effort to prevent him being a baby all his life.

Dogs have come to me at four years old that have never had a day's training and been extremely silly. So silly that their owners have given them away in despair, unable to bear the hassle any more.

Two of these, within six months, were fully trained working security dogs and are now wonderful sensible animals, enjoying life as never before, being adult and useful.

Others, only companion dogs, have been taught all kinds of things no one had bothered to teach them before. They behave like children who have grown up longing to learn but never been taught anything worthwhile. They learn so fast and are so thrilled with their new skills. They become wonderful companions as a result.

Unfortunately those who take them on do have to put in far more work than they would have done had they owned the dog from puppyhood. They are well repaid.

It is much more satisfying to have a dog that waits with wagging tail to be greeted and then may develop some self controlled method of his own of showing his pleasure.

One of mine used to move across the floor like a seal, back legs crouched, making little moaning noises as she came to greet me. Troy sits and waits for me, looking up at me, with an expression on her face that tells me she is thrilled to bits that I am here, but wont indulge in puppy antics to say so as she is now a grown sensible dog.

If we are going out to play, which is extremely exciting, she dances in circles on the spot, but never jumps at me.

The Golden Retrievers I know come to greet me with toys in their mouths and wiggle their bodies and groan with delight, but none of them jump up. Their restrained greetings are just as rewarding and far less dangerous, as a large dog leaping at you may knock you backwards and if you fall and hit your head the result can be concussion or a fractured skull.

In the same way when dogs are ill, it is better to be comforting, do all that is necessary and be there with the dog, but not to baby him or keep telling him what a poor fellow he is and cuddling and overwhelming him with sympathy. Utter misery on our part will affect him and may hinder healing.

Dogs pick up very quickly on our feelings and if we make illness a time for enormous fusses, they may well act ill to get their reward. Children may find staying in bed being ill more rewarding than being well as it is then they get fussed.

They can then use illness as a weapon to get their own way and with some people this persists all through their lives. We have all heard of the woman who has a 'heart attack' every time her daughter mentions leaving her to marry; dogs can behave in exactly the same way.

We have far more influence on our dogs' behaviour by our moods and attitudes than we ever realise. Those that are allowed to mature learn to communicate with us, and if we watch carefully, we know what they are trying to say.

The majority of dogs will ask, in their own way, to be let out, if they need to relieve themselves. Many will knock their water bowls if they are thirsty and if no one has remembered to fill them. They will eye the refrigerator or their biscuit container, or the bread bin, or the cupboard where the food is kept.

One dog, that liked to be in bed by ten thirty, used, if visitors overstayed their welcome, to go upstairs, fetch his mistress's nightdress and bring it down and put it pointedly on the mat. Go home. It's bedtime!

5
THE FIRST YEAR

THE CRITICAL PERIODS.

There are a number of these. They are short weeks of the dog's life in which anything that happens to him has more effect than at any other time. The first three all occur within the first twelve weeks of the puppy's life, which is why it is so very important to make sure we know just how he is being reared by his breeder.

The first period, of his first three weeks, will set the foundation for his future health. Inadequate mothering and feeding at this time can set the puppy back considerably.

The second crucial time is from four weeks to seven weeks, which he spends learning to play, to interact with his litter mates and his mother, and may learn to play fight. Also important at this stage is the way the humans he meets treat him, as the wrong kind of treatment ensures a very unhappy and awkward puppy who does not know how to interact with nice people. Leaving too early deprives him of vital learning experiences.

He wont be friendly if he has been mis-treated as he has learned that people are pretty horrible. The pup that comes from a really good kennels has learned that humans are fun and bring pleasure, such as food and strokes and cuddles and kind voices.

It is at this stage too that the pups sort themselves out into the bossy types and those that are easier in temperament and more biddable. A good mother will prevent the most bossy from thinking he can rule everyone including her; a bad mother allows the dominance to develop, so that by the time the pup is sold, he has won every battle, and thinks he can beat humans as well as dogs and will do his best to do so.

How he does so varies. Few, fortunately, do so by fight and bite, but many do it by wile and guile and we may not even realise that we are being very cleverly manipulated by our dogs. Many owners are unaware that the dog is training them rather than vice versa.

Those appealing eyes can soften even the hardest heart, but we do have to be firm and make sure that we rule the home, not the dog. If we don't take over the pack leader role, the dog will, sensing a gap. He takes the best chair, eats before everyone else, rushes through doors first, and the human who lets him is saying, without knowing it, 'OK, you're the boss. Carry on.'

So that the third of these very sensitive stages, when the pup comes home, and until it is twelve weeks old, can set the pattern for life. This is when we show our puppy that jumping up is not acceptable; it is very appealing when he is tiny, but not when he is a full grown Wolfhound or Mastiff. Even a tiny puppy scrabbling at your legs can easily ruin a pair of tights.

He learns that we go through doors before dogs; we have the best chairs, and sleep in the best beds, and eat the nicest food and also eat before he does. I hear, much too often, some owner say, 'I know we've spoiled him, but you can't help it, can you,' as they present themselves in class with the dog that the neighbours regard as the pooch from Hell.

Research, much of it done by those who rear and train Guide Dogs for the Blind, has proved that the best time to teach puppies about the world and to begin their training is from five weeks to twelve weeks old.

This applies to all breeds, and all breeds can be trained to a high standard if the owner chooses. For some reason, in the UK, the collie pre-dominates in Obedience competitions, as everyone seems to assume that it is the most trainable. The result is that competition has evolved to suit the collie, and it does not lend itself to other breeds winning.

Yet overseas, there are Obedience Champions in many different breeds, and the collie is rarely seen in competition. It is a pity it has gone that way here, as so many other breeds could do very well indeed. Some do have breed only competitions, but on the whole the value of training is not appreciated by dog owners in the UK. In some countries, those who buy dogs are forced, by law, to go to classes until the dog has reached an acceptable standard.

If we play tennis we use the same equipment, technique and scoring as the top players at Wimbledon. There's no other way to play. We can get a lot of fun playing at park standard with our friends without any need to aspire to being a champion player. Our dog gets as much fun from his training and his wonderful time alone with you, as does a high flyer with his skills. But it's still the same game.

Most people don't want to compete. They say, in a baffled manner, that they don't want to learn the routine ring exercises, but to learn how to control their dogs. The problem is that dogs can only learn limited actions, and the competitions, when they began, were simply to see who had the most control over their animals.

Perhaps sadly, they have changed, as so much else has changed in the world of sport, so that higher and higher standards are demanded. The result is that many ambitious people are asking of their dogs far more than they can perform, which is where the constant effort to get a winner starts, with the resultant re-homing of many poor dogs whose only fault is that they weren't born with the ability to out perform every other dog.

In those early days, the dog was asked to sit smartly at heel, not because if he did not he would lose points, but because a dog that sits where he chooses is not under full control, but only partial control. The owner is letting him decide on the rules, and that means the dog is on his way to becoming pack leader.

The dog that refuses to walk at heel and pulls or lags, is also deciding who runs this household; and it isn't his owner. If he is persistent, and many dogs are, then the modern head collars will enable the owner to regain control and once this happens the dog will be easier to teach and there will be a happier relationship.

The ringwork consists of everyday needs taken to a much higher standard. But we need—Keep beside me on the lead and off the lead; come as soon as I call you. Fetch your ball or toy so that we can have a game. Stay when you are told; I want you to sit still while I do up my shoelace, or take off my jacket as I am too hot. Or I want to talk to my friend, who also has a dog. I expect you both to sit still and be sensible, not to pester, however long we may choose to chat.

All these little things enable us to live much easier lives with our animals. Stay in the car till you are told; if you jump out you might be run over. Don't get into the car yet; I put the eggs I just bought on the seat and need to move them.

The Kennel Club, in recent years, has realised that competition has changed to such an extent that the needs of the average owner are not met. Dogs can now take a Kennel Club test, for which they are awarded a certificate and a rosette. These tests are realistic and all dogs could reach that standard if the owners only tried.

In Working Trials the dog is taught to search for lost objects. On one of my courses we were based at a pub where there was a steep drop at the edge of the car park and no fence. One poor man forgot, and slid down the slope in the dark on the way to his car. He lost his car keys. It was a very dark night.

There was no problem. His dog had been trained to search and come as soon as he found what he was looking for. It took him two minutes to find the lost keys. My dogs have found no end of dropped gloves for me, as I often do manage to lose one I am carrying on a walk.

The dog is also taught to follow footsteps, and find something at the end of the trail they laid. This is wonderful if your toddler wanders off at a picnic. No need to call for the police as Bruno can easily find him.

There is no need whatever to go on and compete. If my dog can find a lost child I don't care in the least if she can't beat my friend's dog because she lost a few marks in a competition.

Recently I met the daughter of someone who owned a little crossbred and came to class for a few weeks. They farm and she found it very difficult to come to the lessons so stopped, but unfortunately also failed to realise that the training needs to be kept up, even if it is only insisting the dog sits before going out, before being fed, before coming out of the car. I was told the dog is naughtier than she was before.

It really is a case of use it or lose it. I learned French and German at school, which was many years ago. I cannot follow a conversation in either on the radio now, as I did not continue to practice.

We often expect too much of our dogs. They should come every single time they are called, people say. They may come in normal circumstances nine times out of ten, if they have been well trained. Try calling a dog that has decided to chase a cat or a rabbit.

Dreadful! Is it? How many humans know that if they drink too much they are going to suffer next day, and it may, in the end, if they do it to excess, kill them? Yet they continue.

How many of us start, with all the will in the world, to diet, because we are overweight. And then think, oh the hell with it, and have a cream cake or a bar of chocolate?

How many of us stay up too late, or get up too late, or yell at the kids when we have vowed not to? I'm no paragon. I am allergic to chocolate but recently succumbed as I love it, and bought a chocolate bar and ate it. I suffered extreme misery for the next two days. Which served me right as I know enough to understand that I will pay for my sins.

So how can I blame my dog for not being perfect?

Our dogs don't know what we want of them and never can. They learn by experience what pleases us, but they never know why it does. They may learn by bitter experience that certain actions bring instant retribution, but if we can't make our feelings felt while they are actually killing that chicken or chasing that rabbit we can forget it.

Get hold of the dog with the chicken in its mouth and shake it very hard (one of the few cases where I would do such a thing) and it will know at once that you are angry with what it is doing <u>now</u>. There is very little we can do when it has gone off on a wild chase after another animal, other than to make sure it is on lead and can't do it again in such a place. Don't ever shake a strange dog.

It can't be repeated too often that if he comes back and is punished in those circumstances it convinces our dog he is being told off in a horrible way for wanting to be with us. So why bother? I don't want to go home to people who greet me with yells and hits.

Training makes for much better balanced and happier dogs, as it gives them a role in life. Far too many have short walks, and long periods of doing nothing whatever, while owners are busy. Yet training sessions only need to be of ten minutes, and it should be possible to fit four periods like this into the busiest life. It makes so much difference to our dogs. A half hour spent training will tire the dog far more than a walk.

Time spent with our pup from seven to twelve weeks will prove a bonus for the rest of its life. This is when it should attach: and also discover humans are more fun than other dogs, so that we have complete control, even in a park crowded with other animals.

The pup that is kept isolated from people and other animals until it is sixteen weeks old does not make a good companion. We have to work very hard to make it understand that other people and other dogs belong the world.

EARLY TRAINING

This is best done without any outside distractions at all. Other dogs, or cats, or family members, will make the pup want to go and play with them, or interact with them, so the rule for those first days is puppy and owner and no-one else at all in a place where they are not likely to be interrupted.

Few dogs <u>learn</u> in class. Classes are for the dogs to mix with other dogs, and learn to behave with hem, to meet people other than their owners, to visit new places. Classes are to teach the owners how to teach their dogs, and this needs to be done at home, at first alone with the dog.

As he learns, then he needs to be taught somewhere where there may be a few interruptions. This is when classes become valuable if they are quiet and well run. The dog now practices what he learned at home in a safe environment,with some controlled distractions, at first perhaps one dog walking while all the others practice staying still.

In the past few years I have had over twenty dogs come to me because they had been to other classes where they learned that all dogs do in a group is bark and lunge at one another and try to fight. This is not what training is about, nor is it about playing with other dogs and never settling to work.

If the dogs interact with one another...Smokey wants to play with Timmy...then they will learn nothing. Besides Smokey may want to play but Timmy may want to fight and hurt. All that will teach Smokey is how to fight back, as unless he is a very peculiar dog he is not going to stand still and be attacked by someone else's nasty animal.

Dogs learn by association.

"This is what I do at home: this is what I do in class: this is not what I do in the house next door, or when visiting someone new, as nobody has taught me to do that here. On the other hand when I see a group of dogs together, we always do attack one another, so let's do it in the new class too". They have now been programmed to think that when a number of dogs meet, what they do is lunge and bark and try to fight.

In well run classes they have to learn that people are thoughtful, sensible and kind, and other dogs do not do that, nor must they. Noisy classes are stressful for dogs, owners and the instructors as well. So much more can be taught in a happy peaceful atmosphere. Halls need to be roomy, or to have very few dogs, as dogs too close to one another feel uneasy as do many people in a crowd.

Out of doors there is space and an uneasy dog can easily be asked to work at a considerable distance from the others until he settles down. Once they discover there is no barking from other dogs and no other dog has a go at them they settle, as a rule, surprisingly fast.

If they have been in noisy classes for a long period, it is much more difficult, but it does come in the end. I only had one failure in recent years and that was a Jack Russell, but I suspect his owners did not practice quietening him at home.

Unless we practice the dog's skills in all sorts of places, he is as lost in a new place as we would be if we learned to drive in a disused aerodrome, and never went on to a public road until we had been driving for a year. We would be petrified by the speeding vehicles, and the need to find our way. Yet many dogs are expected to go to shows and win when they have never been anywhere but home and dog club and walks in the park.

A dog can be taught to stay for ten minutes with the owner out of sight in class, and at home. Take him to a show and he will not stay, as he has not learned that he does that anywhere but in those two places. He has to be taken out and about. A dog may stay for ten minutes on the beach at Margate, but if taken to Bournemouth he won't stay there. Everything is different. It is necessary to go back to the early days of teaching the stay and show him that he does it there too.

It takes a great deal of repetition to ensure he understands, and repetition when out with him, not only at home or in class. If he is taught to sit just once a day he won't learn it or remember it.

He must be taught it thirty times a day at least, broken up into several sessions, and also be taught to sit when his food is prepared, when meeting people, when greeting people, at the kerb when crossing the road, and at any other time when it is useful to have a quiet dog under control and not a jumping nuisance pawing at you to get on and walk him, instead of talking to the friend you haven't seen for six months and have just met. Life is easier for both dog and owner if full advantage is taken of this very young stage, and the dog is taught the basic commands and to come every time he is called. We can teach him at any age, but it is never so easy again as in those first six weeks in our home, when he is not yet fourteen weeks old.

ADOLESCENCE

There is another period when the dogs alter in behaviour and this is when they are adolescent. Those who live with dogs all their lives often refer to this as the hooligan stage. It occurs in young humans too, and is extremely tiresome. It is far easier to manage if the dog has had its initial training and learned to obey commands, though this is a stage at which the dog not only decides to try and run free, and does so whenever given the chance, but also the stage at which it becomes 'deaf', and we can call until the cows come home and even afterwards, but come, no. Not till he chooses.

Some people feel that the initial time spent training has been wasted and has failed, but in fact, it is there, and once we begin to have a dog that co operates again, we find that he is very biddable indeed.

I have lost count of the number of biddable pups that came to class that began to be far less biddable at ages between six and twelve months. Some pass through this period without much difficulty, just as some human children seem to weather adolescence without causing the family too much grief.

Others may become defiant, just as human adolescents may wear extraordinary clothes, adopt very bizarre habits, and do their best to test those around them to the maximum of their tolerance. Fortunately the vast majority do mature and become reasonable human beings.

The same thing happens with dogs. They may become extra naughty; they may refuse to obey any command; they become distracted. A bitch just before her season is often extremely silly, and seems to have become a different character. A dog, if he can smell an in season bitch, becomes deaf to everyone.

The age from ten months to two years is the age at which many dogs land in rescue, or are re-homed. Work through this period and we are rewarded beyond anything we expected.

One class member, some years ago, took a dog whose owners gave up on him. She persisted and by the time he was two he was wonderful, and was top of all the class tests. She met the previous owners one day who said if they had known how he was going to turn out they would not have re-homed him, and actually tried to sue her to get the dog back.

They lost the case. Fortunately the judge was aware that with them, the dog would never have matured into such a good dog as they would never have put the time into him that he was given by his new owner.

Both dogs and bitches are capable of breeding by somewhere around seven months, but to allow them to do so will affect their future development. A bitch is not mentally mature enough to have pups then, and she will not develop as well as she should, as much of her strength, which should have gone on growing a good body and good bone, is drained away by the developing puppies.

Most professional breeders wait until the third season, when the bitch is nearly two years old. The dog's strength would also be drained if he stood at stud at this early age.

Both bitches and dogs do their best to escape at this stage; the bitch to find a mate and the dog to find a bitch. We have to be very vigilant. They go through what is known as the Flight Period, and again any thought of coming back when called can be forgotten. They will come back when it suits them, not you.

This is the stage at which time spent calling them on lead, and rewarding them for coming, is time well spent. Forget free running. Let them off and they will effectively learn you cant catch them and they can do as they please. This is usually the time at which people ring up and say 'he won't come when I call him, ever'. What he has learned is not to come when called, as he has got away with it.

Trouble comes because people do forget, or lose control of themselves, punishing him when he does come. That won't do any good either, as he thinks he has been shouted at or even smacked for coming to you; his time is now, and what he did a minute ago is gone from his memory.

Your action, in his mind, said that he has done the wrong thing in coming. So he won't, as you obviously don't want him. This is the start of a very unhappy relationship. This needs to be remembered, all the time, as dogs learn the wrong things fast and one unhappy event is enough to spoil all our previous training.

There are times when it is very difficult indeed. Long ago I was walking the two dogs I had then in the park. They were both very young and I had only just begun training with them. I was with a friend who had two much older dogs, both very well trained.

A young dog ran through a dog flap in a fence, and began to chase them. The older dogs lay down on command. Mine turned and chased him and went after him through the dog flap. There was the most wonderful garden, which three playing dogs soon spoiled completely.

An irate owner yelled at me. I would not have had a dog flap there, but it was no use saying so. Eventually my dogs came to me, with the other dog's owner still ranting. I had to pretend to punish them, but they had come back and were now greeting me. In the circumstances I could hardly say 'good dogs'. I was dismayed and unhappy but did not feel it was entirely the fault of my two dogs. Pretending to be very angry was the worst thing I could do.

I went home and knew what would happen. Come when called? Not they. They wouldn't be such fools as I had scolded them angrily and pretended to shake them.

It was three weeks before my dogs trusted me enough to come happily again. I spent time each day calling them for really wonderful food rewards, to get over the impression that had been caused by behaviour they could not understand. They didn't know it was wrong to chase the dog through the garden, or that the owner had spent hours working in it to produce a wonderful display.

I felt very bad about their action; irritated to think someone would put a dog flap in such a place, and dismayed by the need to work so hard with my own two dogs to overcome their new fear of me.

At the time, both were under two years old, and in the middle of the hooligan period. Since then, even in the park, I have kept my dogs leashed, as you never know whether other dogs about are safe to meet, and if one person has put a dogflap in the garden wall to allow the dog free access to the park, others might.

Some years later, one of my dogs, on lead, was cannoned into by a dog running free, without any owner visible. She screamed, and when I looked at her, she had a great lump bitten out of her side.

I rushed her to the vet and discovered that was the fourth victim he had had that month. He described the dog. It was the same, and that was the last time I visited that park with my dogs. It wasn't a bite; he had taken a chunk out of her, and it happened unbelievably fast. He was away before she even had time to bark at him.

Adolescence is the stage at which we have to be very firm, (not harsh) with the dog, and insist they do as they are told. They need to be leashed at all times when out, and for a few months it is better not to let them free, or they take off. That then becomes a habit, and our dog running free is going to learn some skills we would hate to have him develop, such as the behaviour exhibited that I have just described.

We have taken on a responsibility and it is up to us to ensure that we do not become the kind of owner who does own the dog that everyone else hates.

Sometimes a dog changes character completely when it begins to mature. I once had two German Shepherd litter mates in class. The dog, when they first came, was outgoing and happy with everyone; the bitch was very timid, and hung back. They did not live together, or even near one another and only met in the lesson.

By the time they were a year old the dog had become far less pushy and was apt to worry in new situations, while the bitch became extremely outgoing with everyone. It was difficult to see why from talking to the owners, as both lived in houses on an estate, both dogs went out and about, and both homes had frequent visitors.

It is easier to understand a character change with a rescued dog that has become afraid of people and been ill treated. Within a couple of years the majority settle into wonderful animals, full of confidence and able to accept people without fear.

So much of what we do and how we behave does affect our dogs. The dog that lives with a rowdy city family is a very different animal to one living with a single elderly person in an isolated home. Were the two to exchange homes, they would also change in behaviour.

Unruly families have unruly dogs. Dogs that are spoiled and babied never grow up. Families where there is discipline and consideration for others have well behaved dogs.

THE DEVELOPMENT OF FEAR

A puppy of about four to five weeks old begins to learn about fear, which is necessary or there would be many suicides through ignored dangers. He startles at sudden loud new noises, but if they are repeated and have done him no harm, he accepts them.

Show him a new object, such as a ball, or the toy helicopter I use in puppy testing, the majority of pups are very cautious and may back off, sit and consider, or approach very cautiously, to sniff.

They watch their mother and if she reacts adversely, so will they. This is a protection, as if she sees a snake and reacts to it with terror, they learn at once that they too must be on their guard as snakes may mean death to them.

Some pups seem not to know fear. In the wild, these would probably soon fall victim to some predator, due to their lack of awareness of danger and desire to explore. These pups are a headache to own, as they also seem to have little awareness of pain.

One of mine was so eager to get into a friend's garden that she raced down a flight of stone steps, across the lawn and ran headlong into a tree, almost knocking herself out. She did it three times. After that she had to be taken out on the lead and then let free, as she appeared incapable of realising what it was that was hurting her.

She dug under a fence in her desire to explore, and was caught by her collar and hung there. Luckily I saw her...she had only been tied up for a few minutes while I worked with an older dog...and was able to rescue her.

At eight weeks old she climbed on to the back of the driver's seat of my car while I was in a shop. I came out to find her, fortunately, stuck half way through the window, as she had been determined to escape. A few more minutes and she would have been under a passing vehicle. After that she had to have a crate in the car, as she moved so fast that it was impossible to hold her.

Car windows are a hazard. One owner recently left her pup in her Range Rover with the window ajar and the pup's head through it.

'She'll jump out,' I said.

'She won't. The window's too stiff.'

We went down to the house to get a book that the owner wanted to read. We came back to meet the pup, who had jumped out of the window, having been far stronger than her owner realised. It was lucky she had done it there, in an enclosed safe place and not while they were driving along as she was allowed to put her head out of the window. I don't like that either as I have had windows broken by chippings flung up by another car passing. A dog could be blinded.

This pup, like that one of mine, has an unseen problem, in that she is not sensitive to pain, which seems to go along with a lack of fear. Possibly fear is first induced by pain, and the fear of the animal that caused that pain.

If you press between the dog's pads with thumb and finger, the dog that is sensitive to pain will hardly be able to bear the touch; the normal dog will stand it for a few moments and then pull his paw away; the dog that is pain insensitive will allow you to exert maximum pressure and still apparently be unaware of any feeling whatever.

I could press as hard as I could and that dog still did not draw her paw away. My Golden Retriever hated his feet being touched at all, and he was very sensitive indeed to pain. Others are normal in that they allow some pressure and then withdraw the paw as soon as it becomes uncomfortable, which is with some pressure but not a lot.

Whenever my insensitive pup was ill, as when she had a deep ear abscess, the point at which she showed distress, according to my vet, was the point at which other dogs would be unable to bear the pain.

An hour after coming out of the anaesthetic when she was spayed, she jumped on to the table to bark at next door's cat through the window. I had been told she would not want to move much for a couple of days!

This type of dog is often adventurous, lacks all caution and keeps its owner very alert, having to work out possible dangers that would not exist for other dogs as they would have the sense not to approach whatever it was that threatened them. She had to be cured of chasing bullocks. My other dogs ran from them.

Few dogs are, at first, aware of danger unless they have been hurt. A puppy in a domestic environment has hazards that he cannot have known before he was sold. A dog that has never been run over will race in front of a car. A dog that has never been burned may go far too close to a fire.

A dog is never afraid of sticks until he has been hit hard by one. After that he may be afraid of any stick of any size, especially if he has been beaten in his first homes.

My dog with a badly broken tail had a phobia about milk floats and if we saw one we took off, at speed. My vet suspected that he had been run over by one before I got him, and that was the cause of the tail damage. He remained terrified of electric vehicles for the whole of his life.

Another pup was caught by the shade of a standard lamp. The owner stood up and caught the shade with his shoulder. It flew across the room and covered the nine week old puppy who was terrified. That pup never ever went into any room with a standard lamp in it for the rest of his life, and the standard lamp had to be removed before he would come into the room again.

There are certain periods in a dog's life in which he is far more sensitive to fear than at any other time, and some quite small incident at this time can be traumatic, and remain a problem. It may be apparently cured, but if the dog is under stress and the same thing recurs, then he may go to pieces.

Eight to ten weeks is one of these times, so that it is best to bring the pup home at around seven to seven and a half weeks to let him settle before he suddenly finds common objects alarming.

Pups under about eighteen months old that are attacked by other dogs are far more likely to be badly affected than dogs over two years old who have learned that the vast majority of other dogs are friendly and this is not a normal event. If our dog is allowed to fight, because dogs do, there is something very wrong. Well behaved well controlled dogs don't fight one another.

The start of this period can be very obvious. One of my pups jumped out of the car gaily till she was sixteen weeks old, being so fast that she was out before I could stop her. At sixteen weeks she ran to the edge of the drop to the ground, looked at it, shot back into the car and refused to move. I lifted a shaking puppy.

Somehow, she had suddenly appreciated there was this big drop. I made her get out, kindly but very firmly. Had I been very sympathetic and petted her, she would have thought I approved of her terror, and would have continued to behave like that, sure it was what I wanted. Instead I just said, 'Oh, come on. Nothing to be afraid of,' and put her down on the ground. We battled for three days, as not only would she not get out of the car, she would not get in.

I put the two older dogs in the car and started the engine. That did it. She wasn't going to be left at home, and she jumped in. When we returned, she jumped out after the older dogs. I left the hatchback open and sat in the car, listening to the radio. Presently a small body leaped in and she licked the back of my neck. She jumped in and out several times, as if testing to see what happened, and then trotted off. We had no further trouble.

Two days later, walking in our lane, we met our neighbour on his bicycle. We saw him every day. She stopped, trembled and refused to approach, then threw a fit of hysterics. She was always a dramatic dog, and it was quite a sight.

It seemed absolutely idiotic, but somehow she had become aware of it. It wasn't a car, it apparently wasn't even the thing she had seen daily for the past few weeks. It had changed overnight.

He, having dogs of his own, laughed and said,' Got to that stage have we? Come and sniff it. It's just the same bike as yesterday.' Gradually she relaxed, and once she overcame her fear enough to smell his hand, she inspected the bike, and decided it was, after all, not a fearsome object.

She became afraid of things she had seen daily without bother for the past few weeks. There were cows in a field on the lane; they reduced her to a state of total demoralisation, yet she had happily rubbed noses with one through the gate only the day before. So we walked past the field several times a day and practised sitstays looking at cows.

I thought I could relax, but then she saw horses and panicked all over again. So we practised stays and heeling in a paddock with two mares and a stallion looking over the stable doors. The two older dogs didn't think much of this period at all, as mostly they had to sit in the car and watch while puppy was slowly convinced that these creatures would not hurt her.

I thought we were over the hump when I took them for a walk beside a lake, and she had hysterics when she saw a <u>duck</u>. She was the only dog I have ever had who behaved like a prima donna in a rage when she was upset, though one I had,threw tantrums at the vet, trying to rush out of the waiting room or surgery.

Chita when upsdet danced; backed out of her collar, pulled away, and, most devastating of all, she screamed. It was the oddest noise, not a bark nor a whine. She was apt to do it at home, especially when the telephone rang. It indicated that as far as she was concerned something was very wrong in her world. It upset us, and it upset the other dogs and the cats who all got as far away from her as possible.

I felt somewhat of a fool marching up and down beside the lake day after day until she decided ducks were just part of the world too and she need not dance and scream in fright every time she saw one. I kept her thinking about doing as she was told, with a little bit of heeling, sitting and staying, and not about these monsters who she was convinced threatened her.

That stage lasted about four weeks and ended as suddenly as it had come. On the last day a helicopter flew over, another fairly frequent occurrence. She bolted into the house and hid, and when I reached her, she was trembling.

The next day, not twenty four hours later, she was in the garden when it flew over and she sat and looked up at it. 'Oh is that all it is?' From that time on, she met everything normal with equanimity.

I was always very matter of fact with her. Don't be silly, it's only a...and made her face up to her fears. Had I babied her and taken a lot of notice of them, she would probably have gone on behaving like that as she would have been sure I approved. As it was I made it plain I thought she was making a fuss about nothing.

As we live in the country she was always meeting sheep and goats, chickens and ducks, horses and cattle, and life would have been impossible had I not been able to take her among them as there would have been nowhere to walk her.

All my other dogs have exhibited some degree of fear suddenly at around this time, but none has been as bad as that, though I have met others since who have behaved in the same way. Many dogs exhibit a fear of children, often through having been teased by them when at an impressionable age.

Dogs remember for ever and act as they think you wish them to act. Our old Airedale cut his paw when he was six months old and felt very sorry for himself. Everyone sympathised. For the rest of his life we only had to say 'Poor boy. How's your paw?' and even if he was playing, he'd stop, look mournful and limp across the room on three legs! There was nothing wrong with his paw by then at all, but he had felt rewarded by our attention and was trying to recapture that feeling.

The puppy that is attacked by another dog in this stage of its life will remember for ever, whereas a few weeks earlier, or later, it would not have such a disastrous effect.

Chita, my dramatic pup, at sixteen weeks, was bitten very badly by the village tearaway, a nine to five dog who was the bane of everyone's life. His owner said proudly he was a rogue, wasn't he and he had bitten every dog he met. The dog was well hated.

The bite festered and she needed several injections, Cleaning her face was painful, another occasion for dramatic behaviour, and the result was that she refused to come out of our gate at any time unless in the car. She lay down and took root.

I got over her fear of other dogs by putting her between the two older dogs whenever we went out, using two coupling chains, so that she was attached to each of them. This did work, and for some weeks I had to make sure she was well protected by the big Golden Retriever and my older German Shepherd.

She had then to be re-educated to walk alone, so that I took the dogs to new places, where she had not met nasty animals, and walked her by herself there, while the others remained in the car. By starting with short sessions and lengthening them gradually, her confidence did come back, until by the time she was four she happily came to Working Trials and behaved very well.

That bad attack (it scared me, never mind her, as the dog was very aggressive indeed) at a very sensitive stage affected her for the rest of her life. It was aggravated when at about eight months old I took her on a course where there around a hundred dogs. The course instructor liked them all off lead, and since I was a novice then, I let her free.

I would not dream of doing so now in such circumstances, but one tends to think that those who give courses are very knowledgeable. This is not always so. She was chased three times round the field by a large grey bitch, and only saved from hurtling into the road under a car by a flying tackle from a very experienced kennel maid.

She was so afraid of other dogs after that that she tried to attack them; her idea being 'I'll kill you before you kill me.' Even when she was safe with other dogs on the lead, she was not safe off the lead, and I had to be watchful when other dogs were present, which does not make for a relaxed owner.

I am not exaggerating her behaviour. I went for help to the man who instructed the North Wales police dog handlers. It was three years before he would allow his young children to go anywhere near her if we met, even if she was on the lead.

She could happily sit and stay with other dogs in the showring without any problem, but if they were running free, and one came too near or barked at her, then she was liable to have a go. Once I knew that, she did not get the opportunity.

A farmer neighbour commented that she was very like a bitch he had once had who he could rely on to let him down when it really mattered.

He had judged her rightly, but I realised by the end of her life that the problem was not that she was defying me. She excelled in everything but the stays. She was both nervous and very anxious and her only security was when I was close to her, or in sight.

Out of sight stays were impossible for her; she was brilliant at everything else, but once I had gone, her world collapsed and she had to find me. She was further marred for ever by a bad fight beside her in a competition stay when I was not there to help her.

This was over ten years ago. I had never met a dog like her before, though I have met several nearly as bad since, due to inherited nervousness from their breeding. She behaved so oddly in many ways that I was worried lest I was doing something wrong until I met her niece and nephew who were quite incredible. I hope I never meet any dog like either again.

I had them in class for a year. Both were re-homed, the dog at a year old and the bitch when she was about seven when the owner couldn't stand her any more. She spent most of her life locked in a yard. The dog only survived a few more months in his second home, which was with someone very knowledgeable.

Both were much less intelligent than Chita.

The dog was very dangerous indeed, with a desire to kill other dogs, and the bitch screamed with terror when people approached her. She then flooded the floor. These were exceptional, though at that time, about twenty years ago, there were many like that to some degree due to their breeding.

The bitch exhibited an undue degree of fear. The dog was dangerous because he was totally fearless; he would not accept any form of discipline. He was excessively dominant and intended to remain boss, no matter where he was or who he was with.

All dogs have fear periods, but they rarely demonstrate it so thoroughly as Chita. Recently a friend with a young Boxer pup, that is also somewhat nervous, met one of those people all dog owners loathe, with two off lead dogs that attacked the youngster. This happened twice on separate occasions some months apart. That little bitch has been so badly affected that she has become impossible to take anywhere where there are other dogs, as she attacks at once, because she is afraid of them.

Her owner is responsible, is thinking of others and taking good care to ensure her dog does not make others aggressive; those who know their dogs may attack others and still let them run free with other dogs around are most irresponsible. While fear is developing at this stage, the puppy is also at the stage in which teaching has the most effect. It begins with Guide Dog puppies at six weeks. Every pup at this stage is excited by its new skills and is very keen to learn. It is wonderful to teach a pup as tiny as this to sit and see his happy excited face and furiously wagging tail as you praise him.

If the bond is established as soon as the pup comes home, he will prefer people to dogs for the rest of his life and be much easier to control. The dog that prefers dogs runs off to play or fight with them whenever he is let free, and becomes totally 'deaf' to all calling. This seldom makes for a happy relationship, as it tends to produce very irritated owners.

TEACHING THE PUP TO BE SENSIBLE

The lessons start as soon as the puppy comes home.

'Toby, sit.' This is done with a titbit in the hand, the hand near the pup's face, going back over his head, enticing him to look at the food. He overbalances into a sit and is told what a splendid puppy he is.

Families do have to agree that everyone treats the dog in the same way. It is unkind if the pup is allowed on a chair when father is out of the house and banned when he comes home. The pup, scolded, may appear to look very guilty, It is in fact confused and frightened.

If I am sitting innocently in a chair in my sitting room and a lunatic breaks in, brandishing a knife, I am not going to look calm and collected. I am going to look very alarmed indeed, and that might be interpreted as guilt by someone who hadn't realised what was happening.

The puppy that has eaten half the rug is not aware that that was wrong. It is aware that you are very angry, and shows its fear. It is not reacting because it knows what it has done, but because you are radiating palpable fury, generating a very alarming atmosphere indeed. It is terrified, not guilty. That has nothing to do with the rug. It is you that is causing his problem. He associates his punishment with your return, not with the rug.

HOUSETRAINING.

In the same way, he has made a puddle. Nobody has noticed it for hours, and then, quite suddenly, someone discovers it. The puppy may be asleep. He may be playing happily. Then this noisy giant appears, yelling dirty pup, at him. He hasn't a clue what is wrong, but boy, is he scared.

More dogs are ruined in those first few days because they are expected to know by telepathy what the owners want, than at any other time in their lives.

The new puppy needs to go out after every meal, and also as soon as he wakes. Playing will trigger puddles in excitement, so play out of doors. Housetraining will take for ever if you go out to work and leave the pup on its own. It will also take a long time for it to understand if you push it into the garden expecting it to know what it is there for.

Suppose we are kidnapped by aliens and taken in a space ship to another planet. We have no knowledge at all of their language. They have a ritual that, whenever they go into a room, they bow seven times to the picture of their Leader on the wall. We don't, so we get hit. It is going to take most of us a very long time to realise that this was because we didn't perform the seven bows, which to us, is a ridiculous and meaningless exercise.

Up to now our pup has been able to empty whenever he felt like it on newspaper or the kennel floor. He is very tiny and has little control over his functions. If he were a baby he'd be in nappies. At eight weeks he is the equivalent of a year old child, who we certainly don't expect to be in full control of its bladder and bowels..

The quickest house trained pup I ever met belonged to a family with three children under five. She was clean by day within a week and by night within four weeks.

'How did you train her?' I asked. Most mothers with so many tiny children are extremely busy and easily distracted.

'I set my timer for every hour. And every hour I said, ' Come on kids, puppy needs to go outside' and we all went with her. Whenever she did what she should we all told her what a clever puppy she was and she thought it great fun. By the fifth day she was trotting to the door to take us all out and show us how clever she was.'

The pup learned fast because everyone was so pleased with her. It was, as far as she was concerned, a wonderful sort of game. She learned fast because they went outside with her. They didn't thrust her out on her own into a big cold frightening garden, all by herself, and expect her to know by magic why she was there.

A pup treated in this way sits in misery wondering what it has done to be punished by being evicted from the warm friendly house. It does nothing. But it is desperate and as soon as it is called back into the warm, because nobody knows whether it has performed or not, it lets go and floods the floor or worse. It is then punished.

It soon gets the idea.

Which is not, 'I mustn't do that there.' It is, 'I must never do that anywhere at all. It's wrong and I'll be walloped.' It is very small and those hard hands hurt. So the pup learns to dislike the owner, not to love him or her. There are people who, whenever the dog does wrong, hit it on the nose. Its nose is the most sensitive part of the body, with dozens of very fragile bones inside and this can do great harm, as well as being unnecessary and a sign that you cant train a dog at all.

Even worse are those who have been told by some idiot to rub the pup's nose in the mess it made. All that does is teach it you are a singularly nasty person with extraordinary ideas. You might just as well teach a baby to be clean by rubbing its face in its nappy.

Now the poor pup is very confused, sure that emptying itself anywhere is a crime, and it will be punished by being hit and screamed at. Since its ears are so sensitive it can hear many sounds inaudible to us, this shouting is likely to make it so alarmed it becomes totally incapable of learning. The pup, since you make an unpleasant noise, decides to do so as well, and may snarl back or bark and growl at you.

It is saying, 'I don't like that. Stop it!' The relationship becomes even worse.

If the pup is constantly scolded at the wrong time (the only right time is when it is in mid flow) in desperation, it does its best to do what it thinks you want and holds on until it literally bursts; that may be anywhere at any time, provoking yet more anger.

The result is a thoroughly miserable bewildered mite who cant understand what these horrible humans are on about, and may also have some damage to its inside through trying so hard not to go at all.

We can't expect immediate success. Some gain control much earlier than others. It is some weeks before the puppy has full control of its bladder and bowels by day and even later by night.

Our happy confident well bred puppy is already changing into a dog that people begin not to want. At this stage some families get rid of it, but never say why. Others banish it to a shed or garage where it doesn't matter if it is clean or not.

Very excitable or nervous pups may lose control of their bladders when greeting people. A pup will roll over when approached by an older dog or a person it finds daunting and excrete a few drops of urine. This signals, 'I'm only a baby. Please don't hurt me.'

The majority grow out of this as they mature. It is not a dirty puppy; it is a very anxious one. It has no idea that you don't understand dog language.

Apart from anything else no puppy should ever be smacked. There is still a theory that a rolled up magazine or newspaper should be used to punish the dog. It teaches the dog to be terrified of the rolled up paper. A bold dog will rebel one day, seize the paper and bite the hand that is attacking it. 'You don't do that to me!' With a puppy that makes mistakes, not through wickedness, but because nobody has taught it what to do and what not to do, or because I have missed a cue and not taken it outside in time, I ignore any mistake and praise everything that is right.

Our puppy lives now. He has no awareness of tomorrow, or even an hour ahead. We go and leave him alone and he thinks he has been abandoned for ever. We need to go and come back dozens of times before he realises that we will return. That is why we get such ecstatic greetings. He hasn't been abandoned after all.

I always clean up at once, as pups may eat their own droppings. This is revolting to us but wild dogs scavenge and may be forced to feed on the excreta of other animals. Bitches clean up after their pups, licking away the waste matter so that predators cant smell it, so it is natural to the dog.

Bitches also often regurgitate part digested food for the puppies, which is the only way a wild bitch could wean them. I met one owner who was walloping her poor bitch for her 'dirty habits.' Some people ought not to have dogs, and puppies from this home would not be a good buy.

I have a magic word for my dogs so that they empty when I tell them where I tell them. This saves fouling the streets and it is easy to teach. Most when adult have special times and if these are observed, you can take your dog out secure in the knowledge that it will not cause offence. I don't like dirty streets any more than do non dog owners; my shoes get mucky too from other peoples' untrained dogs.

I once brought out one of my bitches to show a new puppy owner how to teach the pup and how she would sit when told, and stay when told and come when called. Before I did so I said, ' Off you go and widdle,' which she did at once. This impressed the new owners more than anything else I showed them.

It is wise to use a word that is used for nothing else or you may well produce a result you don't want in a place that is highly undesirable.

If house training proves difficult, the pup can be confined in a crate at night; very few foul their own nest. Or many layers of paper can be laid all over the floor, which makes it easy to clean up. Once you have identified the pup's favourite place,all the paper can be removed except for that area.

The paper can be removed slowly to the back door, and then the soiled paper taken outside and put just outside the door. Gradually it can be removed further and further away, keeping it as a fail safe indoors. Then it can be removed altogether and the vast majority of pups realise why, and are now ready to go where they should.

If there is a problem, some people put a bell on the dog; they can then hear him move and take him out at once.

If the problem is with an older dog it is useful to teach a few commands; sit and down and come, which I consider vital for any dog owner to use.

If the dog's stools are very loose he will have more trouble hanging on; diarrhoea is often impossible to control. Looseness, if persistent and the dog is not ill, is usually due to overfeeding, or the wrong food, so it is wise to cut back till the stools are very solid or try a different brand of food.

If they are hard and difficult to pass the dog is being underfed or having too many bones.

Either might make the dog find it difficult to control his bowels.

If the dog is fed at the same times every day he is easier to manage and the times at which he gets rid of his waste will also be consistent. Nowadays most vets recommend two meals a day for several reasons. A big meal might cause stomach torsion (twist; and it can be fatal) especially if the dog runs soon after eating. Waiting so long can make the dog so hungry he is irritable for an hour or two before being fed.

Regular meals in a normal dog mean regular emptying times and once you know the time then he can be let out to relieve himself. My dogs are fed at 9 a.m. and 6 p.m. They empty at about 9.30 a.m and around 5 p.m.

It is usually easier to make sure they do go if they always have one area of the garden reserved for emptying; the rest of the garden is for playing. They should be taken in as soon as they have performed, or they regard that as incidental to going out; and not a reason for going out.

If the floor is very soiled the smell remains and attracts the dog. It will also attract visiting dogs. Ways of removing the smell are with soda water or white vinegar. There are sprays to be found in pet sops which are intended to remove the odour, which is what brings the dog back to that spot.

One dog that I was asked about lived in an old peoples' home. Her bed was at the end of a corridor where there was a lavatory. These were very old people and the area smelled strongly as many of them missed the target. However much you clean up, the smell remains if this is a frequent occurrence.

I suggested the dog was moved to the hall which was right away from this area, and the problem solved itself. If they could do it, so could she. But the hall was always spotless and she respected that. If the dog is persistent a crate is a good idea, as he can be shut there when people are out of the house and only a very odd dog will soil its own bed.

Accidents need ignoring. The dog can be shown his mistake and put outside, but without saying anything or scolding and it should be cleaned up when he is not there. Isolating him won't do any good.

If it happens at night it is usually cured by having the dog sleep by the owner's bed; a bell on the collar will then alert you if he does start to move around and he can be taken out. Mostly this cures them, as they settle happily; which they don't do when left alone.

If the dog is urinating frequently, and it is not due to a physical cause like cystitis, then water can be restricted to just around meal times until he is reliable again.

Old dogs can become incontinent; usually there is a remedy for this. I have always found the homeopathic remedies are better for old age than conventional ones, but you need a homeopathic vet, or a chemist who specialises in homeopathy.

GAMES

Dogs learn much faster through games. Many games people play with their pups are counter productive. Fetch the ball and drop it. Grab the purse and be chased. Chase the cat.

Games need to be thought out and structured, and based on dog instincts.

The most important part of the puppy is his nose. It is very sensitive, able to identify smells that we don't know exist. I once watched a police dog find a tiny cube of cannabis at the bottom of a bin full of marrow bones. Another found one grain of the drug inside a candle.

So our pup will love a seeking game, where his favourite toy is hidden for him. The first few times he needs to see it hidden; then he can be left in the kitchen while we put it under the rug in the sitting room. I hide tiny cat biscuits as well.

Outside he can have toys hidden under bushes (make sure there are no thorns) or in long grass. I have a set of old keys on a big tag and hide those. That has meant that twice when I lost my car keys my dog was able to find them. Another of my dogs found my wedding ring when it dropped in a very shaggy goatskin rug, and I spent some time looking for it without success.

One of the most rewarding games is to teach the dog to fetch a toy thrown for him and to bring it back and put it in your hand, not on the ground. For one thing if you are going to keep this game up, you get a very aching back from constant bending. You can also get a very wet or muddy toy.

I play 'take' and 'give' with various objects, with the puppy sitting beside me. I never throw the toy at first. I tease him with it in my hand until he wants it so badly he takes it. He learns that he takes it from me and then gives it back to me.

When that is perfect, he then sits a couple of feet from me and I call him to me, and he gives it to me, having learned by then to hold on to it and carry it. It takes a few minutes each day but is well worth doing.

It leads on to a toy being thrown and brought back, which you can, if you teach well, do over and over. This is a very useful game if you are short of time or you have a broken leg, as you can play it from your chair. The dog will continue to fetch as long as you can continue to throw and so have a great deal of exercise.

One local collie owner is unable to walk at all, as an illness has paralysed her from the waist down. and her dog is one of the best trained in the area, having learned by lots of games with toys that have been thrown for her to bring back to the wheelchair.

There is no need for expensive playthings. My present dog's favourite fetch toy for a long time was a piece of plastic drainpipe which she stole from the workshop. She adored it, and if we went for a walk near the house, insisted on carrying it with her. People gave us rather odd looks!

I keep my pockets full of little titbits. I change them around as the dog can get bored with only one kind and then they don't work. I have yet to find a dog that doesn't adore liver cake.

Pup picks up my new socks and runs off. I call him, not angrily, but enticingly, and he looks around, sees I have food in my hand, races over for his reward and gives me my undamaged socks as he cant eat and hold onto them. No anger, no chasing, no hassle. Also he has had another lesson, without realising it. Come when called. Boy, that was worth doing!

THE DOG IN THE HOME

In many families life revolves around the dog. We cant do this as Fido doesn't like it. We have to be home by four as he is always fed then and makes a fuss if we are out. He has to be fed first or he jumps up and pesters us while we are eating. The dog has become a spoiled prima donna type, with the whole household revolving around him, instead of having learned his place in the general scheme.

The dog that knows his place is much more fun than the lunatic that rushes around all day barking constantly, upsetting the neighbours. He leaps on everyone he meets, screams at birds outside the window and chases children, cars, joggers, bicycles, and any animal that runs. He won't let you talk on the phone, won't let you settle with a book, won't let you watch your favourite soap on TV, won't let you have friends to visit as he growls and snarls at anyone who dares to come anywhere near his territory, which is probably all of your house and the garden as well.

We can overcome this, if we know the secrets of dog mentality. The next chapter will show you how.

6
THE DOG IN THE FAMILY

HOW THE DOG THINKS

Long ago I took my dog to a vet who had a notice in his surgery, which read...

"DOGS ARE NOT LITTLE CHILDREN IN FUR COATS."

Dogs do not and never can think as we think. They cannot understand today and tomorrow, or even yesterday. They do not understand until they have been shown, not once, but dozens of times, that they don't empty in the house; they go in the garden. They will never know why we make that rule, especially if there is a baby in the family.

They will learn, if we teach them correctly, that they may not steal or destroy our property or attack other dogs, or gnaw our hands, or take the baby's toys.

They need to learn our rules as those protect them, just as children need to learn that if they walk on ice when told it is unsafe, they will most certainly drown. The disobedient and the stupid pay the price.

However, we can never tell our dogs it isn't safe to walk on thin ice. They might learn if they do it once and are rescued, but not otherwise.

Many a pup has tried to walk on a pond covered in green algae. It looks like grass. Few try again.

A neighbour of mine once complained bitterly about my cat, which had managed to get into her pantry. For reasons known only to her, she cooled food by putting it on the pantry floor. She had cooked fish in aspic for her lunch and put it down to cool. Cat was used to finding food on the floor; he didn't know it wasn't for him, and he did enjoy it enormously.

That was before the days of deep freezes, and my neighbour had no refrigerator; I lost my lunch that day as I had to give it to her, and find something else to eat. Cats jump through windows. We have to learn how to avoid trouble, as nothing will change the nature of an animal.

A dog, finding food in the same situation, would also have helped himself unless very thoroughly taught he only ate when given food in his own bowl.

Dogs have no morals and no idea of right and wrong. We can't bribe them, we can only reward them, as a bribe only works if it is offered as an inducement for some future action. A spy might be told 'Give me your country's defence plans and I'll pay you half a million pounds.'

You can't tell your dog, if you sit I'll give you a titbit. You can show him the goodie, but he doesn't know he is going to get it, or when he is going to get it, and may make several attempts to win it before he hits on the right action, as he does not get it if he does not perform correctly.

It is only something he learns when it is done and the correct action has been made and rewarded. He has earned the goodie; not sat because you have said if you sit you get it.

Dogs can put two and two together.Sometimes it makes four but often it makes fifty eight or ninety two or something quite astonishing.

I had a dog that loved to pull a string for my two kittens to chase. They spent hours playing in this way, with him marching up and down with an 'isn't uncle kind?' expression on his face.

One day he couldn't find the string. I heard the most astounding noises from upstairs and when I went up I found him in our bedroom trying to get the girdle from my husband's dressing gown which was hanging on the door. The door was banging against the bedside table as he did so.

I gave him the girdle, thinking surely he doesn't work out that that is like string. He did. He pulled the girdle up and down the hall for the next hour or so, exercising everybody. He had put two and two together and made four.

But the German Shepherd who got a shock from the electric cooker did not make four with her theory. The cooker had become live and as she leaned against it, the poor bitch was hurled across the kitchen. Her owner and her owner's daughter were in the room at the time.

The bitch, who was nearly thirteen and very experienced in what went on in the home, knew that things don't do that; she never went into the kitchen again when either her owner or her owner's daughter was in there. She went in if it was empty or if her master was there, or anyone else. The humans had to be responsible, not the oven. Nobody could disillusion her.

There is a story of an army dog that went out with his handler under fire. A shell exploded near them and blew them off their legs. When they recovered the man thought the dog would not work under fire again.

The dog didn't worry at all about shells and explosions. But they had been passing an oak tree, and for the rest of his life the dog never went near another oak tree. It was the last thing he saw before he was blown over.

One of my owners long ago had a sheltie. While walking down a hillside a large dog leaped the wall, grabbed the sheltie and proceed to shake him like a rat. The little dog's owner managed to get behind the attacker and open his jaws and get her dog out. She had to go to the doctor after her dog had been treated by the vet. While this was going on the other dog's owner stood in front of her dog yelling at him.

A year later the two owners met for the first time since the event. The sheltie raced at the other dog's owner and bit her leg. He had never bitten before and never did again. He ignored the dog. He had not seen the dog. He was seized from behind and was facing the owner when he was being hurt and he associated her with the event. Her fault, so she had to be punished.

One of my dogs used to chase a goat and a donkey, so was never allowed free in their field. Then their owner put an electric fence round them as they were geniuses at escaping, and the dog was allowed to run there.

She made a beeline for the two animals. Her ears met the electric wire and she leaped into the air. Ever after that as far as she was concerned there was an invisible barrier of about twelve feet round every donkey or goat that she met. She would go no nearer.

We never know quite what associations the dog may make. A dog attacked by another dog may react in one of several ways.

a) He is quite unaffected and remains friendly with all other dogs, though he may be wary of the one that went for him and run from it if it is free.

b) He may be fine with all other dogs and hate that one and try to attack if they meet. One dog, long ago, was bitten by the neighbour's dog, through a hole in the gate. He was friendly with all dogs but five years later a tradesman left the gate open and the dog got out. He went next door and killed the animal that had bitten him. He never attacked another dog during the rest of his life.

c) He may, in future hate all dogs of that breed, but not worry about other breeds. I had a dog bitten, when still a pup, by a Cairn Terrier and he had to be kept leashed if ever we saw one. There were no problems with other dogs. One dog that came to my class had been bitten by a GSD when young and could never be put near one in any off lead group afterwards, though he behaved perfectly during the lessons even if the breed was present.

d) He may hate all dogs of all sizes and all breeds, without any discrimination. This quite often happens.

In all cases it is usually curable with professional help and a great deal of dedication.

Life with our dogs is far easier if we understand the way they think and react, so that we can have a harmonious relationship. When this book was first written, in 1978, very little was known about the importance of rank in the dog's life.

Wolves and dogs live in packs. Cattle and deer in herds. Sheep and chickens in flocks. They have a strong social interaction, and in every group there are the high ranking individuals and the low ranking. Mostly, these are born, not made. Like it or not, the animal knows its place and accepts it. Those who live with such units know very well that there is always a boss, and underlings.

Many years ago I spent some time watching a herd of Haflinger mares with foals. Among them was a donkey. The boss mare kept her place by bullying. She kicked any mare who came too close, and also kicked the donkey.

There were ten mares in the herd. The second mare kicked all except the boss mare, and this went right down to the lowliest of all, the tenth mare, who only kicked the donkey, as everyone else did. The poor donkey never retaliated. That was her lot in life. Dogs in packs behave in the same way.

So many people, with several dogs, buy a pup. Within a few months they tell me the pup is far too cocky, and is taking over from the older dogs. Humanly, they feel this is unfair to the established animals, and they intervene. This immediately produces friction, as nobody knows his place. If the newcomer takes over the leadership, the other dogs step down. It doesn't worry them at all. That's life as they know it.

In a hound pack, kept together in a very large kennel, each member knows his place. The boss eats first, and the others wait. He chooses the best sleeping place, and the others wait until he has settled. Then each in turn will select its own place and eat its own meal, the lowliest waiting until last, without any sign of disturbance.

In time, as the boss ages, the next strongest hound will take over, and the old boy steps down. I have seen it happen several times with my own dogs and though being human I never feel entirely happy, the dog that has been supplanted shows no sign of stress.

We need to know this, and to make sure that the dogs sort out their own positions. The only time there will be trouble is if two are of equal rank and vie for leadership. This can be much worse with bitches than dogs.

There is an old myth that a dog and a bitch never fight. That is not true either. I had a bitch that would fight either sex, and went for any dog who thought she might be wanting a mate. That she most certainly never did want, and made her feelings very plain. Some bitches, like some women, have no desire whatever for maternity.

When she came into our home, she was second in the pack of three by the time she was six months old. My older bitch had no desire to challenge. The only time the pup challenged the dog he made it so plain he was not stepping down that she accepted her place. She took over from him when he was twelve, without any sign of a struggle. One day he was top dog and ate first. The next day she was.

The top dog is fed first; he chooses where he or she sleeps; he has the lead put on first; he is played with before the others. Otherwise we give the wrong signals and confuse the dogs and the boss starts fighting the others to keep them in what he considers the correct place. Leave them alone, accept their ranking and there is no problem.

It is not necessarily a dog that rules the pack. It may be a bitch, especially if she lives with several of her own progeny.

Human intervention may well cause fights, as a lowly animal begins to think it has a right to a higher place, because the owner decrees this.

Management of the dogs in the home plays as important a part as training. We need to lay down the rules as soon as the puppy comes to live with us. Our dogs watch us all the time. They know very well who is in charge of the family. If nobody is, they may well decide that it is their role to take over.

To teach our dogs their role in life we need

PATIENCE

PERSISTENCE

PRIDE

The first two are obvious, but why pride?

Pride of owning a well trained dog; pride of owning a dog that regards his owner as the most important person in his life; pride in his health, his attitude to life, his good behaviour. Pride of our own in a job well done. Pride as we very quietly tell our dog to sit and be still and people passing think 'what a well trained dog.'

Obeying a few simple rules soon makes life easier for everyone. Even the pushy dog learns that so far as humans go, he is bottom of the pack, not the one who has the best food, the best bed, and the most attention. A spoilt dog can be very nasty indeed, and may well use his teeth to discipline those who won't obey the rules <u>he</u> has made for them.

It's not fair to say 'oh, it's dad's dog, not ours.

He must tell him what to do.' The dog must learn that everyone in the family, including the baby, is more important than he is. Having said that, the baby must also learn to respect the dog, and not torment him.

The dog understands signals far better than words. We pick up the lead. We don't need to say 'walk'. He knows what the lead means. We begin to prepare his food. We don't need to tell him we are doing so. He sees us take the bowl and open the tin or packet. He will be ready and waiting long before we have put his bowl down. We show him quietly, in a controlled way, how he should behave, without yelling or thumping.

We know what we want him to do. He has no idea. He won't learn by being told once, or twice, or even ten times. He learns by frequent daily repetition, asking him always to behave in a certain way in a certain place.

He needs a great many lessons before he understands and remembers, and performs reliably. Which of us ever passed a driving test after one lesson? Some may after twenty lessons. Others may need a hundred. Dogs are no different.

The reason I find some other dog books are unrewarding at times is because the authors assume that every dog will behave as theirs did. I know very well many of them won't.

Dogs learn by association. They think...'I walk to heel in the dog club and at home.' They do not realise they must also walk to heel everywhere they go. They need to be taught to do so. In time it becomes a habit, but at first each new place requires lessons to begin again at the beginning.

Allowed to pull when out, they continue to do so, because no one has taught them that pulling is never allowed. They have learned it is never allowed in club or at home, but is allowed when out.

Often a dog will win high honours in the Obedience ring, heeling immaculately, and then we watch in utter amazement as the owner is pulled across the showground towards the car park as if the dog had never had a minute's training in his life. That dog is only trained for ring purposes; not for living and I doubt if I would want him in my home.

When the dog pulls us along he is saying he is in command; we are not. It is very little use teaching him not to pull in class and then letting him do as he chooses as soon as the lesson is over. That way, he never learns, as we spend an hour of the week teaching him what is the right way and then go for daily long walks of several hours during which he forgets all he has just been taught. Which is exactly like taking our learner driver on to a motorway after one lesson.

MAKING THE RULES

These differ in different homes. We have to decide what we want our dogs to do and what they may not do. If we decide they may never sleep on our chairs or settees, then everyone must see that rule is observed. Dogs do learn to understand NEVER. They also learn to understand ALWAYS. They cannot understand SOMETIMES. He may not jump up when he has muddy paws, but he can when they are clean. What kind of a rule is that? He doesn't know his paws are muddy. All he knows is that what was OK last time is suddenly quite wrong this time. He becomes very confused.

Some people make hazards for their dog by allowing him to be walked by all kinds of people, most of whom let the dog do as he chooses, and have no idea how to prevent him doing so. The result is a dog that is programmed never to learn, as it is so confused by all the different ways it is exercised, and all the different people.

I once wanted to write a book on the role of the pack in the dog's world. I was taken out to lunch by the editor in charge of dog books.

'But our dogs don't live in packs,' he said. 'They live with the family.'

That was a long time ago, before most people realised that the family becomes the dog's pack. The book was never written which is a pity. We can't change the nature of the dog, but we can adapt and learn how to make sure that the pack rules are obeyed and they benefit us.

THE DOG'S BASIC RULES

Every pack must have a leader. The leader is entitled to the best place in the house (his owner's bed); the warmest place in the house, (right in front of the fire); he eats before everyone else; he is first through the door even if it means pushing everyone else out of the way. If he lies in the gangway, everyone must go round him. He is not going to move. He has prior rights in his own view. The leader goes upstairs and looks down on everyone else.

So how do we prove to the dog that we are the leaders, and not the dog?

We have to think about it. We have to remember. We have to observe the pack rules all the time to stop the dog becoming a nuisance, and training us to defer to him. It can't be said too often.

He does not have the best bed. He is fed after everyone else. We go through doors first. If he is in the gangway he moves to let us past. He does not lie on the stairs and look down on humans. A gate at the bottom will prevent this. They are simple rules but they make the most surprising difference.

EYE CONTACT — IMPORTANT

We don't attempt eye contact with any dog but our own dog as the wrong kind of eye contact is interpreted as a threat. Experienced trainers wear peaked caps which they draw down over their eyes when teaching a new lesson, so that the dog can't be dismayed by direct eye contact in the wrong situation.

I take very good care never to stare at any dog that has just come for the first lesson and never stare at a dog I have not met before. Humans who are attacked, apparently without provocation, have often stared at the dog, alarming him, so that he was afraid they might hurt him. Dogs stare at one another before a fight. If the stare is interrupted, the fight seldom takes place.

I was once on a course where thirty people, with their dogs, were sitting in a semi circle round the lecture room. One dog after another was suddenly triggered to lunge and bark and nobody could make out why. Then my own dog did, and I looked across to find a black dog, quite the smallest in the room, staring at him with unwinking eyes. She looked very innocent to all of us, but to the dogs she was menacing one after another by that direct unblinking stare.

When I pointed out what was happening her owner took care to see that she lay with her back to the other dogs and we had no more problems. The same thing can happen in class; one dog stares at another and the dog stared at reacts, and is blamed for starting something that he most certainly did not start. Nobody realises the other dog is the real culprit.

I try to position the dogs in such a way that this can't happen and also to make sure that if any two dogs dislike one another, they are well apart.

Rescued dogs or very submissive dogs rarely meet our eyes; their own eyes slide away. This is not a sign of a dishonest dog, as some people say, but of a worried dog, anxious not to give what might be interpreted as a challenge. My own rescued dogs, in time, would sit and gaze at me as lovingly as any of those I had from puppyhood, though they never would look at me directly at first.

That long exchange of looks is very meaningful to your dog and he will often initiate it, coming up to ask for contact in this way. Only when they feel that they trust you implicitly will dogs come and regard you with that loving mild eyed gaze. When my dog rewards me like that I feel that the bond is well forged.

With our own loving dog, eye contact is a very different matter.

ATTENTION.

This is the most important exercise we can ever teach our dogs and one that very few people know about unless they are told. I call it the attention exercise.

I have been to any number of classes in my own early days with dogs where I was told 'get your dog's attention' but nobody ever showed me how.

The dog must learn to look up at us, to watch us, to take note of what our mouths say and our hands tell him. He has to be taught to concentrate. It doesn't just happen. We need to concentrate on him too, which is why learning periods must be short, as neither dog nor human can give full concentration for long periods of time.

Puppies have a very short attention span. We make watching us fun; watch me toss the ball in the air; watch this piece of food; if you do watch it, you will earn it. It starts every training session, every walk, and before every meal.

What we are doing by this is to focus them on us, and not on outside events, such as other people and other dogs passing or playing. We are teaching them to concentrate; it doesn't just happen with most dogs, though some rare and wonderful animals seem born to watch their owners and they are the easiest of all to teach.

We need to make watching us exciting; move briskly, not amble along as if we had all the time in the world and needed to drag out everything we do to fill it; be lively and speak expressively, especially if we have a somewhat laid back dog that is difficult to liven.

'Good puppy; great puppy; what a clever puppy', and with a happy voice we can

101

motivate him to work with a will and think that doing as we ask is the most wonderful thing in his life.

It would probably help all those of us who want our dogs to do well to spend a few minutes before each lesson practising being a thoroughly hammy actor! Most of us are far too formal and embarrassed by putting on an extrovert act. I find it difficult as it is not my natural style either.

We must bond to our dog, or we don't have a dog. We have an animal that uses us for his own ends and may end up abusing us by biting us. The majority of dog bites occur in the home, and most of those in the bedroom, as the dog knows he is much more important than the humans who sleep there, and if he becomes really dominant, may refuse to allow them into their own beds. Most dogs, fortunately, are not born boss dogs but if we do have one we have to make sure we are superior to him in every way.

The attention exercise also bonds the lower pack member to us.

We exchange eye signals.

Several times a day we call the dog to us and help him look up to us. We can do that by holding his favourite toy near our faces, or a favourite titbit in our mouths, or in our hands near our mouths. We kneel down as he is very small and tell him 'WATCH ME.' We smile (without showing our teeth as that is a threat to him) and make him realise that he makes us happy when he looks up at us and keeps watching us.

We start by using something that is very desirable, so that he is well rewarded. We work better if we are paid more than 10p an hour. The dog too likes to earn his reward but it must be worth having. Liver cake is wonderful. Pieces of chicken, or of garlic sausage, or cheese, or left over bits of meat from your own meals, can all be used if they don't upset the dog. It's useful to change them around so that there is always a new taste or treat in store.

One class member had a restaurant and used to bring any pieces of steak left on plates; her dogs worked with a will!

I start every exercise I teach, including the attention exercise, by counting 1. If the dog keeps looking at me, I extend the count to 5, to 10, but if he looks away, then I go back to the number before that at which we lost eye contact. Just before he looks away, I reward him by telling him how clever he is and then give the titbit.

In the end the dog should be so well taught that he will maintain eye contact for as long as you choose. You can't teach a dog that is looking everywhere but at you. It is also necessary for us to concentrate as well as the dog.

If we count aloud the dog knows something is happening that involves him and he watches our faces; and it keeps our thoughts from wandering. There is no need to do it any louder than a whisper.

The eye contact, when perfected, says 'You are a wonderful dog and mean a great deal to me and I love looking at you and having you look at me.' It is worth doing daily with your puppy from the time he first comes home, as a game.

PACKLEADERS EAT FIRST

In a family the dog watches to see who eats first. That is, who picks up the knife and fork first. That is the person the dog thinks must be obeyed as no inferior dog would ever dream of starting his meal before the top dog. In some families, mother eats last as she dishes up and the children are served first, so that the youngest member of a family may be the one to start. If the dog obeys one of the children and nobody else, just see what happens at table!

It is interesting when eating out to watch a family. Often mother never starts to eat until the baby has been fed, or the toddler has finished. Any dog, watching this, would assume at once that mother was by far the least important person in the family and she would find him hard to control.

If the dog refuses to obey the mother at all, then the family must all wait until she starts to eat. The dog, seeing this, will think something has happened to change the established order and the mother will assume much more importance in his eyes.

In a hound pack, the lower members wait until the top dog has begun to eat before touching their food, even if it is in front of them. In a family pack the dogs sort out who starts to eat first and the others hang back. One little bitch that refused to eat at all was so submissive that it worried her to have her food put down with the bossier dogs.

She began to eat when they finished theirs first and hers was then put down. Someone interpreted this as her being afraid of having her food stolen by the others: which might well have happened as in their eyes she had no right to eat till they had eaten.

Another dog, offered food before the family ate, puzzled them by lying beside his plate and not touching it until they had all finished their meal. If a dog isn't eating as he should, it is a good idea to work out what the other dogs are doing. He may be so subordinate that he feels he should not touch any food while those more important than him are still eating.

I know it sounds silly to humans, but that is the way the dog operates. We can't argue with him and try to convince him he is wrong by our standards. He is right by his own. That is born in him and nothing we do will change it.

Feeding our solitary dog before us gives him the signal that he is much more important and of higher rank than we are, so he will begin to take liberties. Once we have persuaded him that we are his superiors, the whole relationship changes and everything else falls into place.

With a really very dominant dog, he should only be given food in his bowl, and no titbits or share of our chocolate or what is left on our plate, from our hands. The only titbits he can have are when he is being trained. Once he has accepted that we have the upper hand that can change and we can give him an odd reward; but not a frequent one, or he will once more think he is boss.

If I want to feed my dog before we have our main meal, as we may have guests and I prefer the evening uninterrupted, I make a point of having a cup of coffee and a very small snack when the dog's food is prepared and waiting to be put down. She has to wait until I have finished and choose to feed her. I take my time over eating and drinking.

When I was a child we had far less trouble with dogs as they ate the household scraps, and there never were any until everyone had finished eating. The dog automatically ate last.

WHEN TO GIVE TITBITS.

The dog should never get a treat for doing nothing. This again adds to his sense of self importance. If you do want to give him an extra, such as a piece of meat left on your plate, make sure he sits, then lies down, then walks three steps beside you and sits again. He has now earned it, and also has had a sneaky lesson he didn't even know was happening.

That also stops him pestering for them as once you give them to him whenever he looks hopeful, (and how those brown eyes can control us!) he will start pawing at you, nudging you and maybe even bark until given something, and be a nuisance.

Dogs are cunning. Many know very well that the family does not feed them when at the table, but visitors may be a soft touch. My dogs have to learn that our guests must not be pestered either and I ask our friends not to succumb to those pleading brown eyes.

WHEN TO STROKE THE DOG

We need a rule?

Unfortunately, yes.

If he comes to you to be stroked, nudging you, and spilling your coffee, or knocking your book or pen out of your hands, he is going to be a nuisance. If the coffee is scalding hot, he is also a danger. What he is saying is I want, I want, I want, which becomes his due in his mind. After all, you have to do as he asks, don't you, as you don't make the rules. He does.

The trouble is that some of his rules can cause immense problems. Pulling on the lead down the steps after a cat may result in a fall for his owner and a broken arm or leg. I have known that happen several times.

We have to make sure, all the time, that any action between us and the dog starts when we choose, not when the dog chooses. This one isn't easy, as it is very hard to resist a dog that wants to be petted.

It is one I find hard myself, especially if I am thinking about something else, and my dog comes to be fussed. I have to remind myself she is a dog and if I do as she asks, she will begin to pester.

Mind you, a strong minded dog will still try it on. I have to remind her on occasion that she is not going to win. Since she is trained, if she keeps pestering to be stroked I tell her to go and lie down.

A few minutes later I call her. Now I want to stroke her because I choose to do so, not because she pushes me into doing so. Sometimes during the day I call her and make a big fuss, so that she knows I value her and she has her self esteem. She realises I am more important than she is but she still she has her own place in our lives and is not forgotten.

I choose when I want to stroke her. She does not force me to stroke her when I am busy with something else.

GROOMING MANNERS

The dog that wants to take the brush is a pest to groom. It wriggles. It twists and turns. It grabs the grooming tools and your hand. It tries to run off. In the worst cases it may actually try to bite. It will play with a towel if anyone tries to dry it.

In the long haired breeds, a good breeder will start to groom the pups daily from three weeks on so that by the time they are sold they are used to the procedure and behave very well. The dog that is groomed daily often has a much better temperament than one that only sees a brush once a month.

Grooming removes dead hairs, which come out all the time and are much worse when the hot weather starts. I had one owner ring me in tears because she thought her puppy was going bald. He was long coated and was shedding his puppy coat and developing the adult coat. Fur at this time comes out, often in big tufts. Dogs in centrally heated homes may moult continuously.

Grooming also massages the skin and removes dust and dirt. It enables us to detect any cuts or thorns or cysts or bumps and make sure they are not going to cause problems. It gets them used to being handled all over.

A difficult pup can be tied by the collar, on a very short lead, to a table leg or some other solid obj;ect. I never feel I have control until my dogs will stand perfectly still for grooming and turn and roll over as I ask. Since they accept that I am boss there is never any problem with them. All my dogs have loved being groomed and as soon as I pick up the brush are in position for it.

One of my rescued dogs enjoyed it so much that he would bring the brush and ask for it to be used. Since he was exceptionally submissive I allowed this and did as he asked if I were not busy.

If the pup wriggles while being brushed, try and have someone hold out a tasty bit of food, like a piece of sausage, for it to nibble. It soon learns to stand still, and this also helps when visiting the vet as standing while being examined is then a matter of habit.

Those dogs that need stripping and clipping would benefit by being tied while grooming as many professionals do tie them up while working on them.

Different brushes are needed for different breeds. There are wire stripping brushes to remove thick dead hair; rubber rakes that are excellent for loose hairs as are rubber grooming gloves; combs; hound gloves, which help produce the gleam in the coat and brush the dog after the loose fur has been removed.

Softer brushes are needed for the very short coated dogs like greyhounds. Daily brushing prevents knots and tangles, which not only come in the very long coated breeds but also in dogs like Spaniels and Golden Retrievers which seem to get matted round the fur behind their ears.

I look in the ears and clean the outer parts with a damp tissue, and also clean the eyes of any matter that has formed in the night. Some dogs may have gummy eyes due to wind when walking, and those can be bathed with cold boiled water. If the discharge is coloured, then the dog needs to see the vet.

Claws may need clipping if the dog is exercised on soft ground rather than hard surfaces. Some long haired breeds need to be groomed lying down, first one side, then the other, but the same rules apply and the same methods of achieving control during grooming. A grooming table is an advantage for these.

Grooming should be a pleasure and, especially with heavy coated breeds, it is vitally necessary for their comfort and well being so care should be taken that it is a pleasurable time for both dog and owner. Many dogs enjoy music and this can be played as background as grooming a big long haired dog takes quite a time.

In winter paws need watching. Walking on salt sprayed roads can cause sore pads, as can icy roads.Snow can pack between the pads and make ice balls, so that after walking in very bad weather, paws need washing with warm water.

Oil or tarry substances on the road, or on beaches is another hazard, and can be removed with margarine or butter.

STAND FOR EXAMINATION

Dogs need to learn to stand still to be examined by the vet, or to lie down. Troy used to panic when her anal glands were emptied, to such an extent she had to be sedated as she twisted in circles, crying, and refused to be touched.

Sedation is a not a good idea, unless it is vital. The anal glands are under the dog's tail and there are two of them. They become blocked at times, and the dog may scoot on its tail, trying to alleviate the awful itching this causes.

I have found that some diets seems to cause full glands, while others cause little or no trouble. Troy had to have them emptied every fortnight when I first got her, but when I changed her food that settled and it is well over two years since they last needed to be done.

So, when I groomed her, knowing her fear, I played with her tail and rear end gently, laughing and teasing her to make her think it fun. The next time she needed treatment I told the vet what I had been doing and he played with her in the same way for a minute or two, and then, before she even realised what was happening, he squeezed them. Luckily I have a good vet, as some would think that silly and descend on the dog and empty them at once, which does not help fear.

The stand in class is taught as a stand for examination with owners going over them as if they had been brought to the veterinary surgery; examining ears, eyes, teeth, back of the mouth, the underneath of the dog's paws, looking for thorns, expecting the animal to stand still and not fuss.

It is useful to groom little dogs on tables and to put the pups that will grow into big dogs on a table, as most vets like them up there for examination and a dog that has never been lifted on to a table may panic.

Only one of mine has ever objected. Put on a table to have an injury stitched, she leaped towards me, trying to get into my arms, and the table rolled across the room and cannoned into the vet. I don't think we were his favourite patients that day.

It is a problem for those of us without grooming tables. Few of us want to teach our dog to jump on the dining room table. Hopefully they will get used to it.

Dogs not only have to be taught to stand and be examined but may also have to stand to be bandaged. I have had relay races with the handlers having to stand their dogs still and wind a long length of crepe bandage round their middle and then run to the end. Dogs that played with the bandage were disqualified.

Chita once had an abscess on her paw due to a thorn which had gone in deep. She had to stand with her paw in a bowl of warm water containing medication the vet had given me, three times a day. Luckily by then she had been taught to stand and stay for a few minutes, was several years old, and had become sensible.

I put a towel on the floor and the bowl on the towel and she then had to do her standstay with one foot in the bowl of water. She took it in her stride and after the first day walked over and stood herself in the water, looking very pleased with herself when she was praised. Training helped enormously with her.

Dogs vary so much. Some are very sensible and seem to understand that they are being helped; others panic, and it's difficult to get them to co-operate.

Chita, if she had a problem, till trained, ran in circles, screaming and had to be caught and held while she was treated. A thorn in the paw, or some hard straw which refused to come out when she evacuated could cause an hour or so of hassle in her early days.

Josse, the re-homed dog, on the other hand, came to find me, and presented whatever part of him that was causing pain to me, and stood to be helped. His problems were over in minutes. Other dogs have shown varying degrees of worry but none has been like Chita was at first.

If there is something like straw or string that won't shift itself, causing a problem, then the dog must be coaxed to stand still and the offending object removed with a tissue. Usually it comes away quite easily with a small tug.

DOORWAY MANNERS

There is nothing worse than a dog who rushes through doorways, eager to be in front of you. If small, he may trip you up. If large, he may knock you over. Some never try it. If your dog does, then it is because he is pushy and showing you he is boss, not you.

Going first through any gap, even that in a hedge or a doorway, is one of the easiest ways of showing your dog that he has to keep his place. He is not going to win and dictate to you.

From the very first days in the home, puppy has to learn he does not rush through that opening. He may go through quietly after you. If he does not, he is put on the lead. He may still rush. So the door is opened just a crack, not more than half an inch. As he tries to go through, shut it, hard, but be very careful not to trap a paw or his nose. It may be necessary to do it twenty times, or fifty times, but he must not go first. It is best with a door opening towards you.

With most dogs, it only needs to be done two or three times before they hang back, but it may need to be done every time you go through a door for some weeks before the dog really appreciates that it never goes through any door or gap before you. It is far easier if the pup is taught right from his very first day people go through doors first, always.

In time he decides you can battle with the door and hangs back when it is opened. Ever after, he should follow, not lead. If he leads again, then it has to be done again. He has to learn to make his own decisions in this respect. It can take weeks with a really pushy dog, but that is the type that can hurt you accidentally in a doorway especially if he is Great Dane sized.

Many people teach him to sit while they go through which doesn't show him exactly what you want as the day you forget, he charges in front again. He was obeying an order; he had not discovered the rules.

But circumstances alter cases. I do teach the dog to sit on occasions. I had lessons for some weeks with a large Labrador that raced through the door and knocked the two year old over every time. She could not operate the door to show the dog he must go second.

We taught the little girl to tell the dog to sit and when she wanted to go out of the door to make him sit, every time. It wasn't easy but she did learn and I was entertained a year later when I visited after a long interval.

The tot marched to the door, the dog following, and said 'Susans go through doors first. Bens have to sit.' She had knocked her head twice and this was very dangerous. Now she is six and the dog is no problem at all. She and her two elder brothers can control him, as well as their parents.

There is another hazard with a dog that races through a door. You may be going out of the dog class as another owner is coming in and the two dogs meet unexpectedly. There can be a fight in these circumstances, so that you need your dog quietly behind you while you check that it is safe to go out.

It has major virtues as most dogs learn not to rush out; it can save him running through the gate and under a car, or leaping out of the car the second the door is opened and rushing under another passing vehicle. I have known at least six dogs that died this way.

PRACTISING THE SKILLS

My dog has to sit on the doorstep while I put out the rubbish, and not follow me. She may come if I call her. Or I may go in without calling her to me and not allow her to go out at all. That way, she is never sure what I am planning and waits to see instead of charging out after me. If she does, she goes straight in again.

It is a good way of doing 'stay' practice, without making a chore of it. Stay while I go out to the bin; stay while I make a cup of coffee; stay while we wait to cross the road, the dog of course on the lead.

One recent very young class member horrified me when she told me she practiced stays with her young GSD in the street, making her sit at the end of the road and seeing how far away she could go. It only needs a cat to appear, another dog to come along and maybe attack her, or her to see something that attracts her on the other side of the road. As she dashes across a car comes round the corner, and the next minute there is a dead dog.

The street is not the place to practice off lead work with any dog, however well trained. There are far too many hazards today to risk our dog's safety by practising things like the stays in very public places.

I do not leave my dog on a stay outside a shop; she could be stolen. People might try to pet her, and worry her. Another dog might sniff at her, and make her get up. Or might even attack her, and she would be tied and helpless. I stand in the shop doorway with her, and ask the shopkeeper to serve me from that position, or don't take her to the shops at all.

Meanwhile, once they understand what we want, we can ask our dogs to stay still on the lead while we re-tie a shoelace. Stay while I give this passer by directions to the station.

Many people seem to trust their dogs to walk on the pavement beside them off lead. One day an incident occurs, and the dog is badly injured or is dead. Some dogs pull so much the owners won't bother with leads.

Most towns now have bye laws saying that all dogs must be on the lead and it is essential to teach your dog so that it is safe at all times. This takes commitment. Those of us who don't have it are not good dog owners. We can't be casual in the 1990s; life was much easier twenty years ago, but sadly, times change.

GANGWAY DOGS.

Those of us who have had a number of dogs have probably all met them. The dogs that lie in the doorway, or right in the middle of the passage, watching everything that goes on.

'Don't disturb me. I lie here. You go round me.

If they did this in the wild, when the pack leader came along, the dog would move at once. It is not always the strongest or biggest dog that leads the pack. I used to visit a friend who bred German Shepherds. She also had a chihuahua. There would be three large dogs lying on the rug in the front of the fire, when the tiny dog came into the room.

At once, without, so far as we could see, any signals being exchanged, the big dogs vacated the rug and went to lie away from the fire in other parts of the room. His very small Lordship settled down and had the fire to himself. He always tried to block the gangway and make every person and every dog go round him.

If his master told him off, he gave him a dirty look and quite deliberately walked over and cocked his leg against his owner's briefcase. It is not only the large dog that decides to be pack leader.

Many of us walk over the dog, or round him, but what we should do is make him get up and get out of our way as his pack leader would if he were living with a group of dogs.

A submissive dog that accepts you as leader will get up without being told and move away, and will also wait until you have gone through the door.

GIVING OUR DOGS A ROLE IN OUR LIVES

Those of us who live in the house with our dogs do have to be far more aware of the way the dog reacts. Many dogs live in kennels and never come indoors at all. They are rarely likely to cause this sort of problem as they are very firmly kept in their place...outside...and subordinate.

Those who keep dogs in kennels and never have a house pet may write books; what they tell us is seldom helpful in a domestic situation as they have never experienced a dog around the home all day or the many odd incidents the house dog may encounter that are never met by a dog left in his kennel when not being trained or walked.

We need dogs as well trained and biddable as those for the Blind, as our dogs live in the same environment. If we teach them all manner of skills, they will be far happier dogs.

Long ago I was helping in a class where one member had a little Cairn. Her husband became blind and acquired a Guide Dog. Sue was so fascinated by their new dog's behaviour that she began to teach the little dog many of the same things.

The Guide Dog could take his master to the bank, the chemist, the newsagent, to visit friends, all on command. The Cairn's owner worked in a hospital and one day said jokingly to the dog, 'Take me to Dr So and so.' She did not expect her to understand, but without hesitation the little dog trotted along the corridor of the administration block to his office.

Other class members have also taught their dogs to be part of the household. One, who became pregnant when her Golden Retriever was two, taught her to fetch the baby powder, the peg bag, and pick up anything that dropped on the floor.

Another dog was taught to carry the newspaper, and her tin of dog food; to fetch the letters from the post box which was at the gate of the house; to carry a bucket to the stable for the horse to be fed, and to bring it back when it was empty.

I ask my class members to bring a set of old keys on a leather tag, and we hide them for the dog to find. The day we lose our car keys, the dog can seek them for us.

One of my dogs always carried home the newspaper when we did not have it delivered. They can be taught to fetch slippers; or the remote control, or the portable phone. They can be taught the names of their toys and pick one out of a group of them. Fetch ball; fetch ring; fetch squeaky; fetch tug rope.

One friend had a number of toys that resembled various MPs. Her dog happily fetched each member of the political party she favoured when told the name, and shook those of the opposing party viciously. It went down well at Christmas and birthdays.

We could have so much more fun with them with a little bit of extra effort. All the skills taught in classes lead on to these other actions.

My dog picks up things I have dropped; pens; clothes pegs; the empty margarine tub she has just been allowed to lick clean. She finds things I hide for her, all of which gives her a feeling of belonging, and also extra occupation.

WE LAY DOWN THE RULES

The only time my dog gets her way fast is if she indicates she is about to be sick; then she may reach the door before me, as there is no carpet there, if there is not time to get her safely outside.

The rest of the time she has to wait until I am ready, as she was quite likely, when younger, to run to the door and then bark for a ball game, which was not always convenient for me.

Dominance may be overcome, but it is always there, and if you relax with these dogs, they try for the superior position again.

A friend who was a police dog handler once complained that he had the most disobedient German Shepherd in the country. Why? He had a back injury and was unable to keep up the training, and the dog knew very well he could get away with things that would normally never be allowed as his master was unable to move very fast. Once his handler was recovered, the dog resumed his good behaviour and worked very well.

TO SHOUT OR NOT TO SHOUT.

There is never any need to shout at a dog. Their hearing is thirty times more acute than ours, if not more. They can hear a fly walking. Our yells must be torture to them. All we need is a very firm whisper. It is possible to have a row in whispers, as those who live in places where you can hear every word spoken next door, will know. A firm voice does not mean a loud voice. 'I mean it' has just as much authority in a whisper if the tone is right.

I once took out two dogs in Ireland who had been taught to walk free, but come back to the handler and lie down against the wall when they heard a car. It was the slowest walk I have ever taken as they heard car engines a good five minutes before I did and refused to move until the noise had died away after the vehicle passed us.

Classes must often be nightmare places for the dogs, with everyone bellowing. Dogs may actually be hindered from learning,, as A says SIT after B has said it; and the dog next to that person gets puzzled as it is hearing so many commands.

What they may learn is to ignore commands, as there is a constant shouting of the same one, over and over. Why tell me to sit if I am already sitting?

One of my dogs was very reluctant to pick up a dumbbell. He was a rescue and had been told to drop everything he touched before I had him so he had a conflict inside him.

One day he raced out to pick up the dumbell, and as his mouth closed on it, someone at the end of the hall, tired of her dog's persistent misbehaviour, yelled NO. Mine dropped the bell in horror, sure the shout had been directed at him.

It took another six months to teach him it was fine to pick it up and I would be very pleased if he did so. I avoided that exercise in class after that, as another unluckily timed shout of NO might have prevented him ever touching it again.

I prefer in group lessons to have everyone use very soft voices and hand signals. Dogs don't need those yells. I can often stop a dog from barking by going up to him and saying in a whisper, 'What's all that about then? Hush,' and laying a finger on my lips. A finger on the lips is a useful signal to teach any constantly barking dog. If you whisper NO if it must be said, then you don't upset other nearby dogs.

Not shouting has another advantage as a stentorian yell can be used for a reserve in case of danger. One of my dogs ran free in the park. I did not know children had broken down the fence beside the railway line and she chased a rabbit through the gap and across to the other side. I yelled 'Come' at the top of my voice. She had never heard that noise before and raced back, arriving well before the train that was due.

It is difficult to remember to keep your voice calm. The dog is playing up terribly, you are embarrassed and frustrated, thinking everyone in the room is looking at you, and the word comes out loudly before you have time to think.

I have had to drill myself to remember, as when I first began to train my dogs, I made as many mistakes as the next person.

People feel embarrassed because they make mistakes and don't know what to do for the best. How can anyone know without being taught? I have a vivid memory of being told that one of the 1970s top winners at Cruft's was seen, with her first dog, many years before, crying at the side of the ring at a show because the dog had run away. Nobody would have believed it of her now, but like everyone else she had to begin. We get on so much better with our dogs if we remember we do need to learn.

Every dog I meet teaches me something I didn't know before. Every one is unique, and even pups in the same litter can be widely different in appearance, behaviour and intelligence. Our new dog will be nothing like any we have ever had before.

There is no need whatever to feel ashamed because we have not yet learned how to master this new comer into our lives. The only shame we need feel is if we don't bother to learn or to give it the best life we can. Only those who have lived with a dog that has become a valued part of their lives appreciate the immense benefits that dog can bring.

The dogs I have had have all been very different; one over sensitive to voices; one over sensitive to noises like thunder; one over fearful and another without enough fear to keep her safe. One terrified of traffic; one terrified of men. Troy, who is basically sensible, is the only one that has become afraid of the vet's waiting room and surgery. This began when she had a lump removed with only a local anaesthetic and watched her front leg being cut open.

REWARDS

It is well to remember that dogs don't see rewards the way we do. They can, in their own minds, have some very odd rewards, but they are still rewarding to them. They bark. We come. We may be very angry, but we have noticed them, which is all they wanted, and to the dog's mind, even being yelled at is better than being left alone.

In any case they probably think we are either helping them warn off an intruder by barking too, or are simply making conversation with them. In the same way if we run after them when they are chasing something, we are joining in the chase, and giving them a signal that this is acceptable.

A lonely dog will feel rewarded when his master comes home after a long absence even if he yells at him and beats him. He is no longer alone. Someone is noticing him.

People who only talk to their dog to tell it off, 'Bad dog. I told you to sit straight,' aren't teaching the dog that sitting crooked is wrong. They are telling him that if he sits crooked then he won't be ignored. So he will do it just to gain an interaction, especially if, when he does sit straight, he gets no praise at all.

When he steals your food his reward is a wonderful taste and a satisfied appetite. What happens to him when you discover it may again re-enforce his feelings of satisfaction, as usually he is just ignored.

You are watching a football match on TV and a goal is about to be scored. The dog has been trying to gain your attention without success, so he picks up something he knows you value, like your camera, or the remote control. You yell. The dog has gained his own goal...you have noticed him.

This happens with pups; and it happens with dogs whose owners don't interact with them enough. A game of hide the toy and find it for five minutes before the football programme began would ensure a quiet dog waiting until you had time for him again.

SEPARATION PROBLEMS

Very few dogs enjoy being solitary. They live with the pack and need the pack. Or they are constantly with owners who take them everywhere and rarely go out without them or leave them alone in a room. Being alone leads to anxiety.

The dog that is with a very thoughtful family soon becomes one of the most sensible animals anyone can find, but he is taught from the start that sometimes he does have to be by himself. That won't be for ever. People do normally come back, and he realises that, but only in time.

Dogs that are very rarely separated from their owners often hate being left alone and feel very insecure indeed. One young German Shepherd left on her own for the first time, ripped up the new settee.

Sometimes a dog becomes so distraught when his owner tries to leave him that he will hang on desperately to an arm or leg and actually bite in his efforts to ensure he isn't left alone.

The worst case of this I ever saw was in a Bearded Collie that belonged to someone who owned a newsagents' and had to be out of the house at about half past four in the morning. There was another dog, but that made no difference.

Copper wanted his owner and wanted her so badly that, when I met her, her arms were black and blue with several really bad bites, and he was under sentence of death.

She had tried everything the books said and nothing worked.

She came to me for twelve weeks, and we taught Copper to sit and stay. Nothing else. Sit for five minutes on the lead with her beside him. Then sit for a quarter of a minute with her one step away, which worried him. When he could sit for five minutes like that, we tried four steps away. Gradually she could leave him to ten steps away and keep him sitting until she came back after several minutes.

Then we did the same thing with the down stay.

Next he had a biscuit put in front of him and was told to leave it until it was given to him. He watched the biscuit. She continued with this training at home, and really did put heart and soul into it as if not her husband was insistent that Copper was put to sleep. He was not left alone for more than a few minutes at first.

At the end of twelve weeks his owner hid behind a bush during her lessons and went out of the room and back again at home. Finally we reached the stage where she could tell him to sit, his biscuit between his paws, go out of the room, shut the door, and call to him to eat his reward, so free-ing him from the stay, and then go off without any worry.

Copper became a far more relaxed dog as he had rules now as to how to behave in certain situations and understood them. At that stage we began to teach him other skills, such as lead walking, as his idea of that was to leap shoulder high at every fifth step. Having mastered the ability to sit on command, down on command and stay when told, he soon began to walk sensibly and within a year she had a dog who allowed her to leave him without making all that fuss.

Another owner who had to take a job when her dog was about three years old found he became very upset as soon as she began to put on her outdoor things. She was told to put them on even when she wasn't going out, and then go and prepare a meal or make a cup of coffee, wearing what she normally wore when she went out of the house.

In time those clothes ceased to mean that the dog was going to be left alone and he did not build up panic before she went. When she left, she went out of the front door saying 'I'll be back,' instead of telling him to be a good boy and not to worry and mummy would come back soon, all of which added fuel to his fear.

Often, having gone out of the front door, she came in at the back door immediately and praised him for being sensible. It was some weeks before he accepted her departures without a scene, but by the end of three months he simply went to his bed with a bone or a toy and waited patiently for her return.

The puppy needs to be left alone for short periods, with people coming back constantly. Then this sort of behaviour won't develop.

Dogs left alone too much may do all sorts of weird things, like chewing the wallpaper, or tearing up the flooring, or eating the carpet. The result is invariably an angry owner, who, seeing the dog's fear at the anger, assumes the dog is being spiteful and getting its own back for being alone.

Dogs don't think like that. We might eat a bar of chocolate, go out jogging, or light a cigarette if we feel stressed; the dog has no such option as he is physically trapped in the house.

This makes for a dog that becomes more and more desperately anxious and causes the behaviour to be much worse. We never worked out why Copper behaved as he did as he was a rescue and it must have been triggered by past events in his life. The habit was already there when he was brought home from the rescue kennels. He may have been afraid of being abandoned again.

One of my rescued dogs did the same thing if anyone took his lead from me. He grabbed hold of me so hard to prevent me leaving him that he bit painfully. He had been re-homed six times; I was his seventh owner in six months, as his first owner died and the dog then went from one home to another, with unhappy consequences. He was obviously afraid when someone took his lead that he was being removed yet again.

We learned how to avoid that and if he had to be kennelled he went to the friend who used to train the North Wales police dogs. I dropped the lead, Josse was called across the room and given a titbit, and I slipped out of sight, shutting the door behind me. There was no problem then.

It can happen out of the blue, as it did with one dog recently. His owner couldn't understand why his behaviour had become so odd. Mark had a bitch he had bought to train for the gun, but the older dog lived in the house and the new pup outside in a kennel and run. She came in in the evenings when her owner was at home. Then she was sent for training to a gundog man.

Quite suddenly, for no reason his owner could think of, the older dog refused to come into the house in the evenings, but stayed outside in the garden. I asked when the odd behaviour had started.

About eight weeks ago.

When did the bitch go away for training?

About eight weeks ago.

The owner had not considered that, and kicked himself for not realising it had begun the day the bitch was sent away. The dog was missing his companion, even though she wasn't with him in the house by day. If left there on his own he could see her through the windows, and be re-assured by her presence. Now she had gone, and she had been part of his life for nearly a year. He most probably thought she was dead and was grieving.

A few weeks before this happened, the couple had split up and the wife left home. The dog was possibly now afraid that his owner would vanish too. Once his owner realised what was wrong he took the dog to work with him, and that solved the problem, though it probably has not cured it. Matters may improve when the bitch returns from her training.

A dog that has never shown the least sign of anxiety may do so suddenly. One night I heard a noise downstairs and when I went to investigate found Troy had jumped over a barrier into another room, and was trying to escape through the front door. She refused to go back into the room in which she had slept for over five years.

She bolted up a flight of open plan stairs that she had refused to even try and negotiate up to then and put herself down firmly beside my bed. Terror of that room when it is dark has continued ever since. She will be there happily by day, but never at night. She now has a new sleeping place and is no bother, but the cause of her

115

terror remains a mystery.

People have suggested everything from a would be intruder at the window to a ghost. She does not mind being alone and is not a dog that shadows me wherever I go. Her only sign of unhappiness was refusal to remain in the room, panting and trembling. She is not afraid there during the day.

Chita became, quite suddenly, when she was eleven, terrified of low flying jets which were an irritating part of our lives at the time. She reacted the first time one night when a flight came so low that it alarmed us, never mind the dogs.

She raced round the room, leaped on to the dining room table and defecated. After that I made sure the table was inaccessible but there was nothing I could do about the jets as they were unpredictable. I had to get up and wait for her to stop racing madly round the room, her eyes wild, and, when her fright was over and the night quiet again, cuddle her, give her Rescue Remedy and settle her.

I was about to ask if I could have a tape made of the noise, to play to her softly and then more loudly, when she became deaf, almost overnight. It is the first time I have ever been thankful for deafness in my dogs, as there was no further problem. Her companion was quite unbothered by the din.

That incident had the unfortunate effect of making Chita very reluctant to be by herself, whereas before she had not worried at all.

Noise fear can be dealt with by writing to the BBC sound department and asking for a tape of the noise that frightens the dog. This is then played constantly, very low, as background, and gradually, taking some weeks, the sound is increased when the dog is feeding. Ultimately it should be so accustomed to it that it will not react. Gun shy dogs can be cured in this way.

A dog that has been lost and then found again will often react by shadowing its owners and becoming very distressed if left alone. This usually wears off in time. I have seen it several times in dogs that strayed accidentally, were lost from the car after an accident, or were stolen and then dumped, and re-united with their owners.

Many dogs bark if left alone, or howl, or whine. At one time I could map my neighbours' comings and goings as their dogs began to howl as soon as their owners left and continued until they came home. As they were late nightbirds this was irritating. After I showed them a list of their comings and going over a six week period they took the dogs in the car with them when they went out at night and solved the problem for all of us, as we lived on an estate at the time and the dogs could be heard up and down the road.

There are solutions for some dogs; for others, it may be that they need a home where there are people around them far more. This can be a common problem with dogs that have had owners home all day and then circumstances have forced them out to work, leaving the dog on its own for long periods.

Dogs are active animals and unless well exercised and played with they become bored and find an alternative way of occupying themselves, which may be far from acceptable. The hollow bone stuffed with titbits and sealed with cream cheese can help to keep the dog quiet as can a Buster cube, or a large chew.

The worried dog, like the new puppy, needs to be left on his own, perhaps only for two minutes or so and then rewarded when we release him. Next time it can be five minutes, so that he gradually gets used to being away from the family.

Everything we do with him has to be done gradually, building it up in time, so that he understands. He can't grasp complicated ideas. They have to be sorted into manageable bits for him.

CONTROL THE GAMES

John Rogerson, who is one of the top canine behaviourists in the UK, remains memorable in my mind for his constant saying 'control the game and you control the dog.'

The pup in the nest learns by the games he plays. If he always wins, he becomes packleader. He will control the games and also he will stop other pups interacting with one another and may stop any fights that start. He takes his position very seriously, and is second only to his mother, provided she is good at discipline. If she is not, he will take over her role.

We can teach our dog to play games that in the end are counter productive. The dog runs after the ball, brings it back half way and drops it, or runs off with it. We play with a tug ring and he gets it from us and runs away. He has won. Great. He knows he is cleverer and stronger than we are and more worthy of leadership.

So we play the game on the lead, and the dog can't run off with the ball. We drop it and he picks it up and at once we take it and praise him. Clever boy. A titbit here might not work, as he may drop the ball to gain the goodie.

Many dogs hate to give up a toy. Mine among them. She loves her kong and we play with it daily. Give I say. Nothing happens. I try to get hold of it and she grips harder. I say 'aaa' as if she had just hurt me and she lets go at once.

That came by accident as we had a battle every time for the kong when I first began to play with her with it. She managed to nip my finger and I yelled with pain, which horrified her. She let go at once, and only needs to be reminded of that occasion by a very soft 'aaaah' sound to release it now. It may seem odd but it works very well. Often a growl is more effective than a scolding, so long as you are boss.

She now releases it if I say 'give' as well as she has learned that I intend to win, whatever happens.

Dogs that play with children often turn into dodgers, teasing with the ball, refusing to let go and because the child can't gain control, the dog learns a leadership game and knows the child is lower in the pack than he is. If the child steps out of line, the dog tells him off, and that may be with a bite.

The best game for dog and child is hide the toy and let the dog find it. It is better not to play any game that involves the child chasing the dog (which teaches him to run away, and not come) or to run away from the dog, who may grab him with his mouth when he catches him, not knowing those teeth hurt unprotected human skin.

If children play the right games they too can control the dog and are in far less danger of being bitten. The wrong games can cause immense problems, as again the dog takes over the pack leader position and dictates the rules.

One owner came very worried to class as his German Shepherd had leaped out of the car in a busy car park in the middle of the tourist season, rushed over to a child and jumped at him and knocked him down. What was the child doing? He was about to throw a ball to his father.

The dog played with his owner's eleven year old son unsupervised. I asked the father to watch the game. The child teased the dog with the ball, holding it out of reach until Moss jumped up and snatched it. This boy was considerably larger and heavier than the child in the car park. The dog had not intended to harm the child; he thought he was being teased with the ball in the way his young owner teased him.

That game had to stop and we substituted a much better one in which the dog was taught to find a hidden toy, rather than having one thrown to him.

We did try to have him teach the dog to sit and stay until told he could run for the ball, and not on any account to jump at whoever held the ball. Unfortunately the boy was too impatient and balls had to be forbidden unless father was there too. It took a lot of time to undo what was begun in all innocence.

I can't repeat often enough that dogs don't think the way we do.

When playing ball, once the dog brings it back and gives it to the hand, then the game can continue, though it should be stopped before the dog tires of it, not when he does, as then he will simply go off and leave the ball. Or run off with it.

We once had a wonderful Golden Retriever in class who would retrieve for ever, or so the family thought. The boys in the family took him on the beach one day and threw the ball about two hundred times. He was exhausted, and thoroughly tired of the game. He never retrieved anything again and they lost a wonderful way of exercising him.

The toy should be taken away from him when he is still eager, and put away, He does not keep it. Toys left around all the time cease to be attractive. The dog is as bored with them as strawberry pickers are with the fruit when told they may eat it as they work. After a couple of days it's no longer a treat.

As I said before balls need to be sizeable or they can be swallowed. Several dogs have died that way, choking on them as they tried to catch them in their mouths when thrown. Others have had sticks penetrate an eye or the soft palate.

Toys do need to be vetted and possible accidents considered due to the speed at which a dog can move, or turn when running.

The dogs need their games but we must be in control all the time, and we do have to think hard as the dog has no knowledge of possible danger.

RECALL CONTROL

Once we are in control we have a worthwhile partnership. Call your dog and he races to you, fast and excitedly. What are we going to do now? Will I get a cuddle or an enticing nibble sized treat, or another game?

So when he comes to us we always reward him, not always in the same way, but keeping him guessing which makes it more fun for him.

If the dog never comes when called, you don't have a dog. You have a major problem. You look at your watch and see it is time to end playing in the park because you have an appointment. The dog won't come. There are wonderful smells and a couple of other dogs to play with. Much more interesting than anything you are going to do as that lead will be clipped on and his fun will end.

As you get more and more angry he becomes more and more reluctant to come near you. He may run off and you give up in disgust and leave him to come home when he chooses. One of my neighbours, many years ago, did this often. When the dog did arrive home, as by now he was hungry, he was beaten and shut in the garage without food for twelve hours. He did not have a human time sense.

As far as he was concerned he was being punished for coming home, not for running off when he was called. Coming home was so unrewarding that one day he decided not to come home at all. His owner was amazed. Nobody else was, but she had refused to recognise her mistake and you can't reason with some people. That dog turned up in the dogs' home, and they decided he could be re-homed.

When out in the park with the dog, call him and play with him; call him and cuddle him; call him and give him a titbit. Do this several times. Don't put that lead on at once, as it means the end of freedom.

Then call him and put him on the lead. He will come much more readily if five times out of six he isn't put on the lead and taken home, all his fun stopped.

I do watch where I let my dog off. If there is an aggressive dog about, then I take her elsewhere, as a fight can ruin a pleasant dog's temperament and make it hate all other dogs. After that it is never safe off lead, unless re-trained, and few people ever bother to do that.

At around seven months dogs usually go through what is known as the flight period. The only way to prevent it winning at this stage is to keep it tethered to you so that it can't get away. You have then won.

One man I knew had a gundog bitch who started this during her training. He got it out of her very fast as he needed her to be reliable. How? He told me he went out at six every morning with her on a long line and called her at least one hundred times. Each time she came she was rewarded in one way or another. She went on to be a very steady sensible dog that other people envied.

I was once told by one of my instructors that Success only comes before Toil in dictionaries and nothing is truer. Those who work hard at training get good dogs. Those who don't bother get dogs that can't be bothered either. It is always up to us.

PLAYBITING

All pups do this. They explore the world through their mouths. They teethe for a long time and need things to chew. They tease at hands, trying to nibble them. For some time with one of mine I looked as if I bit my finger nails. I didn't, but she did, and could do it without me even feeling her.

The little nips hurt and if not checked at once, they can become big nips. It does stop, if we insist. It does not stop if the dog is constantly having hands waved around its face, tempting it to grab those enticing fingers.

I keep sterilised marrow bones which I give to a pup who seems to want to chew my hands persistently. The dog does need to chew. I don't keep toys around the floor, but there is always a bone on a low table that she can go and get if she feels the urge come over her.

If the puppy is persistent, it must be ignored. Hands are kept in pockets, and when it tries to mouth the person who is rousing this desire must walk away, preferably into another room, shutting the door firmly.

Every time mine tried to mouth me she was put in her indoor crate and soon learned that such behaviour was far from rewarding as it ended in semi isolation and is no fun at all.

It is also as well to yell as if you were very badly hurt, which is what another pup would do, and continue to whimper and suck at your hand. Most dogs become very sheepish at this point and do their best not to bite so hard next time.

This biting is purely exploration, as the dog learns at that stage through its mouth. Pups that have left the mother too young and not learned that litter mates will bite back hard if they bite are often the worst with this habit.

It is as well to remember that, at first, the puppy will chew on anything it finds. Untidy people suffer. It is no use expecting the dog to leave things alone until it has been taught to do so, so I make sure nothing is lying around that might tempt a small mouth.

Pups can climb; this is something I forgot when Chita was small and as a result I had ten gloves without thumbs, as she was a genius at finding out where I had put them, and would climb onto the backs of chairs to reach them, unless I remembered to move the chairs. I did learn in time and instead of keeping them on the shelf they went into a drawer.

I put everything tempting out of reach, which means out of reach of a pup that can climb on a chair, climb up its back and take something off the mantelpiece. One of mine once sat on the mantelpiece, having followed the cat. She couldn't get down again and scared herself, so never tried that a second time. That same dog, if she heard a cat in the garden, would jump onto the dining room table to look out of the window and bark unless I was there to stop her.

There is always the time we forget and then suffer. I was once on a course with my newest pup, then four months old, with a friend who is as experienced in dogs as I am, but her own dog was then thirteen years old and she had forgotten about puppies.

Without thinking, she put her camera on the ground beside the pup. The case never looked the same again. Luckily the camera itself was undamaged. Her old dog died and she got a new pup, and had to learn all over again about puppy behaviour.

In fourteen years or so, we forget that the wonderful dog we now had started out as brash as any other puppy.

SUBMISSION

We don't want a dog that is constantly challenging

Flat ears in the prick eared breeds may be a sign of fear, or aggression, or of submission. A loving touch on my dog's head results in her ears lying flat, and a very appealing expression on her face.

Contented dogs lie on their backs, and if a rescued dog rolls over and lies happily with his paws in the air, I know that he has settled in and feels safe. Most dogs love to lie on their backs having their tummies rubbed.

When the pup lies on his back at the approach of a big dog, he is saying, 'I'm not going to fight you, Please don't hurt me.' It usually works, but not always, Some dogs seem unable to read the signals given. Often the pup may produce a few drops of urine at the same time, which is again a sign of submission as it will give out its own smell and alert the older dog to the situation.

Very submissive or very nervous dogs may actually flood the floor when greeting people, sometimes people they know well. They can't help this and shouldn't be scolded. Just greeted outside where it doesn't matter. My husband complained that one of our bitches was so bad he needed wellingtons when he met her.

She had a very nervous dog in her background, but as we built up her confidence it stopped and she was able to greet people normally when she was about a year old. I have had dogs in class that we have been unable to touch as if so we precipitated a flood.

I have always found the most difficult animal to train is an over submissive dog. This seems mainly to happen among collies. Those I have seen seem to need to be as close to their owners as possible, leaning against a leg, unable to stay away from the owner for even a second, lying down and rolling over if spoken to by anyone. It doesn't seem to be nervousness; just an immense desire to please which is overdone. I have never met anyone who managed to train a dog of this type for competition.

CONTROLLED LONG DOWN

We use every means in our power to establish leadership over our dogs. Many a time I have heard people say to someone, including, in my early days, me...

'Your dog loves you but has no respect for you at all.'

We know our dog respects us when he ceases to push through doors first, comes when he is called, does as we ask willingly and fast, and stops pulling on the lead.

Sometimes our abdication of responsibility means the dog sees a gap and tries to fill it, but not being born to authority he becomes confused and unhappy, longing for someone to say 'Do as I say. At once.'

When a dog first comes to class I watch it closely. Does it play up all the time, wanting to play with other dogs, ignoring the owner? Is it restless and a nuisance when they are sitting waiting for class to begin? Does it twist and turn on the lead, jump up and pester its owner?

That puppy is going to need more work than the pup that comes in, surveys the scene, decides nothing is happening at present to interest it and lies down quietly beside its owner, watching what goes on. This is the easy pup whose owner has perhaps without even thinking about it, made rules that the dog must obey and made sure that they are kept. A dog that has a few rules made and has them enforced is much happier than one that has no framework at all for its life.

Does the pup lie down when shown how?

If there is a dog that won't lie down even after several lessons I know we have a very dominant dog indeed. Lying down is a sign of submission. It is often very difficult to get terriers to do so. One young Australian Terrier looked as if he never would, but after a few months he suddenly showed signs of going down with a will. His owner was surprised and delighted because he was becoming more biddable.

But she was telling him by making him lie down that she was top dog and he was not.

We had one cross bred terrier belonging to a fourteen year old girl who never would lie down at all. One of my colleagues decided that he would make the dog do as he was told. I thought it unwise, but was told the dog had to learn people were boss, not him. Paul was very badly bitten.

The dog was put down soon after for biting the child. The child's mother described the dog as trouble on four legs from the day he came home. I very much doubt if anyone could have taught that dog he was not boss.

Another girl the same age arrived with a little bull terrier cross that was very nasty indeed, and, had I not jumped out of the way, would have bitten me. His owner made him lie down, and he stayed like that for the whole lesson, not taking part. He came for several weeks, learning to do nothing but lie still.

I discovered he was a stray from a gipsy encampment, and they had taken him in after he had a road accident outside their house that broke his pelvis. His first owners couldn't afford the vet bill and were going to have him put down, but he had apparently been visiting the house and the girl had grown attached to him.

She did everything she was told, including the long down. Within two years he was the star of the club and became a wonderful dog, living to a great old age. I often met him when walking with his master as by then his child owner was away from home and married with children of her own, and was always greeted fervently.

The long down is not a stay exercise. The dog has to lie still for at least twenty minutes. It can be done while watching TV so long as you make sure that if the dog gets up he is put down again. Lie still and be good. Lie down. Good dog.

It's useful to practise during those wallpaper programmes that we all watch and never remember afterwards and wonder why on earth we wasted our time. I find my dog more interesting than any 'soap' on the box.

We aim at one minute to start with; then two: then three, and increase the time until the dog will lie still if told for at least twenty minutes.

It is extremely useful when the family is eating. It is another way of saying 'I'm boss and you do as I say' without confrontation. One extremely pushy dog that we despaired of, now, as soon as he sees the table being set for a meal, lies beside his owner's chair, ready for the 'lie down and be good' command.

MAKING LIFE HAPPIER FOR THE DOG

One of my rescue dogs, who had been taught very little, and had many changes of owner had at some point been taught a very useful action. As soon as I started to fill the kettle, or prepare a meal, he curled up in a corner out of the way to watch, and never moved again until told.

He was one of the most rewarding dogs. He had so little affection in his early days that he adored the tiniest attention and would lie for hours with his head against my leg and his paw curled round my shoe as if hanging on to me.

We can do so much with our dogs just by the way we behave ourselves when they are around, and by management. I find I never need to raise my voice to my dogs. They are watching and listening, waiting for me to instigate some fun. A soft whistle will bring them.

I have had two dogs of my own that were very much boss dogs, but once I realised this and showed them what I expected, they became every easy to live with. People thought I was very lucky to have dogs that behaved so well. But it didn't come by accident. It takes time.

You may feel that this is all nonsense but let me tell you about Klaus before you make up your mind.

He was a West Highland White, a breed that has been abused by puppy farmers as they are so appealing, so that some of them are most undesirable They must come from good breeder. Over breeding produces bad dogs.

Klaus was well bred but his owner had been in and out of hospital in his early days, which did not help, as he was looked after by different people each time. He had learned that when he wanted something and pestered, he got it. The house he lived in backed on an alleyway that led to a school and the children threw things at him.

When I met him he was a snappy snarling nasty little mess and was eighteen months old. He had bitten several times. Nobody could go near his bed; nobody could go near him when he was eating; nobody could touch his toys as he not only grabbed them, he bit. If he wanted to sit on his owner's lap he did, or she was bitten.

I made rules and she kept them, as like so many people, she had a love/hate relationship with the dog. When he got his own way he was adorable, but she was becoming afraid of him. She did not want him put to sleep.

New rules were made. He was never to go upstairs. A gate was put at the bottom to stop him as he liked to lie halfway up and look down on everyone. Top dogs look down on other folk.

As soon as he was out of his bed in the morning something was to be put in it; the broom, or the vacuum cleaner, or a box of tins from the supermarket. It was not his. it belonged to his owner who allowed him to sleep in it when she said he could. Not when he chose. It was also moved around so that it was never in the same place in the kitchen.

No one was to speak to him for three weeks except for absolute necessities.

All his toys were to be put away. He could have his bone when his owner chose to give it to him, not when he begged for it.

If he tried to jump on her lap, she at once put down a tiny biscuit on the floor, said 'off' and then praised him when he did get down. A few minutes later, she invited him to jump up.

The garden was divided so that a solid fence hid him from the children, and he had about eight feet to play in near the house. This stopped his constant barking as there was nothing he could see to bark at and nothing was thrown at him as the new area was well away from the alley fence.

There are circumstances in which you do have to change the dog's environment as the sort of training to overcome the problem is far too time consuming. In this case with children racing by, some not very nice children, he was constantly being upset again.

He could go in and out to his part of the garden from the kitchen door with easy access. This routine helped with angry neighbours and as they ceased to yell at him for barking, he began to be a much nicer dog.

He was given one tablespoonful of food, and when that was eaten the plate was removed and he was given another. He began to learn that people near his plate meant more food, not that it was being taken away and he stopped guarding that.

He also stopped guarding his bed, especially when his owner began to stand in it at times. My bed; not yours. I allow you to sleep there when I choose.

He became a charming little dog and nobody was bitten again. He did not pester for food or toys or games, or to go outside. He waited until his owner gave permission.

Few dogs are really easy or problem free. With all those I have succeeded with, my own as well as others, it took patience and persistence, before anyone could feel pride. I had two of the most difficult dogs I have ever met, but both turned into very nice dogs indeed after a year or so.

It took time and patience and persistence and a great deal of energy and thought. Once that it is achieved and the owner and dog live on happy terms life becomes very rewarding. Klaus's owner was so pleased with her little dog, but if she had not been determined to show him once and for all that she was boss, he would not be alive now.

Incidentally, she was disabled, so had problems of her own to overcome. She was determined to change him as she was so fond of him and he was a very young dog. She persisted; she used lots of patience and in the end she was very proud of him. So was I.

There have been many others exhibiting some of those faults, but he was quite the worst I have seen although he was so small a dog.

It is not only big dogs that wish to lead the pack. The little ones can do it just as well. Some do it by fight and bite, but as I said before many do it by wile and guile and they are much cleverer than we are.

No wile in a dog? One of mine was an adept. If both dogs had a bone, the other dog's, she was sure, was always nicer than hers. So she ran to the window and barked. The other dog left his bone to see who was there. Nobody. Puzzled, he went back to find her happily chewing on his bone. He took hers. There was never any fuss. Just a piece of cleverness which gave her power over him.

They do the same to us and often we don't even recognise what they are doing. So we have to exercise leadership all the time, and make sure the dog knows its place. A very dominant dog can be a very dangerous dog and nobody wants to live with that.

7
THE ADULT DOG

WHY TRAIN OUR DOGS?

The vast majority of dog owners don't. Some think it cruel to make the dog do anything other than what he chooses. I hate washing up. Is it cruel to make me do it? I would soon live in a horrible sort of home if I never cleaned any dishes. I don't suffer any traumas from doing it and nor does a dog that is being taught good manners. Most dogs delight in having something interesting to do other than lie around waiting for someone to notice them.

If we buy a dog we have a responsibility, not only to care for it, and keep it in good health and exercise it, but to make sure it does not give offence to anyone. There is only one way to do that and that is to teach it from puppyhood how to behave in a manner that will make other people admire us and our dogs, and not detest us both. Also training the dog can save its life in many situations.

Often people come to class saying 'I don't want to compete, so I don't need to teach my dog those requirements. I just want him to be sensible and do as he is told and not be a nuisance.'

This is about as useful as someone coming to a tennis coach and saying I don't want to play at Wimbledon so don't teach me the rules. I just want to have fun.

Whether we play for fun or aim to become top world players, we still need a tennis racquet and the right kind of ball, a court marked out in a certain way and a net at the correct height. We have to be taught how to hold the racquet, how to get the ball over the net and the various shots and how to score.

We don't have to excel. We can still have a lot of fun and exercise. We need the right equipment, and we need to know the rules; we can't change them and suddenly say 'OK, today we will score points even if the ball goes out.'

The exercises we teach our dogs can be life savers. If we can stop the dog running away with one command, then we have a major asset in controlling him.

I was out with one of my dogs when he saw a cat on the other side of the road. He lunged suddenly and the lead broke at the clip, leaving the dog free. He bolted towards the road and I yelled ' DOWN' at the top of my voice. He did lie down, with his paws over the kerb, within a foot of a large lorry that was passing at the time. Had he not gone down, he would have been dead.

Another dog, not taught that 'down' command, did the same thing and was killed under his owner's eyes.

The stay exercise is also a life saver, and can be used for all kinds of situations.

When competition first began it was merely common sense. Those who devised it merely wanted to see how well a dog had been taught, and give people some fun and an incentive to teach their dogs to be sensible. Could he walk on the lead without pulling, or lunging, or lagging? Could he walk as well off the lead? The lead might break and you need the dog beside you. It always worries me when I see dogs off lead on pavements in towns, or in lanes with no pavements at all, running ahead of their owners. It is silly if the dog is not trained and it is merely showing off if he is, as no dog is ever one hundred per cent safe.

It is inconsiderate even if your dog is well trained, to allow it total freedom unless in a very large secure place where you are sure it will not give offence to anyone.

CONTROLLING OUR DOGS.

The 'come when called' is vital as we can't control a dog that doesn't come when we want him and doesn't know his name. This is the first basis of all control so that time spent on this exercise is better spent than going for long walks when he is off lead and disobeying all the time. That comes later, when our dog is obedient.

We need, by law, to be in control of our dogs twenty four hours a day. No one can be in control of a dog that is out of sight, and even in a garden there is room for a dog to vanish and commit mayhem behind a bush.

He may be digging up your most precious plant; or biting someone who has come unexpectedly through the gate, not because he is vicious, but because he is startled. Or killing next door's cat. He may be digging his way out of the garden under the fence. Or being let out by children who think it funny to open the gate but then are terrified when he runs after them, and they trigger him to bite.

NEED FOR VIGILANCE

Dogs, every year, are stolen from their gardens. It is easy enough with a placid dog, and then it's a hundred miles down the motorway, ending in a pub where the thief tells some unsuspecting person he is devastated as he has been sent abroad, or has to move to a flat, or has been divorced and has to sell the dog.

Recently someone not very far from where I live left her Yorkshire Terrier in the car while she went in to the garage shop to pay for her petrol. She came out to find an empty car. Someone else getting petrol told her a man had taken the dog out of the car and driven off with it. He had thought at first this was her husband about to take it for a walk, and did not realise what was happening. I now lock my car even if left for only a moment in case the dog is removed.

In both instances a hundred pounds or more changes hands with no questions asked and an innocent person is now in charge of a stolen dog which might be identified and returned to the rightful owner, with no repayment of the money.

OUR RESPONSIBILITY AS OWNERS

This does not only apply to teaching our dogs to be safe in all circumstances, to ensuring they are in good health and well cared for, but in our attitudes to other people. We must respect their rights. Our dog must not cause harm to anyone, or be a nuisance, in any way.

Mine comes to the hairdresser with me, where she is fussed and petted by almost everyone, but two ladies are afraid of her so that when they are there I take extra care to ensure she does not go anywhere near them. She can't understand their attitude as that is one of her favourite places. Everyone who works there has one or more dogs.

I took her in as a pup to socialise her and now if I go without her they all grumble. Where is she? If I have left her in the car as it is not a hot day, I am asked to fetch her in. She curls up and lies down all the time I am there, unless someone wants to pet her.

Some peoples' attitudes can be remarkably unrewarding, and it is not only those without dogs who suffer from them. Those with dogs can suffer even more.

I remember one nightmare course when a friend and I both had very difficult dogs. Hers had had a bad puppyhood and was technically a rescue; mine was a rescue, about two years old when I bought him. We were in a hostel where we all had dogs. One owner allowed hers to roam up and down the corridors and left her door open.

I had only had mine a few weeks and my friend had not had hers in such a situation before. Both were nervous and uneasy and we were afraid might attack the other dog, which we definitely did not want to happen. Both would sit on command, but the roaming dog triggered them, as the corridors were very narrow indeed.

Almost everyone else made sure their dogs were safely in their rooms, as they recognised our problem, and knew enough about dogs to realise we were in the process of curing it, which takes time.

I could take my second dog in without worrying at all. The owner of the roaming dog, asked to keep her dog in while we brought ours in (which only took five minutes) gave a short and very unpleasant answer. It revealed to the rest of us that not only had she no consideration for others, but also knew very little indeed about dogs.

After that, since we had to run the gauntlet every time we took the dogs in and out (they slept in our rooms at night) we took it in turns to go first and make sure the coast was clear. Those who were knowledgeable helped us. Then, one dog secure behind a shut door, the other owner made sure it was safe for the second to come in. It added a lot of unnecessary stress. Also, we were being considerate in the face of totally lack of consideration on someone else's part. It did not endear that person to us.

I doubt if she ever realised that her safe easy well trained dog was a hazard to other people, as she could easily have been attacked had we been careless. Two years later both our dogs were safe in all circumstances, but we were overcoming built in fears which we had inherited through someone else's treatment of them, not through our own.

With the co-operation of other dog owners these problems are overcome quickly; with lack of co-operation from those who know little, but think they know, there is one setback after another, making it far harder for the owner to remedy the faults that have been wished on him.

The most dangerous people in the world are those who are sure they know. But in fact they don't know. Experience teaches wisdom and we then know how little we do know... all those millions of dogs we have never met; the behaviour we have never seen. No one can ever know everything.

Much of what I know I have learned from people older than myself with more experience in the dog world; much of it the dogs themselves have taught me, hundreds of dogs over the years. What I do know would take more than this one book. What I don't know would fill volumes.

Considering others, and ensuring our dogs do not upset them, whether they have dogs or not, is a major part of our responsibility as dog owners. Nobody forces us to own them. Many people consider that they are an unnecessary and dangerous luxury and it is up to us to prove they are neither, as they contribute to our well being.

I visit friends who have kennels. There is a rule in all of them that we never take our own dogs out of the car until we have checked with the kennel owners that it is safe; that there is no loose dog about to come out from behind a buildings, or being let out into the yard for exercise.

The dog comes out on its lead.

In a police dog training area where all the dogs are well trained, if a dog gets loose, (and accidents do happen) then there is a shout of ''ware, loose dog' and every other dog is at once put in either a kennel or a van securely until the loose dog is under control again.

The Kennels where my pup was born is very rigid about loose dogs, and those boarding are always walked and exercised separately so that there is no chance of an accident. Unfortunately people are not always either thoughtful or observant.

On one occasion a client came in with his dog, and did not see the Kennels owner in the paddock with a boarder. The visiting dog was a fighter. He jumped the four foot fence and attacked the boarder. The Kennels owner tried to separate the dogs, as it was possible there could be bad injuries.

One dog snapped at the other, but instead caught a human hand. The result was a finger that was, at first, in danger of being amputated. Luckily there was a good surgeon and the bite did, eventually, heal without causing too many problems afterwards.

It only takes a moment.

Even a well trained dog can be unreliable.

One high level competition dog always sat by the car while it was unloaded, and then went into the house at the end of this exercise. For nine years there was no problem. Then, one day, a cat raced out from next door and the dog was triggered to chase. She died under a car.

I put my dog safely in the house before taking in the shopping if I am in a place where that could happen. Rooms have doors that can be closed even if the front door has to be left open.

In class I expect everyone to be considerate. If someone has an exceptionally difficult dog I point it out and all the class members are expected to co-operate and help to teach that dog that nothing nasty is going to happen while it is there.

Often these dogs are rescued, and have a sad story behind them, which everyone is told, so that a dog that has been brutally used by youths is kept away from anyone that might remind him of his past; a dog that has been bullied by children only meets very carefully chosen children; a nervous dog is allowed to relax without being asked to do more than play for few weeks.

Other dogs are kept away from them, unobtrusively, and those with brash dogs are expected to be ten times more vigilant. Since we work out of doors, if their dog starts to play up, they can walk away from the class to the other side of the area and calm the dog without a scene that might upset a more timid animal. Bolshie owners often have bolshie dogs. I hope to change their attitudes if they come to class, but I have only had two I would have preferred many miles away in twenty five years, so there aren't many of them around; or at least, not in dog classes.

You can meet them when out with your dog. One woman's dog chased one of mine, who turned, barked, and began to chase the intruder. I called out 'down' and to my delight in spite of being chased my little bitch went down and stayed down. To my astonishment the other woman went up to mine and began to thrash her with her lead.

I took the lead and said 'what are you doing?'

'She was chasing my dog.'

My companion pointed out that her dog had started the problem. Since the woman had every intention of continuing to thrash my poor dog I took the lead, and she finally went off, still very angry. I discovered the lead in my car two days later. I never saw her again, much to my relief, as the fault did not lie with my dog at all.

I was surprised that she lay still while being hit, but I think she was as astounded as I was. Nobody in her whole life had ever used a lead as a weapon to harm her. Luckily she did not associate that lead thrashing with me and did not become afraid of leads, as that can give immense problems when it happens. Rescued dogs are often afraid of leads, hands and feet, as well as rolled up newspapers. With good reason.

STARTING TO TRAIN

One of the most worrying things I find about many breeders is their insistence that the puppy must be allowed to grow up and not be trained at all before six months old. People think they mean do nothing whatever; the breeders do not realise that the first time dog owner has no idea that the breeder is talking about competition, not about civilising the little animal which they do automatically.

Equally worrying are those keen competitors who teach the puppy so much that they can enter obedience competitions at only a few months old. There are people who have won with eight or nine month old pups, but that seems very hard on the youngster.

Over the years, I have found that many pups that have been brought to such a high standard, cease to perform well by two years old as they are tired of being forced. The requirements for competition today are very high indeed. A dog that sits half an inch crooked will be penalised.

One of my friends tells how he, at the age of seventeen, entered an Obedience competition with a young bitch of less that a year old. He came third. He listened to the judge congratulating the winner and the person who came second and waited happily for her praise.

What she said was:

'As for you, young man, you should be ashamed of yourself. Go away and play with that poor baby and let her be a puppy as she has never had a chance.'

There was one aspect of that that the judge had not considered. When he told me this story he said. 'Actually I was just a kid playing games with my pup, only they weren't the sort of games most people played. We were both having fun.'

Now, some thirty years later, he does not recommend teaching very young dogs to that standard and does not start on his own until they are a year old, though for their first year they are taught to be sensible and not start any habit that will be a nuisance when they are older, and they have games that are training in disguise.

Whether they are destined for high competition, as police dogs, or dogs for the disabled, deaf, or blind, as sheepdogs, or those engaged in bomb and drug detection, or search and rescue, or household companions, they do need to be taught manners. All young things, including human babies, are savages when born, and have to be guided into behaving in a way that does not damage other people or cause immense problems. Otherwise what we have is a vandal in the house.

Pups learn, whether we teach them or not. They chew, whether we like it or not. If not checked they chew our hands, our clothes and the rugs, carpets and furniture. Dogs have even been known to chew doors, and pull off wallpaper.

They howl, bark, cry, chase the children and the cat. If out and off lead, they may chase squirrels, rabbits, cars, bicycles, children and joggers.

They steal if food is within their reach. They don't know it is stealing; how can they distinguish between food put down for them and food left available?

So, from the day the puppy comes home, we teach him to be sensible. If we don't, there will come a time when we will regret it. Between about eight months and two years most dogs and bitches go through a hooligan stage. They riot; they rush everywhere. They do everything we don't want them to do; they are so full of their new strange adolescent feelings that they stop listening to us.

If they were teenagers they would drink, swear, take drugs, and rebel in every way they could imagine. They would play strange music very loudly, take the stairs three at time, slam the doors, and generally exhaust everyone else in the house.

Like human youngsters they suddenly find that the adult in charge of them has faults, forgets things, isn't foolproof, or the wonderful person they thought. But is merely human and imperfect. They try their wings to see how far they can fly before we bring them back to earth and draw lines beyond which they may not pass.

We need guidelines for them. Dogs and children alike.

THE INDOOR KENNEL

There are often times when we need to be able to put our partly trained dog in a safe place rather than struggling to control him while we deal with an emergency. The answer to this is the indoor kennel, sometimes known as a crate. It can also be useful even when the dog is fully trained if you have a visitor who is terrified of animals.

It is also a boon when we don't have time to watch the puppy and ensure it does no damage.

I couldn't do without mine. It is wonderful to be able to put the puppy in a safe place with its toys, and then relax, knowing she can come to no harm and do no harm.

There are a number of firms that sell them. The pet shops usually only have those for small dogs. They come in all sizes. I have found the suppliers are very helpful if you ring and tell them the breed, and will advise you on which you need.

There are collapsible models which can serve both in the house and the car. Also it is an advantage if you wish to travel with your dog as hotels and such places are much happier if they know you have a secure place in which the dog can be put and that there won't be any damage to your room.

Some people, with two or more dogs, use them to keep the dogs, while waiting for showing or working, safe at unbenched shows while they are competing with another. It is also useful at dog class if you have a new pup and want to bring it in. The pup will be secure, no other dog can get at it, and it can lie quietly and watch what is going on, leaving you free to work with your older dog.

I like to put my pup in an indoor kennel while I am busy. That means I can iron safely and not have to watch for a puppy chewing the flex, or pulling at it if I go out of the room, and bring a hot heavy iron down on himself.

I can open the doors to the garden without worrying that he may get out. I can vacuum without a pup that is in the way, trying to attack the cleaner, or even my legs, as that is good fun to an untaught puppy.

I do not like my dog outside in the garden without me. I have no idea what he is doing. He may be able to escape; or chase next door's cat, bark at birds and my neighbours, and produce ill feeling between us, or dig huge holes in the lawn, or pull up plants. He may eat something a bird has dropped and be poisoned. Children may tease him over the fence and undo all the good I am doing.

In the indoor kennel, he is near me, is safe, and when I have finished my work, which I do quickly without my small hindrance, I can let him out and have time for games. These are learning games and I have never met a pup that didn't think them enormous fun, and be ecstatically pleased with its small self when praised and cuddled and told what a clever little animal it is.

The bitch I have now, when my young grandchildren start rioting, as small boys will, puts herself in her kennel with the door open and lies there out of the way until they settle down again to a quieter game.

If I sit in the chair beside the kennel, she lies down inside, as that is close to me, again having put herself there. It is a place of safety, a sanctuary, and at night she often sleeps in it, although she has a bed outside as well. The door is not shut. She can leave it at will.

She regards it as her own territory, and not a place of punishment.

It has another virtue as if a pup has to be left on its own while you go out, it is much safer there than left to wander the house, and feels much more secure. It can have its bed, and toys to chew, and there is no danger of the furnishings and carpeting being damaged.

It is important to make sure the kennel isn't used to keep the dog secure all day;

he must come out and interact with people and have freedom to run and stretch his legs. Also it needs to be big enough for him to stand in and to turn round.

Like everything else we need to introduce it slowly. Put the pup in with its food; leave the door open. Then put it in for a few minutes with its toys, but sit beside it and talk to it.

Gradually the time can be extended until you can leave it there during a party, avoiding having it under foot or thrust into the garden or a shed.

Children need to be discouraged from treating it as a Wendy house. This is for the dog; not a family play place.

THE TRAINING TOOLS

Dog trainers often say that there are several AIDS to dog training. Apart from the fact that the word 'aids' has an unfortunate meaning today, I prefer to use the word tools, which seems to me much clearer to those who are just beginning to learn the skill.

We have a number of tools which we can use, two of which cost nothing and are part of us. Our voices and our hands. It is also important to watch the way we move; and the way we behave. Amble along without much attention and the dog will also amble along with no attention at all.

Teaching a dog requires a great deal of concentration and very swift reactions, so that you can guess what he is about to do before he actually does it, and to prevent it at that stage is far better than to do so after he has done the wrong thing.

If you see a pheasant or a rabbit before the dog does and at once take action to prevent a chase the result is success. But once the dog has seen it and begun to move, even with a trained dog there may be failure.

If we play tennis, there is a point at which the ball can be hit with maximum effect. Hit it too soon and it may go into the net or out of court. Miss it, and the point is lost. This is the secret of good timing. It is the same in dog training, which is why it is much easier to teach with toys or titbits than to rely on a movement to check the dog; it is usually done at the wrong time and if the checking is being used in teaching the dog to walk at heel, all that happens is that you have a dog with no fur round its neck, that has learned nothing as it has been given the wrong cues.

WHAT IS TIMING?

Timing is very important whatever we are doing with the dog.

The dog is pulling, and is in front of you, towards the side, and about a foot away from you. You say 'heel', and then give a jerk. Nothing happens. The dog associates the word with what he is doing now, and what he is doing now is pulling. So 'heel' to him, means 'I stay where I am. This is heel.' The jerk mystifies him, as it can't be explained to him that it happened because he was pulling.

The wrong command was given at the wrong time for that action. Timing of the command is vital in any exercise but is worth considering in great detail when teaching the dog to heel correctly.

I teach people to stand still, when the dog pulls, and tap their thighs, so that the dog looks round, having stopped pulling at that point. He is waiting for something else to happen. At the thigh pat the vast majority of dogs come in to your side and then you say 'heel' because now they are in the right place.

If you do this every time he pulls in time you only have to tap your side and he thinks 'I'm wrong. I ought to be back there,' and back he comes. You haven't said 'heel' when he is in front so he doesn't learn that 'heel' means pull; and he hasn't learned either that a jerk is meaningless as it hasn't had the result the handler wanted, and so the dog can't associate it with anything that is wanted from him.

As soon as he is in the right place when teaching him, he gets his praise and then his food reward. So that the timing of the word is very important, or the dog learns something you did not intend to teach. Once he walks properly beside you without pulling he is not rewarded with food, as he has now learned that particular skill.

Timing commands correctly is vital in every exercise we teach the dog, and even more important is the timing of praise. If we say 'Good dog', as the dog gets up from a 'stay' instead of waiting for you to return and tell him he may move, then we have praised the dog for doing the wrong action, not the right one.

Good handlers seem to know by instinct when to correct. The rest of us have to learn it. I find it far easier nowadays when I have twenty or more dogs of many breeds each week to watch and work with, as I get so much practice.

It can be so wrong. For instance, we tell the dog to sit which he does so briefly that we say 'good dog' as he gets up. Our timing was wrong as we should have said 'good dog' while he was still sitting. Now he is convinced that what you were really trying to teach him was to sit for a second and then get up again. The praise which actually teaches the dog to sit and stay sitting has to come almost before his tail touches the ground. The corrective jerk works very well for skilled people because they use the correct action, which is a snatch and release, not a violent tug and towing action, and it is used at <u>exactly</u> the right moment. This is just before the pull begins; not when the dog is way ahead and we are off balance.

Timing praise and action correctly is a major skill. Some people never achieve it, which is why it is much better to use food rewards, as they can be given when the dog is doing right and most owners understand that. Many classes never teach timing at all, which is why people are unsuccessful.

THE VOICE

The human voice is one of our major assets. It can indicate approval, especially if a smile is added.

'You good dog.' 'You clever dog.'

It can indicate disapproval.

'Bad dog. What do you think you're doing?' The tone conveys our meaning, especially if we frown as well.

I live in Wales and many of my owners speak in Welsh to their dogs. I forget and praise their dogs in English. The owners are surprised to find the dogs understand me, and look happy and wag their tails. In fact it is not the words they are hearing,

134

but the <u>tone</u>. The Welsh for good dog in my part of the country is Ci (key) da; bad dog is Ci drwg...if the last word is prolonged and the r is rolled, it sounds very like a growl and is much more useful, I find, than 'bad dog.'.

The dog, hearing enthusiastic praise, understands very well that he has just done something clever and earned your approval. This re-assures him. It's one of the most important tools we have.

I believe it is the RAF dog handlers who say that praise is the good dog trainers' secret weapon. It is certainly true. A praised dog is always happy and confident. He knows that when he does right he gains immense approval and since he likes that he tries hard to be right all the time.

It is not only dogs that respond, but people too. Years ago I went on an unusual course. In one session we had to pair off. One partner was blindfolded and had to be guided through an intricate maze on the floor made up of upturned plastic mugs. There was only one path and a penalty was earned if any of the obstacles was touched.

It is very tempting to say, 'no, not that way...be careful, there's a mug within an inch of your foot...'

The winner was an experienced handler who said, 'That's fine. Just stand quite still and move your right foot one inch...oh brilliant...you're doing very well...'

Whereas the negative commands produced tension, the praise relaxed the blindfolded person and gave confidence. Families who appreciate mum's cooking are much more likely to have interesting and varied meals than those who grumble all the time; don't like this, want chips, not new potatoes...lack of approval switches people off and does exactly the same to dogs. I love visitors who say 'that was wonderful,' when I have spent hours cooking, and next time try even harder to produce a good meal.

We do have to remember that the dog has a different time perception to us. We can praise even a small child for an action he performed yesterday or even days ago.

'Your grandmother tells me you made her a lovely daisy chain when you visited her last week. She was so pleased. It was very thoughtful.'

We can never tell our dogs that they did well last Saturday and we are delighted. The praise applies to what he is doing at the instant it is given. So if he is shaking in terror because he has seen something that scared him, or another dog he is afraid will attack him, if at that moment we use a pleasant re-assuring voice (which is human and natural) unfortunately he assumes that what we are praising is the action we definitely don't want.

What we need here is not the soothing voice, but a matter of fact, 'oh come on Bennie...that won't hurt you. Here... let's play ball,' and we distract him from his worries.

Maybe he is growling at someone passing by. Many people will try to re-assure him and comfort him, and pat him saying, 'It's all right, lad. Nobody's going to hurt you.'

That is a message he can't understand,. He interprets it, 'It's OK to growl. I approve.' Which is not what we intended at all. So many people teach their dogs to be anti-social by trying to comfort them. If he is growling at a passer by he needs to

135

be convinced that won't do. The correct thing to do here is to ignore the growl and distract the dog with a toy in your hand or a titbit. Not occasionally, but every single time it happens.

We can use our voice to rebuke the dog, but again it must be done at the right moment...while he is actually eating that piece of steak he pinched...not when it has gone. A sharp 'what do you think you're doing?' can produce results. If we find the steak has vanished, it is no use whatever scolding the dog. He does not realise why. The past is gone; he lives in the present.

With an obstinate puppy, a growl is often effective. If it bites you harder than you like (it will nibble, they all do) puppy noises of misery usually alert it to the fact that it has hurt you. That is how its litter mates would react. With an older dog that may accidentally hurt with its teeth (you both tried to get the ball at the same time) a 'that hurt,' in an indignant voice is enough to make most dogs realise what happened, but it must be said immediately, not seconds later.

A soft soothing voice has an enormous effect on a terrified animal. I was once at a horse show when a pony got loose as its owner had not tied it properly. It panicked and raced round the arena, with people and ponies all jumping out of the way and several people running after it, shouting.

I stood at the side of the arena, saying over and over very softly, 'Don't be afraid. come to me.' After a few minutes it heard my voice and did come to me. I soothed it with more words, and tied it again, this time safely.

I heard someone say , 'Did you hear that tomfool woman telling it to come to her?'

They plainly had not noticed that the pony had come to the tomfool woman who it trusted not to yell and scare it even more. I used to spend a lot of my time when I lived in Cheshire being commandeered by horse breeding friends to come and talk, very softly, for an hour or so to a new foal or a frightened animal brought in for schooling for the first time.

At first the poor animal cowered at the back of the stable. I stood by the half door, just chatting. I might recite poems or nursery rhymes, anything to keep my voice going softly and comfortingly. Usually within an hour the pony or horse would come towards me, curious, obviously listening.

I quieted my terrified horse on the Windermere ferry by talking to it all the way across. On another ferry that served the Highlands and islands of Scotland, a farmer stood for several hours beside a large container inside which was a very big bull. The old man sang hymns non stop. I can still see him, grey haired, red faced, dressed in tweeds with a pork pie hat on the back of his head, singing 'Rock of Ages', while the animal stood quietly, without panic.

They used to 'break' a horse by very cruel methods. Much better ways are used now by the really skilled, and so they are with dogs, as the old jerk and yell methods also 'broke' the dog. We want to school him and teach him to trust us all the time.

I have trained fox cubs and badger cubs just by talking - and also you train a hawke by non stop talking.

We must be fair, It worries me when an instructor demonstrates the use of the voice to a class by first praising his or her own dog, and then shouting at it and making it cower. This isn't fair as the dog has done no wrong and all that happens is that the owner appears entirely unpredictable. I would never scold my dog unless she had done wrong, and if I wish to put over the point, I merely say that if I were to use a very angry voice on her, she would be most upset and know that I was not pleased. I explain it is unfair to her to use a nasty voice just to prove a point.

Our voice is a major tool and if we abuse it, we don't succeed at all. Classes where the dogs are praised a lot by everyone learn far quicker than those where yelling and shouting and blaming the dog is the order of the day. If an owner forgets to praise her dog when it has done well, I always do so at once and the dog responds to my voice in the way it would to its owner's.

If a dog has difficulty in performing some action, when it does right I ask everyone to join in and praise and this really does have a terrific effect on an uncertain dog. Suddenly everyone likes it enormously and it is happy to repeat the action that brought that wonderful result.

One party piece I have often seen is for the handler to praise the dog with words that definitely are not praise, such as 'bad dog,' 'awful dog', 'stupid dog.' 'wicked dog,' but in a very happy voice. The dog still responds as if to praise if the tone is right. It's not what you say, but how you say it. So many people say 'No' with a 'Yes' voice and are surprised at the result.

FOOD REWARDS

There is still, amazingly, in spite of all the research done in the past few years, a group of people who believe dogs should work for love, not for rewards.

It takes time to build both love and trust. It does not happen overnight in either the human or the animal world.

Suppose we rescue a dog and bring him home. How are we going to teach him? He doesn't love us; he doesn't know us; he may actually not like us very much. How in the world are we going to get through to him that he must obey us? By shouting and hitting him? That, with a rescued dog is very likely to get us well and truly and deservedly bitten, as well as being extremely cruel.

Josse, the dog who had six male owners before me, hated men, probably with very good reason. Whenever we saw a man he tried to lunge and attack. I took him out just before a meal so that he was hungry. I had in my hand a piece of cooked garlic sausage, (the kind good butchers make) about an inch long; something he could really see and smell and taste.

I kept this in my cupped hand, right at the bottom by the little finger. Whenever we saw a man I held out my hand to him and let him bury his nose in my palm, trying to get at the food, which I held tightly. He forgot the passer by, and concentrated on trying to reach the food.

Had I done as was suggested, and every time he saw a man jerked him so hard he almost came off his feet, he would have associated men with a very unpleasant experience indeed. As it was, he learned to associate them with something pleasant; being fed with a very tasty treat. We went every week to my ex police dog instructor friend who lined up men with titbits for him to meet.

With some dogs a toy works very well, but rescued dogs rarely know how to play and have to be taught. It was a year before Josse played like a normal dog.

Two years after I bought Josse he sat quietly beside me in a big hotel where there was a convention of barristers. Two hundred men in evening dress filed past us from the lecture room to the dining room and he did not attempt to move. Nor did I have any food in my hand. We had been coming in to go to my room and our way was barred as the men filed out.

There are dogs that only want to please themselves and never care about their owners. The only way to train them is to keep them slightly hungry and give a food reward. One dog, who became a Working Trials Champion some years ago, was so dominant that his owner, who is one of the top trainers in the UK, could not get results without food.

I was once invited to sit in on a lesson with a Bull Terrier, given by my local police dog instructor friend with two other police dog handlers present. The dog had been sent to be trained professionally as his owners could not cope with him.

He obeyed every command except 'sit' and that he would not do.

All three men tried every way they knew to get the dog to co-operate. He stood, rock solid, looking up at them, defying them to make him do as they wanted.

I was invited to try.

I took a piece of cooked liver out of my pocket and held it to his nose. I moved my hand so that he overbalanced trying to look up at the liver. I said 'sit' as he did so. He had no option, in that position, to do anything else. I at once gave him the food.

Within minutes all I had to do was to say 'sit' as I put my hand in my pocket and he sat without any bother at all, looking very pleased with himself. Being rewarded for the right action was wonderful. So why not do it again and get the same result?

'Cheating,' said one man.

'He'll only do it with food. You haven't taught him anything,' said one of the others.

His trainer, who had set up the situation, took over, and showed that the dog now understood what 'sit' meant. That little reward had helped him learn. Within minutes he was sitting on command without a treat, having learned the action without any stress whatever. He did not like hands on him forcing him into position.

Many people seem to fail to understand when to discontinue food, sure the dog will only do as asked for food. We teach a child a,b,c, and are very pleased indeed when he learns it for the first time. We show immense approval as he completes his first reading book. We don't have to praise him extravagantly when he is able to read the bible. Now we transfer the praise to the much greater achievements. But we may offer him five pounds if he reads a particularly difficult book that he is finding difficult to master.

It would be silly to give the dog a treat every time he sat once he knows the word very well, but it will keep him very keen if we go back to our first lessons occasionally and do reward him for sitting. It will speed him up and make him even more willing.

Dogs need highlights in their lives just as we do. We can have a night out, or a visit to friends; the dog can have an extra tasty treat, or an extra game with his favourite toy, to brighten his days. Sometimes, if we have taught him something new and he has mastered it, he can have a jackpot. A whole sausage instead of a tiny piece!

It isn't cheating or bribery, any more than it is cheating for us to collect a week's wages for a week's work. We know we will only be paid if we do work; that is hardly bribery. We have earned it and the dog has earned his reward.

We reward with food every time he behaves correctly while he is learning. Once he has learned, we discard the food. I have occasional training sessions with my dog where I go back to treats and I always have a toy to reward an exercise that is done well with a game. She plays as much as she 'works' when she is being taught.

When I had Josse I used to play follow my leader with him, with a piece of food in my hand. He loved to shadow me closely, so that if I dodged he was there with me, and I couldn't get away. Another instructor, watching him one day, said to someone beside him,

'That dog is being trained, but he doesn't even know it.'

As a result, he worked with a tremendous will, as this, to him, was not work but play.

THE HANDS AND HAND SIGNALS

I found with my deaf dog that hand signals work extremely well, so well that I have used them on all dogs ever since. A lot of dogs don't respond to words at all; they stop listening, especially if they live with a constant background of people talking, of non stop radio, or TV.

I can do a display with my dog; I ask her to sit, but I don't use the word sit. I might say 'Fish and chips' and she sits. Or 'Bananas and Custard' and she sits. Or give the names of people in the news, or pop stars, or furniture and she still sits.

She is not listening. She is watching my hand. When I give her a signal, she sees it and performs the right action. One of my class recently did not believe me. She tried it with her own dog and as she lives in a hotel which her family run, she entertains the guests now with that particular routine as her dog will do it too. As will any dog, given the correct signals.

The most difficult team to teach is often a collie with an owner who gesticulates a lot when talking. Collies that I have known, and there have been many, seem particularly sensitive to hand movements. Those hands are saying, go there, lie down, don't do that, go right, go left, come here, and the dog behaves like an eel on a line.

I had one man so bad I made him teach his dog with his hands in his pockets. He was amazed at the improvement in his Dobermann.

I had a letter once from three people who lived in the same house. At a certain time each evening, they said their dog went berserk, and rushed around and bit their ankles.

What were they doing then?

There was a commercial break on TV which they used every night at the same

139

time. One laid the breakfast, hurrying to get it done before the action began again; one filled the hot water bottles and put them in the beds and the third made a drink for everyone .

Three people rushing round fast so as not to miss their programme when the advertisements ended. Six hands moving rapidly in all directions and a bewildered dog desperately trying to interpret and obey those hands without the least idea why.

I suggested that they used three breaks, not one, and only one moved at a time, while the other two played with the dog and kept him from watching those fast moving hands. It worked wonderfully well, and a year later I had the pleasure of meeting them and their now beautifully behaved dog and being taken out to lunch as a thank you.

I use different signals for different actions. It is easy to invent your own, but make sure that the same one is always used for the same action or again there is confusion. If someone has a signal of their own I don't change it, as that puts training back and bewilders the dog.

One of my best handlers was sent to Australia for ten years as part of his work. He took his dog with him. They joined an enormous dog club, but he was told his signals were wrong. He could not progress until he had changed them to those used by the club. I can't see that it matters, but maybe there was some reason that escapes me. Perhaps others might have become confused through watching him.

That club had five grades, and the dog went through them in four months, as he had in fact achieved a higher standard than even their top grade during his lessons with me. Most people took eighteen months, so I was pleased to know my pupil had done so well. Sadly he couldn't compete, as only pedigree dogs can out there, unlike here where any cross bred can take part in the working side of the Kennel Club shows.

We need to think very carefully about signals as dogs do confuse so easily. I have done it myself which is why I realise its importance.

I have a signal I use for the dog to go out and fetch something I have thrown. With my first agility dog, when I tried to teach her to jump, she wouldn't. She kept running around desperately, hunting the ground. I couldn't understand why until I realised I was using the same signal for 'fetch' as for 'jump'.

She couldn't understand why there was nothing there to bring back to me. I expected her to go over a hurdle. Once I realised what was wrong (and it took some thought) I invented a different signal. There were then no problems

One useful exercise is to teach the dog to lie down when it is coming towards you. It may be on the wrong side of a road, and suddenly see a friend. To be able to stop it before it dashes under a car is an enormous benefit.A lot of people won't teach this as they say it slows the dog when you want it to come fast. It only does if you are a poor trainer.

There are also problems in teaching a young dog if owners call the dog when it has been told to 'stay'. It doesn't know what is expected of it at all. In the early stages the dog is never called off a 'stay'. The owner returns to it. It is only the well trained older dog that understands that sometimes he has to stay till the owner comes back and sometimes he is going to be called.

People tell me they use 'wait' if they are going to call the dog, and the dog knows the difference. And then I watch them use the same hand signal for 'stay' and 'wait', and they wonder why the dog can't tell the difference between them.

I have three signals for those exercises; not just one. If I want the dog to 'stay' and intend to keep it there until I return to its side, I use the flat of my hand, and hold the hand in front of the dog's face, being very careful not to flash it before the poor animal and startle it. It is a slow considered movement, which the dog soon understands.

If I intend it to come to me, from the stay, which is one of the competition exercises, I use a different signal. I use the middle three fingers, slightly spread, which means, sit there until I call you and then come to me.

If I am going to ask the dog to lie down half way to me then I use one finger only. My dog is then well aware that at some point she is going to be told to lie down before she reaches me, and does not become confused at all. Nor does she slow when called to come without a drop.

I am not very happy about the exercise in competition where you call your dog off a sitstay as many clubs teach this too soon and the result is a very confused dog.

Some people use their hands to cuff the dog across the face. That is unkind, unnecessary and with a tough dog could be dangerous as one day he'll have had enough and will bite the cuffing hand.

I was appalled one day when a new owner came who had been to another class. She had a large German Shepherd and a riding whip. Every time he did something wrong she brought it down on his back. I removed it, took her very unhappy dog from her and showed her how fast I could get results with titbits and praise. She wasn't getting any results at all except for a cowed dog that was terrified of her.

As she had also been told to shout at him and scold him I made her keep quiet and only use signals, not her voice. Within two weeks the dog knew what was wanted and began to be much happier.

WHISTLES

I have taught with a whistle, but a neighbour and I both bought pups at the same time and both used whistles. Baffled dogs would run to the fence and try to come to the wrong owner, or I would give a down signal with mine, which turned out to be his sit signal, and the dog would do the wrong thing. Once we realised what was happening we stopped that. I only use the whistle when I am sure no other dog is within hearing.

The silent whistles have different settings, but it is never possible to know whether yours is unique or someone else has the same one. A whistle trained dog could be more easily stolen as it responds fast to the sounds it knows.

I discovered accidentally that one of my own re-homed dogs had been whistle trained at some point in his life. He was about two when I got him and had spent much of that time in various kennels. I had a bad cold and lost my voice and as I had taught the other dog to work to the whistle, I used it on her and then set about teaching the newcomer. He responded very fast but not in the way I expected. I use

141

a long blast for down; that to him meant sit. It took me several goes to find the come signal that he knew; that was three short blasts.

It is quite odd to work with a dog trained by someone else who does not respond as you expect, but it was easy to work out his code.

Had I known it in the beginning, teaching him would have been far quicker.

CLICKERS

There is a very useful booklet by Karen Prior called Dog and Dolphin which comes with two clickers of the sort children play with.

Taught with a clicker, the dog can be given his reward much faster than by voice, as the click is the reward and it startles them into instant attention.

I find it very useful, but it can't be used in class, as all the dogs would be triggered by the same click. I use it mainly to get the dog's attention, as they love the noise, but it has much wider uses.

These are well explained in the booklet. The address for its purchase is given at the back of this book.

THE IMPORTANCE OF PLAY

We get on very much better with our dog training if most of it is play. It must be controlled play, with the owner having the upper hand all the time, but we have a much more willing dog.

Why is play important?

The dog is an animal; not a human, and even with us they say all work and no play makes Jack a dull boy. We all need time off work to relax; to have fun. A dog that never knows play is a deprived animal. Sadly many rescues and many kennelled dogs have no idea how to play and have to be taught. Some people fail to realise its value.

I once met a man who told me he had been on Concorde when it was searched by a dog handler and his dog for drugs.

'That policeman was an absolute idiot,' he said. 'I don't know why they didn't sack him.'

'Why?'

'The dog searched one block of seats and then, would you believe it, the man played ball with him. The dog charged up and down the gangway for about five minutes before he searched another block.'

Plainly the speaker knew nothing abut dogs. There may well be a ball or a squeaky toy or some other precious (to the dog) object in a police dog handler's truncheon pocket. No dog can search for anything for hours on end and Concorde is a very big plane. I tried to explain that this was the sign of a brilliant handler but I don't think my hearer understood.

The game here was a reward when the dog had completed a few minutes search. Obviously there is not going to be a cache of drugs in every bank of seats for the dog to find, so he needs to be kept eager and happy in spite of that, so that he continues to search when asked.

The games we play with our dogs can either reward them for good behaviour or further their teaching. There are training games, which make the teaching much more fun and much less of a chore. No one is very successful who thinks, 'Oh, blow it. I'd better do ten minutes with the dog,' and goes out and trains as a chore to be got through.

The attitude for both needs to be, 'Hey, let's go and have that wonderful game.' As with everything else, the time to stop is when the dog wants more, not when he goes off to the house and his attitude says 'let's go in. I'm sick to death of that.'

If we expect him to concentrate we have to concentrate too, putting all our energy into whatever we are doing with him, being overjoyed when he does it right and refraining from fury when he gets it wrong. If we feel irritated, the dog soon knows and that is when it is wise to stop teaching, have a game and go and do something else.

If he is making constant mistakes in an exercise, it is not because he is disobeying. It is because we have not made our meaning clear. It is very easy to feel totally frustrated and very angry. I have often done it myself, but have learned that that does not give good results.

An owner comes to me and says, 'Poor Bennie got so upset yesterday and I couldn't think what was wrong. I suddenly realised that I was giving him the wrong messages...' Then I know that lessons are paying off and someone is well on the way to becoming a dog handler who knows what to do and gets results.

THE TEACHING GAMES

Everything we teach the dog can be part of a game. We have far more control if this is done, as games that begin to get out of hand can be stopped at once. So many people say 'I can't control my dog when he's excited. He's ever so good when he's not.' But the time he could be dangerous is when he is excited and that is when I want to be able to control my dog so that she doesn't harm herself or anyone else.

My dog is leaping to get at her kong, which she knows I am going to throw. I pretend to throw it and then say 'down'. This is part of the fun and she drops like a stone and waits eagerly to be released. She is practising 'down' at a distance, on command, and 'stay' till she is told to move, but she doesn't know that. She is having fun. I am improving her skills. I always think about the game, so that part is fun and part is training, and nothing is going to lead to a problem later.

The wrong games can cause problems.

One little pup was thought by her owners to be vicious as she barked and snarled and snapped and growled at only nine weeks old. I went to see her, and found that the games played, while fine for an adult dog, were overwhelming the puppy. She was becoming over excited and exhausted and complaining in the only way she knew. Many dogs need time out and space, just as we do, away from the family hurly burly, just to relax in peace. She was constantly stimulated and had no rest.

I suggested they stopped rough and tumble games and rush and chase games and concentrated on hide and seek. Also when she showed lack of interest, instead of stimulating her to more fun, which is nice for humans, she was allowed to go to bed and rest as little pups need lots of sleep and if they don't get it are bad tempered, like small children.

Many of the games we teach the dog are training games. There is one I teach every pup I have, which has untold benefits if done thoroughly. This is described below.

THE COME GAME

If there is more than one person in the family the come game can be played with everyone taking a turn to call the puppy. In a short time, the sound of his name will bring him running eagerly to find out why you want him, It is never fair to call him and then ignore him when he arrives or put him straight on to a lead and restrict him. With only one person in the household, the come game quickly becomes a bonding game, the puppy longing to reach his owner for a game or petting, and it teaches him his own name.

Donnie, Donnie, come, and we squat down and hold out our hands with something in them to attract the dog. Maybe food; maybe his favourite toy. Sometimes nothing, but when he comes he is cuddled and petted and fussed and told what a great guy he is. In this as in all else when training one can run into major hazards.

I was told a story about a very famous dog.

Many years ago, some of my readers will remember, there was a dog on the children's TV programme, Blue Peter, called Shep. This collie was bred by one of my friends. John Noakes, who was presenter then, rang her up one day in dismay to say the dog refused to come when called and wasn't answering to his name.

The breeder spent a day at the studio and discovered that when not on view, Shep was kept in a big pen. Everyone who saw him said 'hallo, Shep,' but did nothing else. No pat, or food, or cuddle. Just say his name and pass on which was not really at all rewarding.

It was meaningless and his name became meaningless.

He spent a month in the Kennels where he was born, learning a new name. Every time it was called, he was rewarded. Only a very small number of people knew that name and it was only used when he was needed, and he was rewarded for obeying. After that there was no problem as those who did not know how to treat him were never told his new name.

Years later, I was one of the judges at a temperament test for Rottweilers and German Shepherds. We had twenty four dogs that day, all lovely happy friendly animals. Some of the dogs seemed very slow to obey commands, and to come when they were called. Some seemed not to know their own names. In every case we found those were dogs that lived with big families.

Think of the dog in a family. Everyone is busy with their own affairs. People talk at once, interrupt each other, laugh, quarrel, shout, run around. Doors bang. Radios blare. The TV may be on quacking away in the background.

The dog, surrounded by din, blanks out, just as we may blank out a boring radio programme, thinking our own thoughts and not hearing a word of it. Or cease to listen to the sort of person who talks about nothing non stop.

Sometimes the dog is called something different by every family member. Mother calls him Brunie. Children call him Brun. Father calls him Bruno. Call him, and he won't come. He has no idea that he is wanted, and often just his name is used, without any command at all.

Try saying a friend's name and nothing else.

'John.' 'John.' 'John'.

John looks blank. Do you want him? Or do you want him to do something? If so what? He isn't telepathic. In time as you never say anything else, he stops responding.

The other type of dog that pays little attention often belongs to someone who lives alone and talks continuously. Little of what is said bears any relation to what is expected of the dog, and has little to do with him. His name becomes meaningless because it is used too much and not only when the he is needed.

The pup needs to be kept on the lead out of doors when the 'come' is being taught, as if he escapes all he learns is that come means 'run away and make everyone mad'. If he is allowed in the garden whenever he chooses to do as he chooses, and won't come in, then keep him slightly hungry always so that food will bring him fast. I like my dog with me, then I know what she is doing.

One of my dogs, when only two years old, running free in the garden with me, found a cat in long grass and chased it. The cat went over a wall into the lane and so did the dog. Luckily the cat then went up a tree, which did end the chase.

I had to teach the dog that whatever happened she did not go over that wall. The lane led to a busy main road, and was bordered by fields of sheep, with gates that could just as easily be climbed. I planted bushes outside the wall, but in the meantime she could still clamber over it.

I put her on her lead, took her ball, and threw it over the wall. As she went to jump after it, I stopped her, called her back and we went through the gate and collected the ball. I did this twenty times, twice a day, for six weeks. This was simply another version of the 'come' game.

She thought it a new and interesting game as she always did have the ball, although we went out of the garden and collected it. She never went over that wall again, even if a cat did. By the end of six weeks whenever she went to that spot, I called her back and we had a game well away from temptation.

This is a useful exercise at the garden gate. Every time the dog goes through, it is stopped, and brought in again. In time you have a dog that, even if the gate is left open, will not go outside.

When I want my dogs to come fast, I always slap both thighs with my hands and then lift them to chest level, clasped. This signal is soon learned and can bring the dog to you even if at distance. When I taught my deaf retriever I had a problem, but it was solved because he loved to fetch almost anything. I only had to hold a toy in my hand and he raced to me, eager for it to be thrown.

Even when a very old dog, almost unable to walk, he adored bringing back his toys and asked for a game, though he could only totter. As long as he wanted to play and was eager for his food and little walks, I reckoned he still was able to enjoy life. Only when he stopped eating and asking for a play did I decide it was now time. He was then nearly fourteen.

HIDE AND SEEK

This is great fun for the dog, and it helps to bond the dog as he is having more fun. It is a lesson but the dog does not know it is being trained.

The game can get more complex as the dog becomes more skilled. At first I shut him in one room and hide his toy in another and then take him and help him search. Once he knows what he is looking for, I can hide it and send him without me.

This becomes part of our daily fun. At night I always hide a biscuit for my dog to find, as part of her goodnight ritual. It may be under a cushion on the settee, or under a corner of the rug, or on one of the dining room chairs which is pushed under the table; or under the blanket in her bed.

Her tail never stops waving as she hunts around, becoming more and more skilled at looking in unlikely places and so delighted when she finds her treat.

I hide myself in another room behind a door or a piece of furniture, at unexpected times. (I do make sure I am alone in the house!) A whistle and she's there, hunting for me. I play it in the garden, hiding behind a bush or a tree or a shed. This re-enforces the come game, coming when called, which soon is a habit, and no longer a problem.

The dog learns nothing from one or two repetitions; everything we teach him needs to be done over and over, a number of times each day, before it is part of his skill.

Hide and seek with the family is even more fun as one member can hold the dog until it has learned how to stay without moving until told it can move, and then release it to find the other person.

Once the dog has learned to use its nose in this way, then toys can be hidden outside. At first you have to have the dog on the lead and show him where they are hidden. Once he is skilled he can do a free search.

Dogs live through their noses, which tell them all kinds of things we can never know. Whether the dog that walked the lane before them was a dog or a bitch; whether there were cats, stoats, weasels, foxes or pheasants in the garden last night.

A running dog, that has caught an interesting scent, checks and turns back in order to comb the ground carefully with its nose, seeking out the smell that has caught its attention. Hidden toys need to be well scented and it is a mistake to do as one of my handlers did, which was to wash the dog's toy every day, with the result that it never did learn to find it as it had no recognisable smell.

146

The dogs will examine a visitor carefully, and know whether there are dogs in that family; or cats, or maybe birds, and how many as each has a different scent. One of my bitches, who adored pups, if I had handled any, would come and smell me off and on all evening, with a rapturous expression on her face.

In the same way your dog knows if you have stroked or cuddled a cat, or been near someone else's dog. Mine could not leave me alone one evening when I came home after cuddling a frightened foxcub all one afternoon. He was in the animal sanctuary and there was a helicopter display. That terrified him, so he spent two hours tucked inside my anorak. He had been found at only two weeks old. Fox cubs behave very like puppies in some ways though they move more like kittens.

There are many games we can use to develop that sense, and give the dog more fun in his life, but unless he has a foolproof attitude to coming to you, we can't play them, and do miss so much.

One of the Working Trials requirements is for a dog to find four hidden objects in long grass in a large square marked out by a pole at each corner and walked round to keep a boundary of human scent. The dog learns to search inside this. The handler must stay outside. As always, we do it at first with the dog on the lead being shown what to do.

It is in fact a way of teaching a police dog to hunt for clues when working, but for our dogs it is enormous fun, and mine will happily bring me six or more hidden objects, loving the hunt and the pleasure she has knowing she has done well. I don't compete any more as Wales is so far from all the Trial venues, and overnight stays are now very expensive, but I still teach the various exercises, to give her extra 'work' and to prevent boredom.

SEEKBACK

This is a very useful game. You play with the dog, using an old glove, or a discarded purse or wallet, or a set of keys that you don't use, on a large leather tab.

With the dog on the lead, you walk a few paces, and drop the object, trying not to let the dog see you do so. Having walked on past the dropped article for about ten paces, you say 'LOST', and lead the dog back and encourage him to pick up whatever it is lying there.

In time he can be sent back on his own to find the trophy and bring it to you. This game has saved me endless money in that my dog always finds a glove I have dropped as I walk, or his lead, which I put down and forgot.

Many dogs I have known have found lost car keys, so that this is very useful game to teach. It is necessary to check the place you teach in. I once tried to teach one of my dogs in the forest. I dropped a glove and she fetched it back with enormous pride. Then I dropped an old purse, but before she reached it a charming elderly lady ran after me and said ' Dear, you dropped your purse!' and handed it to me. That stopped our game, as the dog didn't see why she should bother when other people did the job for her. We started again in a much quieter place with her favourite toy, so that she was excited about trying to find it, and then progressed back to purses, keys and gloves when she understood what she was supposed to do.

CHASING GAMES.

These need care.

Dogs are contrary animals. Run after them and they run away. You are the hunter and they are the rabbit and they are much more skilful than you at escaping. This is the quickest way of teaching your puppy never to come that I know.

We all do it until we know better.

With one of my early pups, many years ago, I used to run after her when she had a glove, to exercise her. She was remarkably difficult to teach to come as a result. Then, I didn't know why. Now I know I had taught her she didn't need to come as I would chase her.

This is a game to ban, especially with children.

The pup won't come.

Run away from <u>him</u>!

This turns him into the hunter and you into the rabbit and he will rush after you, partly triggered by the chase instinct but also because you are leaving him and pups hate being alone. You might vanish and he is not going to allow that.

I have vivid memories of one Christmas Day when we walked three large dogs in the dunes at lunchtime as we were eating in the evening. We did not expect anyone else to be about but one family had decided, as it was remarkably warm for the time of year, to have a beach picnic. The cloth was laid on the sand and you never saw so much food in your life. There were ten people.

Our dogs, off lead, saw this bounty and ran towards it. Food! On the ground! Imagine! All I could think of was to race back towards the car yelling, 'come on dogs, car.' They were so sure I was going without them that they turned at once before reaching the party and came towards us. I was able to leash them before any harm was done.

Again, I was thankful that I had taught them all to come fast when called, and knew enough to run away instead of chasing them which would have ended with them in the middle of the food. I hate to think what would have happened then. They had all been taught to chase me.

On another occasion I went to a training group I had not visited before. They ended the session with all dogs playing off lead. Mine was a stranger to the group and also a bit of a fighter, and I didn't let her off.

'Come on. Trust her,' the instructor said.

I pointed out that these dogs knew one another; she was an intruder into an established pack, but I was told not to fuss. So, knowing perfectly well what was going to happen, I let her off, hoping my training would pay off.

As she approached another dog, it curled a lip at her and she went right in. I was afraid the fight might escalate with other dogs who knew one another joining the first.

I ran fast towards the car, calling her, and at once she left the fight and chased after me.

'O wise one!' the instructor said. I resisted the temptation to say 'I told you so!'

So, never run after the dog, Run away. It can get you out of all kinds of awkward situations.

Remember too that if you allow dogs to chase squirrels and rabbits in their early days, they will go on doing so and may escalate to cats, small dogs, children, bicycles, joggers and cars, none of which will make you popular. The rule is, never let it start.

At one time I had three dogs and two Siamese cats. Indoor games and chases were never allowed, and the dogs knew that they greeted the cats quietly.

The first dog I had without a cat in the house did chase them, but since she was obsessive about playing with her favourite toy, I only had to throw it and she forgot the cat and came at once to play with me. She was not off lead where there are likely to be cats outside our garden, but there are about ten neighbourhood cats which all trespass.

So, chasing needs to be controlled, and I don't allow my dogs to chase other living creatures. Once a dog has killed, it will kill again, given the chance, as ancient instincts are brought to life which we have been trying to stifle.

Any instinct that is unrewarded, dies away. Any that is rewarded flares up again and it is then twenty times harder to get rid of that urge.

THE SKILLS A PUP NEEDS

There are a number of skills that all dogs should have for their own benefit and those of others. Today with the Dangerous Dogs Act looming over all of us, every dog should be an asset, and not a nuisance to non dog owners and neighbours.

Will he come when called and sit in front of the owner and not jump up? Also will he meet other people and not jump up? He may be muddy. He may claw new tights, or damage tweedy material. He may jump at a small child and terrify it, or knock down an elderly person who suffers from lack of balance and cause injury.

He may jump and snatch at a ball and miss, and instead catch the hand reaching for the ball at the same time. That is interpreted as a bite though it was not. Under today's law it could still mean the end of our dog.

Can he fetch back something that was thrown and bring it to his owner without dropping it? And put it in the owner's hand.

Will he stay when told without getting up and running off to play with other dogs or chase a running child?

I take my dogs regularly to a big tourist attraction and walk round so that they become used to children doing all kinds of strange things

One day I was there with one of my pups, then only about four months old. An enormous Old English Sheepdog came running towards her. He was far bigger than she was and she was very alarmed. I wondered what the dog would do and was afraid he might attack her.

Suddenly, from a considerable distance away, a voice called out. 'Major. STAY' The dog stopped dead, and stood quite still and did not move until we had passed and the owner called out to release him. I walked on with an unalarmed puppy who knew she had no need to fear this dog. That was a well trained dog with a very considerate owner who realised the pup might be scared.

I was fascinated long ago when a friend and I travelled together to a show with our dogs. I was in the lowest classes and finished well before she did as she was in the top class. While waiting for her I took my dogs to the exercise area and let them play.

By the time she had finished, there were about twenty dogs, most of them working top classes, all having a wonderful time.

When we wanted to go we called our dogs (she had three with her) and they all came and jumped into the car, which was a large estate. Behind us we could hear voices calling frantically and we stopped and watched as not one dog took any notice. All those dogs that could win in top competition and wouldn't come at all when they were playing!

That is one of the reasons why I don't like some of the puppy classes. The pups all play together and learn that when they see another dog, then its fun and games. So they don't come at all when let off lead if another dog is around. The aim in the controlled pet class is to ensure they learn that, even if with another dog, they come the second they are called, as the owner is much more fun than any dog.

Many small shows now have the opportunity to take the new tests, which are to see if the dog will behave in this kind of situation. One part of it is to let the dog off with other dogs all around, on lead with their owners who are watching and see if it comes as soon as called. The reward, apart from the satisfaction of knowing your dog has done well, is a very nice rosette and a certificate.

There are no winners. It is a major asset to have a dog that can pass. Some groups have different grades of test, so that the dog can perform at three different levels, learning more all the time.

It provides fun for the dog, occupation for the dog, and also is a way of preventing boredom as the dogs love working with you, instead of spending their time lying listlessly waiting for a walk.

One of my owners wrote to me after she and her dog had left, as he was now well trained. He had been an abused pup, who had then been dumped and run wild for six months until caught by the RSPCA inspector. He never overcame his fear of men in motor bike gear, even without the helmet.

Her letter said:

'I had no idea what a benefit I was storing when I brought Bran to class. The training calmed my dog so much and he now knows how to behave in so many different situations. If he gets alarmed, I just settle him down and we do a few of the exercises and it soothes him. It's wonderful.'

I met Bran again when he was nearly ten years old, a very different animal from the terrified dog that came for his first lesson. In that case it definitely was the owner, not the dog as he was a charming fellow once he overcame his fears. But which owner? Those who saw him at his first lessons and didn't know he was rescued, would have drawn very wrong conclusions.

8
TEACHING THE SKILLS

THE ADVANTAGES OF TRAINING

Dog training really is a skill, and people who say it is easy are not telling the truth. It takes a long time to learn and very few people are born with the ability. No one expects a medical student to perform an operation on his first day in college, yet many owners seem to expect their dog to behave after one lesson, and many instructors seem to expect the owners to learn equally fast.

Since that doesn't happen, many don't come back, which is about as sensible as the medical student refusing to come to the next day's lectures because nobody let him take out an appendix at the end of his first day.

Those who instruct teach very well if they are competent but not even the best of them can perform a miracle and turn an untrained dog into a trained dog in an hour.

Those owners who do stay all say exactly the same as the rescued dog's owner.

'He's so much better behaved at home now and when I take him out. He does listen now. He does do as he's told. He's so much calmer.'

Those training sessions fulfil a number of needs. They show the dog who is boss; not him, but his owner. They give him something to look forward to as most dogs enjoy their training periods enormously; it is so much more interesting than just lying still waiting for something to happen.

I am told over and over that they all know the day of their class, and are ready to go when it is time, becoming more and more excited as they reach the venue.

Once our dog is trained there are so many more things we can do with him; agility is fun, with the dog exercising himself, as he runs and jumps, though it must be carefully taught. Avoid any class where people laugh if the dogs make mistakes, as that is not fair to any dog. They need to be taught with care and consideration.

Young dogs should not be taught to jump until over a year old, when the bones are hardened. Dogs with physical disabilities can't be taught either. A session should start with the dog running around to warm up and loosen his body, otherwise he could pull a muscle or strain one, and should not go on too long, or he will be stiff and sore next day through over use.

If he is to go on a long sponsored walk, of a distance beyond that of his normal walks, he needs preparing as do marathon runners, or horses, by gradually increasing his exercise until the target is reached. Dogs taken on a ten mile walk when they have never done more than a mile or two before may well suffer as much as their owners would without due preparation.

Nothing could be more unpleasant than being pulled along with an outstretched arm for ten miles, so that here careful lead training is a must.

BREED DIFFERENCES IN TRAINING

Some breeds are much easier than others. There are breeds that are born to walk to heel and love it; others are bred to walk behind a man with a gun and not get in front of him, and may lag. No one with a gun walks with his dog at heel; it is just behind him. Most gundogs learn to stay much more easily than other breeds as they are selected for their ability to behave well in exciting situations.

Some are bred to quarter a field or hunt a hedge and normally would not be expected to walk on a lead with the owner. but we turn them into pets and have to manage as best we can.

There are dogs with an inbuilt desire to chase and run, such as greyhounds and lurchers, and for them to be successful pets, the need is to discourage this unless taking part in some form of racing tests with them.

Control is the essence of the Lurcher tests, so that the dog that suddenly races nine times round the field and refuses to come when called, is not going to excel. It is fascinating to see all these different breeds responding to training.

EQUIPMENT FOR TEACHING YOUR DOG

It is as vital to have the right equipment for your dog as it is to have a good racquet for tennis. Playing with one that is badly sprung will make a good deal of difference, and do little for your game.

At one time everyone had a slip chain, which is sometimes referred to as a choker. This has been abandoned now except in very rare cases of extremely difficult dogs, and even then it must be used properly. It is very easy to put it on wrongly, which does choke the dog.

Many are badly made, with swivel links that catch and prevent the chain working at all. Few are ever properly fitted so that either they are too small, or far too long. Some have links that are far too small; others are large and clumsy. The very fine chains can cut.

If a chain is used... and I never advocate it for novices... it needs to slip easily over the dog's head and have about three inches of leeway when tightened.

Chains have a major defect, as they are far from easy to use correctly. In professional hands they work extremely well, as they never actually tighten on the dog's neck.

In the wrong hands they can cause damage, and rarely do any good at all. So often one sees dogs panting horribly or half choking and coughing. In either case, some damage is being done to the throat. Some people tow the dog, the lead constantly tight, some are towed by the dog in the same way. Some give constant nagging little jerks which do no good at all, and must upset the dog, who can't understand what is happening or why.

If the corrective jerk is taught, some people are much too fierce with it. In time the dog becomes used to it, and becomes hard necked. It then needs a far stronger jerk. Also if the dog has been trained by a man, when a woman takes him out, there is no way she can use that amount of strength and everything she does is useless.

Once maximum strength is used and the dog still doesn't respond, there is no way to go. The dog is now impervious to any form of correction and will never change using this method, which is why it is discarded by those who keep up with modern research.

Apart from this, vets have found many neck injuries due to overuse of the chain and time after time I have dogs come to my classes, from a class that has used chains, with no fur at all round their necks and the beginnings of a very sore area.

What we use instead is a collar known as a half check. This is made of a strip of webbing, which goes round the dog's neck. There is a ring at each end of the strip, through which a small length of chain is passed. This will tighten round the dog's neck like a chain, but being mostly soft, it does no harm. Those I use, made by a retired police dog instructor, are adjustable so that they can fit exactly and grow as the pup grows.

They can't possibly be put on the wrong way. Even the police use them as the man I buy from supplies police forces with equipment. He calls them combi collars. They do not need to be changed if you walk your dog on the right after training him on the left, as a slip chain does. If that is on the wrong side, or on the wrong way, it chokes the dog.

I find that the majority of leads sold in pet shops are also inadequate. The kind with a loop of leather and a chain all the way down is very rough on human hands and the dog needs to be taught not to play with the lead, not allowed to bite on it all the time. I find plaited leads also can hurt hands, as can nylon.

I use a lead made to match the collar. It has an added advantage in that it has a ring about eight inches above the clip so that it can be reduced to half length. There is also a ring in the hand loop which can be attached to the clip. The loop so made will anchor the dog to a post or tree if it is necessary, or loop the lead so that if you take it off you can slip it across you, and not lose it.

There are a number of different kinds of clip. The scissor clips have big disadvantages as a strong dog can pull them straight if he lunges, and then he is free. They can also catch in fur and ears, and be painful.

The best clip is the trigger clip. This can't pull out, and can't catch any part of the dog if he is wriggling and fussing, which is when accidents happen as you put the lead on. The lead must be strong enough for the dog. It is essential to have a good lead, as the stitching may come undone, or a cheap trigger clip break and then your dog is free, perhaps in a very dangerous situation.

Good leather leads are very expensive, but the webbing leads which match the collars are very strong and can also be bought in rainproof material if you are out in all sorts of weather.

Though expensive to buy, good quality equipment lasts for a very long time if cared for. I have one lead that is twenty years old, made of good leather, and a harness that is over forty years old, passed on to me long ago by its first owner. It is still usable. Regular cleaning prolongs its life.

Dogs like whippets and greyhounds often have special collars as they have no fur to protect them, but those that come to me for training, and the lurchers, seem to do very well on the combi collars, which can be bought in different widths.

Sometimes people will put a dog that pulls badly into a harness. This needs to be tailor made, as if they fit badly, they can cause sore places.

Various types of head collar can be used. There are several different types on the market. These have also to be carefully fitted, or they may ride up towards the dog's eyes, or cause sore places on his nose. I would rather see the dog taught to walk

153

sensibly than have one of these fitted, but they do have their place with a very difficult animal and an owner who may be disadvantaged in some way by disability or age.

TEACHING THE SIT

The old method was to put your hand on the dog's back near the tail, the other hand under the chin and place the dog in the sit. I discovered on the courses I gave that many dogs taught this way think that sit means the owner is going to put them in position and never learn to do it on their own without being touched. They don't understand they have to make the action without human contact.

That may sound incredible, but I would take the dog from the owner, walk forward and ask the owner to call SIT. A surprising number of dogs did not sit. They had never learned what the word really meant.

So we do it with food in our hands. A nice tempting titbit, not something that is a bit of a bore. Remember to change the titbit often, so that the dog never knows if it will get cheese, or a liver tablet, or a piece of homemade liver cake, or perhaps chicken.

With the dog in front of you, facing you, you put the food to his nose so that he can smell it, but keep a tight hold so that he can't snatch it. Then lift your hand over his head, towards the back of his neck. He will follow the hand, and look backwards and literally fall into a sit.

The reward does not need to be bigger than a nail paring; just a taste. At the end of the session he can have a big piece as reward, and I sometimes give a bonus unexpectedly so that the dog becomes eager to win that and works much more willingly.

Any form of teaching that is stress free has advantages over one that compels the dog to perform out of fear. That may confuse him as well. He learns that when he does this he is rewarded; he has his wages. Few of us would work for a boss who refused to pay us at the end of the week, or yelled at us if we made a mistake.

This is the easiest way of teaching sit that I know. I have never known it fail except when people get the action wrong. I use a clenched fist to hold the food, and later on can ask my dog to sit, just using that as a signal and I need no food in it as now he is proficient. I take it for granted that when the command is given the dog will understand and obey.

We now try to make the dog sit straight at our side, or in front of us. Why? You may be told that if the dog doesn't then you lose points in the ring. But you don't intend to compete so that is silly.

There are several reasons.

We have told the dog what we want. He thinks 'OK, I'll do it, but in my own time and where I choose to sit. That'll prove that I'm really boss.'

In fact we haven't imposed our will on the dog; he has imposed his on us. So we try again until he realises he must get it right. Now, if he sits in the wrong place, he does not get any reward at all. Nor blame. Just start again and try again.

It is useful if he sits crooked at your side to practise with him between you and a wall.

If he sits crooked in front, call him between two chairs, so that he can't twist.

154

Why insist? Does it matter? Suppose we are out and ask him to sit as we approach the main road. He does, in front of you, in the road, turning away from you, and the next car goes over him.

We are waiting for a bus; the dog sitting tidily by the owner,under control. He won't trip anyone up because there isn't a length of lead between him and his handler. It looks wonderful tosee him sitting quietly beside his owner.

One little collie that was a joy to watch belonged to someone who has had many dogs before her. At sixteen weeks old she was brought out of the car in the carpark to meet four of us, and to play her latest game.

Trot over to a newcomer...lovely...and the pup is dying to jump up. But every time she does so she is gently put in a sit position, and then rewarded. All of us had a little treat for her and as she approached us we held it out.

She knew she only got it when sitting, not when on two legs scrabbling at our clothes and muddying us. So she had a little game there and then, coming to each of us several times in turn, sitting and being told what a great girl she was and being rewarded. She was so proud of herself, this tiny mite, only up to our ankles in height, but delighted because she was doing what the big dogs do.

Within a very short time she learned never to jump up at all because it had never been allowed. If it is allowed sometimes, then she won't learn. No dog understands sometimes. Only never or always. If strangers approached, her owner always told them politely that the pup is being trained and please don't encourage her to jump up, or she won't learn. So many people love petting puppies, but it can make the training very hard when they encourage them to do the wrong thing.

It may take up to ten weeks to teach; and it can all be undone in five seconds.

The sit is so useful. Sit beside me while we wait for a bus, or a train, or a taxi. Sit beside the car and don't jump in until I have moved that box of eggs off the front seat...Whoops... whose dog hasn't learned and has jumped on the eggs and broken them? That actually happened. Two dozen eggs make a mess!

Sit in the car and don't jump out until told, which will save a dog leaping under the next car or lorry. Many die that way.

Sit while we talk to a friend, or read a notice, or window shop. Sit no matter what happens. Sit at the kerb while waiting to cross. There is no danger of being pulled suddenly into the road and under a bus or a car. I ask mine to sit even when there is no traffic, so that they don't form a habit of crossing without me looking hard to make sure it is safe. Guide dogs are taught to judge for themselves and watch for traffic, so our dogs ought to find it easy when we are able to command them to stay and not rush over.

Years ago in the height of the 1970s IRA campaign on the mainland, I walked through a crowded shopping centre with my dog. A police car tannoy asked everyone to leave the area fast, as they had been told there was a bomb in one of the shops.

My young Golden Retriever was alarmed by people racing past him, and I knew if I joined in there might be an accident as he would try to bolt. I stepped into a doorway and made him sit and stay still until everyone else had gone, praying nothing would happen while we were there. He was trained, which was a godsend. As soon as everyone else was out of the area I ran at top speed, the dog keeping beside me, until we were safe, when he sat beside me in the crowd.

It was a hoax that day...but we can never be sure. I have never been so thankful that I had taken the trouble to train my dog to do as he was told and sit and wait and walk beside me at whatever speed I chose. Training can save lives; never mind trying to win red rosettes. That is a luxury, not a necessity. Many dogs perform wonderfully in the ring but are a hazard to themselves and others everywhere else. I will explain why in the chapter on Situation Training.

THE DOWN

It is always interesting to watch the dogs that come to class on their first lesson. Those that learn to lie down fast are submissive dogs, but those that resist, and are very difficult, are dominant, and have to be taught at home that they are not boss of the household. Once this has been sorted out, then they will behave far better and learn well.

Once the relationship of dog and owner is established, everything else falls neatly into place.

Often, if we ask the owners, we find the resistant dog does as he chooses; no one can go near him when he is eating or in his bed, or has a toy or a bone. Until this is changed, training is going to be very difficult indeed, and life with him is really not much fun.

To get the dog down, he is first put in the sit, which he should now know. This time, the hand holding the food goes right down to the floor and keeps the food there. Most dogs collapse at once, and lie down to gain their reward and eat it. It is given at once, again with a lot of praise.

'Good dog. Clever dog. What a good boy.'

The praise is so important and can speed up training fast if used at the right time, in every exercise we teach.

I like to teach the dog to go down from a standing position as well. It is very useful if he can do this. He is running after a rabbit, call 'down' and if well taught he drops at once. This too is a life saving skill.

LEAD TRAINING

The dog I dread meeting is the year old dog of a large breed whose owner suddenly needs to take him to the vet for his booster. The dog lives in an area where he has plenty of space to run in and has never been on a lead at all. The result is a nightmare for everyone, including the poor animal who doesn't understand why he is suddenly being restricted in this way. He usually comes from the type of ill informed breeder who says 'don't train your dog till he is a year old.' By which time he has trained himself to do everything you don't want him to do. All dogs are very good at that.

Those who constantly walk with pulling dogs end up in need of physiotherapy to cure the pain induced by all that stress over a period. I know that only too well as my Golden Retriever pulled until I discovered how to cure him. The physiotherapist even told me what type of dog I had! Dogs such as Rottweilers and German

Shepherds do not move in the same way as the Goldie and the stress is on different muscles in the owner's arm.

The little puppy is very likely to object to everything new you try to do to him at first. He will scratch at the collar, trying to get it off. He will either sit down and refuse to move when first out on the lead, or try to grab it and play with it, and resist walking.

If he is very obstinate try walking backwards with the pup walking towards you, so that he is also learning to come to you; bend down and entice him with a titbit or a toy; most puppies will start to move then, as they enjoy being with you and being cuddled and petted.

It is vital to prevent him becoming terrified, as he will if you try to tow him around on it.

When I choose my new puppy, as I said earlier, I take a little soft cat collar and ask the breeder to put it on for me. By the time the pup comes home the collar is already part of its life. The lead goes on when he is put in my arms, but it is not used. It is just there, and it can help restrain the pup he makes a sudden dart for freedom.

During the day, when I am playing with my puppy, attach the lead, and let him drag it around. Once he is used to that, I pick it up, being careful not to apply any pressure, and let the pup walk around with me following. Within a few days the lead is part of his life.

It is no use forcing it. This has to be done gradually and gently, so that the dog actually wants to be on the lead, and is not terrified that he will be nagged and jerked, as he will then try to escape and pull all the harder.

TITBIT SKILLS

One of the reasons some people are against titbits is that they don't use them correctly. They hold them in the air where the dog can neither see nor smell them, and expect him to know what they are for. When teaching our dogs we have to consider every action we take, as they can come to surprising conclusions.

One of mine apparently always came before I called her. I discovered one evening, facing a window that acted as a mirror, that her signal to come was not her name and the command, but my lips opening. She was not disobeying, as everyone thought. She had decided that lips opening was a command. After that I used hand signals with her, and not my voice.

When dogs first come for lessons, we teach them with food all the time. Once they have learned a skill, there is no longer any need for a reward. After all, we praise the small child extravagantly as he begins to learn the alphabet and to read, but when he is ten years old and reading fluently we don't give him a reward every time he reads a page.

We teach the dog to pay attention in his early lessons to the hand with food in it, and then we walk with the dog beside us, the lead as loose as possible, and hold the food right up against his nose. It is no use holding it in the air as he will jump for it, or holding it where he can't possibly smell it as it will have no effect. If we hold it in the middle of our bodies he learns to walk bent round, which must be very

157

uncomfortable and could trip us up.

We start the titbit rewards with the tiny pups at their first lessons, so that they learn that walking beside the owner is fun and has its own rewards. No rewards at all come if the pup starts to pull or bounce about or play silly games with the lead.

In a surprisingly quick time the dog is walking close to his owner, scenting the food. At first we only take two or three steps at a time; then we walk on longer, but never very far. Once the dog does this really well it can be tried without a lead in a very safe place where he can't come to harm if he runs off. I start mine on this indoors.

When we can get about ten steps in a straight line, it is fun for the dog if we begin to turn right, and then left and then turn round and walk in the opposite direction. The more variation we can put into this the more fun he has. It is also more fun if we walk briskly, if we vary the pace so that it may be slow or fast, and keep on with those exciting twists and turns. Straight lines are boring and encourage pulling.

We can walk in circles, or turn left every few steps, which will make him think twice about pulling ahead, and even try dance steps. A musical background is as encouraging for the dog as the owner. Well trained dogs form country dancing troupes with their owners, and there is a new form of competition, called Canine Freestyle, where dog and handler work to music together. It looks wonderful and the dogs love it.

So many people start by taking the pup out for a long walk without ever teaching him how to walk on the lead. This is like taking your first driving lesson on a motorway.

The result often is a puppy that pulls nonstop and this becomes worse as habits started now persist.

PROBLEMS THAT CAN ARISE

THE PULLING DOG

This is the most common fault there is. It starts because nobody knows how to prevent it, and allows it to go on. It is worse in those dogs walked by a number of people, none of whom know how to teach a dog. Often the dog does not come to class until it is over a year old, and the habit is well ingrained. The problem is that no one realised that walking on the lead is a skill that must be taught. It does not just happen.

So often in class you see people who walk more or less with the dog, but never look at him and don't really have any idea what he is doing. When teaching we need to be able to anticipate the dog's actions, to read him as we would read a book. Which is how he treats us; he is well aware of every movement, and knows if we are concentrating on him or looking vaguely around at other people and their dogs, or wondering what on earth to get the family for supper.

Nobody should expect the dog to walk to heel in a precise way when out for a walk, but the lead should not go tight with the dog way ahead. He needs to be reasonably close or we take up too much space on a busy pavement. We can relax and let the dog sniff around occaisionally in an appropriate place. Many male dogs are allowed to mark every post and tree and walking them is a total bore. This again can be stopped when it starts. It is easily cured by refusing to allow it. Well trained dogs don't do it.

Training my first Goldie not to pull was extremely difficult. Because he was deaf, my instructor put on a large crepe bandage which went through his collar and round my thigh so that he found it impossible to pull. It was a bit painful, but we kept our walks very short, only increasing the number of steps when he ceased to pull.

After six weeks of that, for ten minutes twice a day, she took me to a show and he won two rosettes and the cup for the highest percentage of all dogs of his breed on that day. He scored 96%. He never pulled again when with me.

With dogs that won't learn any other way, it is useful to find a wide space, in a field or empty car park. The dog is allowed to go to the length of the lead and you pretend you don't have a dog. You have a large heavy bag on the end of that lead. You don't speak at all, don't say 'heel' or 'come' or anything else. No praise. No blame.

Timing is all important here, as you change direction the second the dog starts to pull, not when he is well away from you.

If the dog starts with you and pulls in front, you at once turn round fast and walk off in the opposite direction. If he goes East you go West. If he goes North, you go South. When you are out of breath (and you should be if you do it properly) you stop and rest, but ignore him. Start off again in the opposite direction to the way the dog is looking and pulling.

Watch the lead doesn't catch under his body. If so, just stop and release it, without speaking. You need to watch the dog all the time, which is why you need a large empty area. It can be done on a long line, but I find it more manageable on a four foot lead, as the long line can snarl round both of us .

Most dogs seem to think that this is not much fun and that it is far better to walk beside you than to keep dashing off, and doing as they choose. It usually takes ten minutes twice a day for about five weeks to cure a really difficult dog. It can be done in one session. I once taught this to a very persistent man with an enormously energetic German Shepherd. He went on for an hour. The dog never pulled again. I was tired just watching them. They were exhausted at the end of the time, but it worked.

Another very useful exercise which cures pulling teaches two things at once; it teaches the dog to come, and it teaches him to walk beside you. You start out, and when the dog pulls, you turn, and walk backwards, calling the dog to you. The dog is now in front of you and facing you.

When he reaches you, you turn again so that you position yourself on his right side, and him on your left, in the correct heel position. He may walk two or three steps without pulling, and then start to pull again. So he is then brought to the front, you walk backwards, and as he reaches you, turn again to the correct heel position. After doing this a few times, the dog may walk as many as ten steps before he begins to pull. With this exercise, you do talk to him. When he is coming towards you, you say 'Fido, come.' This has the added benefit of using his name, as some dogs don't seem to know that! In time he learns to walk beside you.

THE DOG THAT WON'T MOVE AT ALL

There is a school of thought that believes in putting this type of dog on the lead and dragging it. That might work so that the dog walks out of fear, but it often results in such abject terror that the poor animal appears to have taken root.

The worst of these that I have ever met was a little Corgi bitch. Her owner was retired and recently had lost his wife and bought the dog as a companion.

He rang me up to say that the puppy wouldn't walk on the lead at all. He had rung the breeder who said, 'Tie the so and so to the door with her lead. Open and shut it violently. Then she'll b---- well move.'

Should he do it?

My feeling was that that breeder was not fit to rear puppies and heaven knew what the poor little animal had suffered before she was sold. She was car sick, which didn't help. She was so petrified when she saw the park that she lay and shivered and wet herself. All that enormous space when all she had obviously known was a kennel. No one had shown her anything of the world before she was sold. I hate people who don't earn the money they ask for the pup and skimp its care in order to make a bigger profit.

There was little to be done at that stage so we went for a walk with the owner carrying the puppy, then about twelve weeks old and small for her breed and her age. I suspected that food had also been skimped. Rearing pups is expensive.

I suggested he did that daily. It took about three weeks before she would even sit on the ground without shaking.

Move? Not she.

But by then she was bonded to her owner. So I held the lead and he walked three steps and she ran to him. More than three steps and she froze. He was much too far away. They made an odd sight as he was tall and she barely came above his ankle. He was a very nice man but he was very shy and felt silly talking to his dog so he had to use food to reward her all the time.

We had some very odd walks for the next few weeks, but each time he was able to go further ahead and she would run after him, each time a few more steps away from him, so that she became used to the feel of collar and lead and ceased to be afraid of it.

It was twenty weeks before he could hold the lead and she would walk, after a fashion. So I walked a step behind him and she walked so as not to lose him. After four weeks of this I passed the lead to him and they walked on and I stood still.

I met her a year later, a happy confident little animal bounding around her owner when off lead, and walking perfectly when on. He went for long country walks with a friend and the Corgi now would walk miles.

She was very young when we began, which helped overcome the problem but we also had to teach her to trust people. I wondered what had gone on in the kennels where that poor pup was bred.

It is much more difficult with an older dog. I met a bulldog some years later that had been taken to a big show for the first time at ten months old, having never been out of his kennel and yard. He should have been taken out daily, and learned to

160

walk around the village, and then a town, and then taken to tiny shows where he was not daunted by enormous spaces and huge numbers of people and dogs.

He froze when put in the show ring and had refused to walk on a lead ever since.

He had the biggest chain I have ever seen and a very heavy lead. I took these off him and put on a light collar and lead. Move? Not he. We tried food; we tried games; we tried coaxing. He lay still and shook.

What did he like doing? Playing with his owner's five year old son. So the little boy came to lessons and we did get the little dog to play. Then I held the lead while the child called the dog. In a few weeks the owner could walk round the area with him. A year later to my delight he was Best Of Breed, (ie the best bulldog in the show) at a big show, and had shown no signs of fear.

He should have been taken out and about from a few weeks old, and taken to little shows, where there was not so much excitement and activity, to accustom him to the scene gradually.

One little chocolate Labrador was very reluctant to walk on the lead unless the family's older dog was with her. On her own, it seemed to scare her. So her handler, who was experienced, didn't attempt to get her to walk beside him, but bent down and walked backwards, with her coming towards him, which was something she enjoyed. She had food to attract her and after a few moments, he turned so that he was beside her and she was walking alongside. As soon as she realised and stopped still again, he started walking backwards with her coming to him.

At no time was she forced in any way, and the gradual coaxing soon enabled her to walk normally with her owner, without needing the other dog to give her confidence.

9
THINKING ABOUT TRAINING

THE INFLUENCE OF STRESS ON TRAINING.

WHAT TO WEAR

It is necessary to think about ourselves when training our dogs, as we can stress our dogs just by wearing the wrong things.

Hard shoes bang on wooden floors and cause vibration. High heels can be dangerous as owners trip easily, or may turn an ankle. Flip flops have been known to come off, and leave their wearers barefoot. Some floors are slippery so that the type of shoe can mean the difference between success and failure. Soft soles or trainers are ideal.

One parent was angry with me because her child came to class in a velvet suit and went home covered in dog hairs. Fabrics that do attract these are best avoided. The synthetics seem to have a knack of picking loose hairs out of the air.

Long skirts may trip their wearers up. They billow over the dog and put him off. Out of doors they can be impractical if it is windy as they not only blow over the owner's dog, but over other people and their dogs. Puppies have torn long skirts by grabbing them, as they move temptingly past.

The wrong length skirt may brush against the dog's ears all the time he is walking, and so irritate him that he plays up.

A straight skirt that is either above or below the dog's head is fine, as are trousers. Materials that make strange noises, like corduroy or some of the waterproof fabrics, can also put a dog off.

Tight clothes are a disadvantage, as we need to be able to move freely and comfortably.

It may sound pernickety but it can make all the difference between failure and brilliant success.

THE DOG'S HEALTH.

A dog that feels off colour will not work well. Antibiotics or other drug treatments can affect them.

It is not fair to expect them to train when they are lame, or have a cut paw, or are in pain from a sore ear.

If they are not infectious they can benefit by coming to class and lying quietly watching what goes on. The handler will also learn by watching.

Before we blame them for being stupid or unco operative, it is as well to be quite sure that there is nothing physical bothering them.

OTHER FORMS OF STRESS

Twenty five years of dog training for Obedience, Trials and for sensible controlled pet dogs have made me very aware of many situations that can cause stress, which do not seem apparent to some people.

When a brand new owner comes to club, the dog may be stressed, the owner may be stressed, or both may be stressed. Often, it is both, as the pair interact.

Few newcomers to dog clubs know what to expect.

For pet owners the essence should be on control. The handlers learn how to control their dogs everywhere, not just at home, or at the dog club, or maybe in the show ring.

To say, as someone did to me, with great pride, as I watched her unruly dog behave abominably, "My dog is an Obedience dog, not an Obedient dog," is a sign of stupidity. This was an ill trained dog, and an owner that appeared to be proud of the fact that her dog was boss, not she. Nobody liked her dog.

There is no denying that teenage dogs are difficult. Everyone has to go through those months, when nothing seems to work, the owner despairs, the dog seems out of hand. At about two years old, if training has been faithfully done, a change occurs as the dog matures.

Few owners are aware that some of the symptoms their dogs exhibit are due to stress. There are a variety of reasons for this.

Owners who are consistent and manage to avoid stressing the dog unduly by constant nagging, have much better behaved dogs at a far younger age than those who are constantly shouting and losing their tempers with the poor animal. This alone stresses the dog.

Some owners do not concentrate. They chatter to their neighbours, so spoiling the class for everyone. That results in stress for the dogs as they pick up the feelings of the rest of the class, who are now also stressed, as they are exasperated.

This situation is made worse because the instructors are now also stressed because those thoughtless handlers are making their lives very difficult. Some owners are sure they know it all and won't change even though their dog is not progressing. Some do no homework and might as well stay at home anyway.

Few people bring pups to class. Few clubs run puppy classes, yet six weeks of a good puppy clinic could avoid many of the problems that beset adult dogs, and that cause the clubs to be filled, not with dogs in need of training, but with dogs in need of re-habilitation owing to the lack of guidance from the owner in the early days.

The dog may stress easily, due to his breeding. He may be stressed by a multiplicity of conflicting commands from a family with different requirements for the dog, who have never got their act together.

Mother allows him on the settee; father yells at him if he is on the settee. Mother calms him when he gets upset; everyone else tends to over-excite him, often to a degree beyond his control.

The puppy, now terrified out of his wits, bites. He is then either put down as vicious, which he is not, or taken to a rescue association for re-homing.

From the many letters I receive from owners, some clubs can add to the stress, but the newcomer to training does not realise it, or understand why.

Stress shows up in a number of ways, some of them rather odd. The obvious ways are constant lip licking, panting, a rapid heart beat, if you feel the animal's heart. The dog's eyes look very anxious.

He may lunge and bark at other dogs, often in fear of them due to an adverse interaction with an older dog when a pup. He may play up, and make the owner feel a fool; the owner then gets agitated, the dog gets more agitated, and causes class disruption.

This upsets other owners, and promptly a surge of stress goes round the class, making training completely impossible.

A bitch near to her season will act up; and may cause the males in the class to act badly, especially as these are untrained dogs, far more instinct than training. The result is frustrating for everyone.

I find a new class makes no progress unless the dogs in it are relaxed, at ease, happy with one another, and the owner is also at ease.

Sometimes a class progresses wonderfully: another group may seem to go nowhere, the instructor feeling as if he or she is trying to swim in thick treacle, with every lesson producing problems. Dogs allowed to play together before a class never settle to learn.

Stressed people and animals don't progress; a stressed dog won't learn and a stressed owner is resistant to learning. The dog makes no progress, classes are a waste of time, and the owner leaves, blaming the club.

Sometimes the clubs blame the owner, and shrug off responsibility, but I now feel that the first group of new dogs and new owners need to be handled very differently from subsequent classes.

This again can cause problems, as many people have come to expect dog club to be very active when training; on the move all the time. This with a number of untrained dogs results in barking, perhaps even fighting, fear puddling, which is a pest, but the animal is overstressed, and general confusion results.

New owners need time to get their bearings, to know their instructor. It is no use bawling out commands at someone who doesn't know what recall and retrieve mean; and it is no use asking them to sit their dogs, when they don't know how and maybe won't be shown as the class is too big and the demonstrator is inaudible.

The dogs need to be calmed. A great deal of progress can be made by just teaching dogs to sit still while owners are told the purpose of each exercise.

I give one to one lessons; these, over six weeks, give progress of a sort never seen in club. I find that something I have carefully gone over several times can be forgotten by the time the owner gets home. The rule then is, if in doubt don't do anything you are unsure of, wait till next week, or ring and ask advice.

It is easy too in these individual lessons to see when stress begins. At that point we lie the dog down quietly, and I talk to the owner, giving him a chance to settle. He has had more than he can yet take.

These lessons give me a bonus as often they are with a breed I have not yet handled in class; and I can study the dog as an individual and see where his breed characteristics make him differ in behaviour.

Concentration in a stressed dog is nil. His fears overcome his intelligence, and his trainability. Ideally, I would like to see a ten week instruction course, explaining the meaning of all the exercises and letting the dogs learn in class, just to lie quietly, no matter what else was going on.

The exercises then are practiced at home, without any distractions. Some of the best classes I attended taught voice control and hand signals and how to walk, and nothing else. The dogs were outside in our cars.

Owners need to come every week without fail. Those who do that, do progress. Those who don't can cause problems as the lessons have to be more elementary for them than they should be, as their dogs are behind and can't catch up in a few minutes. When dogs progress the lessons are much more fun, as more ambitious games can be taught.

The dogs that have made most progress in my class often started off very stressed; so obviously that the even the owner was aware of it.

These dogs don't join in the classes. Owners sit with the relatives of those working, who have come to learn. The dog can lie and watch, without being made to take part when he is wary of everything around him; and until the day he comes in happily, greeting me with a wagging tail, he does lie and watch.

The owner, unworried by having to concentrate on a misbehaving dog, sees how each exercise is done and trains it at home. A number of these dogs, when they do come into the class, have won the end of term test, having had far less stress in their training than those that have been forced to participate.

Many dogs work at home. They are very good at home. But the owner does not recognise that away from home there is bound to be stress.

Some dogs can take it; some never can; others can be trained to take it. I think too that what is classed as nerves is more likely to be a dog that stresses easily, or has had too many adverse experiences when young.

An excitable dog is also a stressed dog, and the best way to calm excitement is to sit the dog, stroke it, speaking soothingly, and keep it sitting until its eyes look normal again. An excited dog may be dangerous so it is essential to work with him in places where he does excite, to learn how to defuse him. A good dog class is the safest place to do this.

Once the dog has become relaxed in class the training can start, but it is necessary to watch those eyes, which soon show anxiety. Also to watch the dog's behaviour, and never take him beyond a point at which he is likely to react badly.

The old fashioned basic club training for a dog that lunges and barks at other dogs is to bring him in and check him savagely every time. This made my re-homed dog worse; he associated other dogs with a very unpleasant training session. It has made several dogs I have met bite their owners when they tried, for the first time, to discipline them in this way.

I stopped that sort of training for my dog and left the class that insisted it was right. I brought him in to the top class I taught, at the end of the evening, with my hand full of titbits, just before he was due to be fed.

He was hungry enough to ignore the other dogs; and he only stayed in for five minutes, other dogs being kept well away from him.

I never allowed him to get to the point where he was triggered by another dog. I watched for that tell tale lip licking and the odd look in his eyes, and the second I saw it, out he came, back to the sanctuary of the car to recover.

When I had had him three years I found a good dog class, as it is not easy to train one's own dog when instructing others. He could stay for a whole lesson, but it took time. He rarely attempted to lunge and bark, though he still reacted if another dog was triggered to lunge at him. I knew him so well that I could anticipate a problem and move him fast away from the offender.

Many dogs come to my class via the RSPCA. These are bound to be stressed. Not only have they often been abused, but they have to meet new homes, new owners, new rules. Often there is total inconsistency on the part of their owners who don't understand the dog's need for absolute security so they don't set rules which he can understand and obey.

Sometimes too it is easy to spoil a dog like this, feeling sorry for it, but it then begins to take over, finding with glee that it is now important for the first time in its life.

Often owners fail to realise any odd behaviour is often not naughtiness, but the result of extreme stress.

There needs to be a lot more thinking about training as applied to the dog and its behaviour. Some dogs put into competition would be happier left at home, as they simply cannot take the situations involved and go on from week to week enduring what to them is a form of torture.

The owners suffer constant frustration as they don't realise they are expecting a dog only capable of a GCE standard to take a high degree. Not every child can win high academic honours, but sensible people realise that and don't force them. They have other skills. The dog that fails in competition is often a very rewarding companion. Apolice dog that excels in his work may do very badly in competitions.

SITUATION TRAINING

Like every other form of training, this can't be done with a stressed dog, so it is essential to work on calming him and making new places fun rather than daunting. The best way to do this is to play with him if there is room and it is a sensible sort of place in which to have a game.

One of the top handlers of all time always said 'If your dog won't play, he won't work.' One of the best training books I read advocates playing with the dog for a month in any area in which you wish to train in future, without exerting any pressure.

Having mastered the basic exercises in class, it is now time to apply them to using them for situation training.

This, quite simply, is training your dog for living, so that you can take him anywhere, and know that he will not misbehave. There is no hidden secret; once the dog has learned sit, down, stand, come, fetch, stay, he knows the keywords that will influence him in any situation.

One of my dogs developed a lump on her front leg. As she was trained to stay when told, she did not need a full anaesthetic and all the trauma and the risk that that entails. She was told to sit on the table in the surgery, and to stay.

She was not happy: she was trembling and looked very worried, but I was with her, and told her how good she was being. She sat, holding up her paw, while the fur was shaved off and a local anaesthetic injected. She did not move while the lump was cut off, then stitched, the blood washed away and the injury bandaged.

The whole procedure took about five minutes and went very smoothly indeed, because she has been well trained to stay when told, whatever is happening.

Provided we are totally consistent and always behave in the same way, working out what commands are sensible under the circumstances, we can ensure that our dogs become partners in our lives, and not extraneous nuisances that we sometimes wish we had never bought.

A dog that knows exactly what is expected of him in certain circumstances is a very happy confident dog. The pup that is taught to lie down while the family is eating is far less of a nuisance than the pup that pesters, going from person to person, begging for food.

Family and visitors often need training in this too as they are tempted to give the dog a little piece of something from their plates. This ensures he becomes even more of a nuisance.

It is useful to teach the dog that he keeps beside you at whatever pace you choose to walk.

It is icy; the dog may cause you to fall over if he pulls, so he is taught to walk very slowly, at heel. I teach this by having the dog do one step, then sit, at first. Show people will say that this spoils him for fast work, but it isn't true. A properly taught dog does whatever you wish when you wish at the speed you wish.

When I was showing my German Shepherd bitch, I always did about a hundred yards at slow pace with her before she went into the ring. She moved very well at the necessary fast pace in contrast, as she preferred fast pace to slow and was glad of the opportunity to show how well she could move.

Normal pace walking is no problem, but suppose you are told the kitchen behind the hall where you are working is on fire. You need to get out fast without a panicky dog beside you, so he is taught to run at speed, still without pulling, to enable you both to get to safety. He knows the drill so he does not panic.

You are out with your dog and come across a football match or a Sheepdog Trial that you would like to watch. If the dog as been trained to lie still beside you whenever you aren't moving, there is no problem at all. It must also, of course, have been taught not to run after every ball or sheep it sees.

In advanced class stays the dogs are taught to sit still in two lines while another dog is called to the handler, running fast past all of them, in front of all the dogs.

I may have a ball with me, or a toy that the dogs like, and walk past them throwing it up in the air or bouncing it, or throwing it to the handler to catch.The dogs learn that they must still stay without moving. It takes time to get to this stage.

We are walking through the town, and see something in a shop window and want to stop and look. The dog sits beside us, close at heel, so that no one can trip over him or his lead or tread on his tail.

We wish to cross the road, but it is busy. Again the dog sits at heel, until we say 'over'.

We have one of those cuddly looking dogs, rather like a teddy bear, and everyone wants to stroke and pet him, or they want to fuss our new pup. This can cause immense problems as every time the dog is stroked he is getting a terrific reward, and we end up with a dog that has only one idea in his mind and that is to mug everyone he meets, in order to be petted.

The dogs' response delights the person who has instigated the action and the dog becomes more and more of a nuisance to the owner, leaping at passers by, or jumping up, which is fine on a nice day with the right person, but not on a muddy day with someone dressed for an interview who hates dogs.

We feel mean if we say 'no' and stop the action, and the person who was about to greet the dog is then left feeling hurt and rejected.

I take handlers with this problem to a busy tourist centre, and everyone who comes to pet the dog is told, 'we are trying to train this dog not to jump up, as an old person might be knocked over and on a wet day clothing could be ruined. Please don't stroke him until he is sitting quite still.'

I have not found anyone who objected to this approach. With their co-operation we can turn our hooligan into a sensible dog that, on meeting people, will sit quietly and wag its tail.

With a particularly difficult dog that has had too much of this kind of interaction with other people, we put the other dogs in the cars at the end of the lesson, and the problem dog's owner stands with the dog beside him or her.

Then each person in turn comes up, ignores the dog completely and shakes hands with the owner. When the dog is sitting quite still, it is petted by stroking the chest gently. They do learn, but this can take a long time with a dog that has been used to having people rush up and try to cuddle it.

Golden Retrievers and fluffy dogs like Chows and Samoyeds seem particularly to suffer from this type of attention, but any dog can become addicted to petting.

At home, if the dog pesters for attention it is ignored, either by picking up a book and reading it, or going out of the room and shutting the door. A few minutes later you can return and offer to pet the dog; you begin every action. The dog does not.

Training helps both owner and dog, as there is a right way to meet every situation, and there is a wrong way. I have known people who think dogs ought to be allowed to be dogs, to jump all over people, to chase cats and rabbits and squirrels, and generally be a nuisance to everyone but the besotted owner.

We live in a world that has changed dramatically even in the last twenty years. People are apt to sue far more than they ever did before, and also, being out of touch with the animal world, will interpret a bark as an attack, or a nip as a major bite. The next thing we know, we are in court accused of owning a dangerous dog.

We have to train our dogs for their own protection. A child leaps the fence for fun, or for a dare, or to get his ball, ignoring the dog in the garden. The modern child apparently does not dream of knocking on the door and asking politely for the ball.

The dog sees an intruder who is invading his and his owners' territory. He sees his role as protector of that territory and attacks. Nobody says the child ought not to have trespassed. The dog is blamed.

168

No matter how secure a garden is, there may always be someone who manages to break in; so that to have dogs roaming free even on our own property is no longer wise. I teach my dogs that even if the door to the outside is open, they do not go out unless I say they may.

This is simply another situation for which we take time to train.

I practise downstays near a sheepfield (never in it, but outside the gate.) Stay when you see a sheep. Stay when the sheep run. Then the dogs are not triggered to chase and kill. I do not do this at lambing time.

I would never dream of taking even a trained dog on lead through any field with farmstock, unless it was essential, such as visiting farmer friends. Sheep are timid animals and afraid of dogs, and if we, walking across the field, trigger a ewe in lamb to run, she may lose that lamb.

This is the farmer's work and his profit. The ram lamb the ewe loses could well be worth several thousand pounds if from a particularly good breeding.

To let our dogs off lead in such circumstances is criminal. If we do, the farmer is entitled, under the law, to shoot the dog, even if we are in the field too.

Once we are aware we have a problem we must stop it, by training the dog in the situation which causes the problem. He chases joggers. So he is put on the lead and walked where there are joggers, making him sit and stay every time one passes. The same with bicycles, cars, or motor bikes.

It is time consuming, but we have a responsibility. No one forced us to have a dog that could be a danger to other people. Those who let their dogs out to form packs and harry passers by are guilty of gross misconduct. Those who allow children to play with dogs unsupervised are asking for trouble.

We must ensure our dog is under control at all times and that we know exactly where it is twenty four hours of every day. The first time a dog misbehaves it is an accident; we could not know.

Once he has done something wrong, he will do it again, and this is where we now have to take steps to ensure it can't happen, either by never letting him off lead, or by teaching him how to behave in those circumstances. If we can do neither then we must think very seriously about keeping him.

I had to do a great deal of situation training when I got Josse, my re-homed dog, as he was not used to going for walks in busy places. He had been kept in kennels and only walked in quiet farm lanes. He was terrified that I was going to dump him again.

He had been put in a car or van six times, and handed over to strangers. He felt very insecure if we went to friends' houses, or places where we might stop overnight.

He hated being taken out of the car. He felt safe there, and if we went for even a short walk, we went back to it at a speed that almost had me flat on my face.

I was told to walk him past the car, over and over and not allow him to go in until he went slowly. Only he went faster than ever, pulling back to his sanctuary.

I sat down to think. What did he suppose was happening? He thought he was not going to be allowed back in the car at all. How could he know that he would be allowed in when he slowed down?

So I took him and his breakfast to a remote car park, where few people ever came. I opened the car door, stood beside it and held out the food. 'Josse, out.' Out to get a piece of food. 'Sit.' And then immediately... 'Josse, back in the car.'

For the first day I did nothing else. Out of the car, food, back in the car. Over and over until all his food had gone.

This became a game. By the end of the week he was coming happily halfway across the car park and then walking beside me back to the car. Within a year he would come for a walk and we could go back to the car at a sensible pace.

New places always worried him. Whenever we stayed anywhere that he had not visited before, I spent about half an hour walking him around outside, getting him used to the area and the smells. Then we might have to learn how to negotiate a flight of steps and a swing door, so we would do that several times, always with a food reward.

Once, staying in a particularly busy hotel, he was exceptionally bothered by the noise and bustle and all the people. I walked him round the grounds for an hour before bringing him into the reception area, where I sat with him at my feet for another hour, just watching. Someone asked what I was doing.

'Training my dog.'

'That's training?'

Yes, of course it is. Training him to feel secure in new places; training him to learn that people won't harm him; training him to accept new situations.

If a dog creeps around with his tail tucked under his tummy, or licks his lips frequently, or pants heavily, or tries to bolt, that dog is very worried indeed. Our aim is to remove all those symptoms, and have the dog secure with us, trusting us in every new situation as well as those that are familiar.

Forcing him or becoming impatient will only add to his stress.

It's up to us to work out what situations do cause us problems and then teach the dog in those situations to be sensible. Would it be best to ask him to sit, to stand, or to lie down? Then, always in the same situation, he performs that action and in time will do it without being told. Many dogs, if their owners stop for a chat, simply lie down quietly until they are ready to move off again.

It has to be trained first and insisted on every time for maybe years before the dog realises that in this situation I lie down; in that situation I sit. I stand at the vet's.

There are other situations which we need to think about.

TRAFFIC SHYNESS

The dog is afraid of traffic?

Walk round a car park where all vehicles are stationary. Go out early in the day on a quiet road and get him used to passing cars, re-assuring him and giving him a titbit if he behaves sensibly when they pass.

I had to do this with one of mine. First we played around my parked car in the drive of the house. Then we walked up and down our very quiet road early in the morning and late evening. Then we walked when it was busy. Once he could accept that without a problem we went to the corner of a busy main road, at a bus stop where there was a seat, and sat there, often for an hour at a time.

We trained within two hundred yards of a bus station, and then when he could accept that, near the railway station, I was very glad I had taken the trouble as when my father became ill with cancer, I was able to take the dog with me and visit my parents, going by train from Manchester to Euston, then taking a taxi to Victoria and continuing by train to Bexhill.

Taxi drivers admired him and all of them, when I told them why we were travelling, took me to a place where I could exercise him without problems and did not even charge waiting time while I walked him. He lay quietly on the train and slept all the way. He was then just over a year old. He was a very boisterous dog if left to do as he chose.

By the time he was two he was coming to book shows and schools, and would lie quietly at my feet all the time I was talking. Again, it had to be trained.

There are sometimes very odd situations which again need thought. One dog that came for lessons was a two year old Newfoundland that had never been trained at all and was creating major problems for his owners, who ran a large caravan site.

When he came out of the car, the dog leaped on the owner's back and put his paws round her neck, clinging to her. Nobody had worked out how to put him on the lead and get him on to four legs again.

I met her with a piece of sausage in my hand which was more attractive than leaping on her, although it usually ensured I was pinned against the wall until his lead was on.

We taught him, with considerable difficulty, to walk sensibly on the lead. We now had to create a new situation, in which the dog learned that he had to forget about pulling and about jumping on his owner. It didn't happen overnight.

The Newfie was taught to stay. This meant as soon as he got out of the car, he sat still till the lead was on, and we no longer had to contend with a dog either pinning me against the wall, or embracing his owner from behind.

Another of his tricks was to grab towels from holiday makers he had chased, and rip them up.

So I went over several times a week, out of season, and the dog was taught to stay first without anything happening: then with all the staff filing past him at a distance of about a hundred yards. During the lessons they gradually came closer.

Once he could sit still until they could come right up to him and tickled his chest. Then they began to walk about fifty feet away from him, waving towels.

Again, as we gained a better reaction from him and he could sit quite still, they came nearer and nearer until in the end they were passing him so close that they were almost flicking the towels in his face.

By the summer, he could walk past people with towels and neither chase nor snatch.

It does take time, and commitment. We can never cure a dog of something he has been doing for some time in a few days.

I find the stay is more useful than almost any other exercise as the dog can be taught to stay whatever happens. When a gate is open, or a door is open, or something alarming is happening, the dog is put on a stay to keep it out of danger.

He stays and watches motor bikes, bicycles, joggers, running animals, and does not dream of moving as he has been very well taught. After all, gundogs are expected to stay while guns are fired, birds fall in front of them, other dogs race out to pick up, and they do not move unless told.

Gamekeepers will have large enclosures thickly planted with shrubs in which they keep pheasants and rabbits. The dogs are trained in the enclosures. We can't do that but if a dog chases rabbits then we train him, on lead, where there are rabbits, until we can trust him not to run when he sees one.

I train my dog with three friends and their dogs in a park where the squirrels are afraid of nothing, and run close to us. The dogs now ignore the squirrels.

The only reason a pet dog is not so well trained is that most of us don't take the time or the trouble to ensure our dogs are safe at all times in all places.

The stay has other uses. Someone falls in the street with a heart attack and there is nowhere to tie the dog. He must stay while you cope with situation.

I was once in a dog class when some idiot fired an airgun through the window and showered us all with glass. Luckily it was the top class. We put the dogs on a stay while we took the shards out of their coats and then swept up.

One or two people had scratches due to flying glass, but no dog was hurt. It could have been very serious, as the glass splinters were extremely sharp and very small, and could easily have cut a leg artery in a dog.

It is a matter of working out how you want the dog to behave, of ensuring he does as you want always in those circumstances and insisting that he does not sometimes do as he is told and at others create mayhem for everyone around.

Many people who have a dog, and become disabled, have found that their own well behaved dog can be taught to do all that is expected of an assistance dog. So many of us keep a toy pet that is never allowed to grow up, and we miss so much by doing so.

The bond that develops has to be experienced, as it is far stronger when the dog is trained than between an owner and an untrained dog. It is wonderful to see our dogs becoming older and wiser and doing as we expect them to do without even being told. They know now how to behave in all kinds of situations.

10
CARE AND MANAGEMENT

FEEDING

There are probably more dog foods on the market than there are breeds of dog. It is very difficult indeed to know which to feed. Many are excellent, but there are some that it is better to avoid. Cost is not any indication as to merit, as some of the cheaper brands are very good. I like to be sure what is in the food I give my dog, and I read the nutrition advice on the packaging very carefully.

Dogs, like people, can have food allergies. I have known dogs allergic to beef, to liver, to wheat, or to gluten. There are a number of specialist diets on the market which help with these problems. You can buy foods which are lamb and rice only, or chicken and rice; or are gluten free, or even vegetarian. Most good pet shops can advise on these.

There are foods for pups as soon as they are weaned; for the junior dog at the maximum phase of his growth; for the working dog, who needs far more food than the dog who only has short walks. There are excellent low protein foods for the older dog, which are worth changing to at about six years old, as they help to stave off the kidney diseases that can affect the veterans.

If the dog isn't thriving it is worth trying a different diet. If he is hyperactive, and racing around all the time, without much sense in him, it can again be his food that is giving him far too much energy. He may be having one that would be more suitable for a working sheepdog covering around forty or fifty miles day. The fact that a diet doesn't suit your dog does not mean it is unsuitable for all dogs.

Chita was very difficult indeed until she was three, when a trade magazine I wrote for decided to give its contributors a dog food as a Christmas bonus and I received a large sack of a food I hadn't tried before.

The new diet calmed her within six months, and I had a very different dog. I changed a number of other over active dogs on to the same food, with the same results.

Aggression may also be due to diet; constant indigestion makes the sweetest tempered person irritable; dogs are no different.

The puppy needs four meals a day up to about four months. The breeders should give diet sheets when the pup is sold, but if not, most of the big food manufacturers have leaflets to help with this. The amount of food obviously needs to be increased as the puppy grows.

Many of them will stop eating the first meal of the day and put themselves on to three meals at between four and six months, at which age they can be put on to two meals a day.

I have found in recent years that many pups go through a phase of not wanting to eat well at around seven months. They become faddy, and may refuse one or two meals during the day.

I am beginning to suspect that at this stage they need to come off the very nourishing puppy and junior food on to an adult food, as they are being overfed, and are sensible enough to know it and adjust accordingly. Owners worry at this stage, but the pup comes through it and begins to eat well again within a few weeks.

I feed my adult dogs twice a day, as they may become extremely hungry if only fed every twenty four hours. A hungry dog is not very co-operative as all he can think about is how empty he is.

Also that one meal a day means a very loaded stomach. Any dog exercised on that or allowed to run, may get a stomach twist which is very nasty indeed and can be fatal. We would suffer if we ran a marathon immediately after eating our Christmas dinner.

One modern problem among dogs is the same as humans. Many of them today are much too fat. This brings problems just as it does with us. A rough guide to how much food to give is half an ounce of food per pound of body weight for a dog that does not gain weight and a quarter of an ounce per pound of body weight for a dog that gains easily. There are special diets for overweight dogs.

Dogs that are given frequent titbits gain weight easily. One digestive biscuit from a packet, given to a small dog, is the equivalent to us of eating a whole packet of biscuits. Remember the difference between his weight and ours. It is such a shame when a dog is overweight as they are such beautiful shapes when in good condition. It is so sad to see them struggling and panting instead of racing freely.

Although the food manufacturers give guide lines on the packet, this is not necessarily right for every dog. I once visited one of the Guide for the Blind centres. There were eight Labradors in eight kennels, all weighing around fifty six pounds.

There were instructions for feeding on each kennel door. The dog in kennel number one did not gain weight at all easily, and was having two pounds of food per day. He still looked remarkably slim. No two amounts were the same. The little bitch in the end kennel looked plump on only half a pound of food (the same food) each day.

Most vets like dogs to be on the thin side rather than too plump, as this ensures a longer life without too many problems. Any dog with hip dysplasia or arthritis needs to be kept on the low side of his correct weight, as extra weight will put to much stress on those painful joints.

People do have to be asked not to feed them with snacks. There are dogs that go round the household scrounging at meal times. In other households where everyone has snacks at different times the dogs can be overloaded with sweet biscuits, a share of potato crisps or a sandwich and even chocolate. Human chocolate should not be given to dogs, as it contains theobromine, which is far from good for them.

Many people use doggy chocs as rewards when training: they do have one drawback, as does cheese for the same purpose, when we have very hot summers. There is nothing more disgusting than to have melted chocolate or Welsh rarebit in your pocket, even if it is in a bag!

The liver cake whose recipe is given at the back of this book makes ideal rewards when training, but even that has hazards. Troy and my friend's dog are both allergic to the wholemeal flour. We have to make it up using gluten free or potato flour. Rye or rice flour would probably make it too. All these are available in health food shops.

Some breeders advocate raw meat, but I feel there is a danger of salmonella poisoning with this. If I feed meat I cook it. I don't feed raw eggs for the same reason. I feel that the foods on the market have been well researched and contain all the nutrients a dog needs, while my own diet for them may not.

I use one of the dried foods for Troy; but other dogs of mine have done better on tinned foods. It really does depend on the dog. I have to be careful with her to avoid additives and colouring, which upset her.

Pups can run into trouble if fed in the kennels where they were born on goats milk, or one of the proprietary puppy milks. Changing them to cows' milk can mean an upset tummy, as the formula is different. Ask the breeder what kind of milk they had, and, if necessary, either find a supply of goats' milk, or a puppy milk from the vet, which will come as a powder and need making up in the same way as a baby's milk. Many health food shops have goats' milk, and it can be bought in frozen packs.

There is only one make of dog biscuit that I can give Troy, so if your dog is having any minor health problem, or scratching unduly, it may not be that his food is disagreeing with him but just his particular brand of biscuit. Changing brands may be all that is necessary. The coloured biscuits and those with flavouring do not suit all dogs.

Foods on which some dogs thrive may not agree with other dogs and there are many households where each of several dogs is on a different diet. When I had three dogs at the same time, each had its own brand of food. Janus, with pancreas problems, was on a diet of a special tinned meat with added biscuit. This had to be very carefully weighed to get the right proportions, as the least variation upset him. He couldn't digest any biscuits, but I cut wholemeal bread into thick slabs and then into biscuit sized chunks and baked it hard in the oven. He enjoyed that, and could have it when the other dogs had their biscuits.

Puma put on weight on nearly every food I tried, until I found one that suited her. Chita needed a diet that did not spur her into hyperactivity and the very best foods on the market disagreed with her.

Household scraps don't make a good diet. They may fill the dog but they won't nourish him. Like pups, whelping bitches need a very good diet indeed to ensure they produce healthy litters.

There are dogs that can take almost any diet, and seem unaffected by changes, but most dogs can be badly affected by a sudden change. One dog had violent diarrhoea because his owner ran out of her usual dogfood and bought a different brand, and fed it to him without introducing it slowly over a period of several days.

If changes must be made, they need to be made over a period of about eight days; first of all one quarter of the new food is mixed with three quarters of the old one for three days; if this causes no problems, then the dog can be given half and half for another three days.

Then three quarters of the new food to one quarter of the old, and then the complete change is made. Dogs do not need variety.

Dogs can form very odd habits. One we had when I was very young preferred to steal the cat's food and left his own. My mother overcame this by putting his food on the little shelf where the cat was normally fed and the cat's food in his bowl on the floor. They fed like that for the rest of their lives, never being aware that in fact

175

they weren't stealing from each other.

Rescued dogs also may have odd habits, due to the way they were treated in their first homes. One dog would never eat if anyone else was in the room. Another would eat nothing from his own bowl; he needed a human dinner plate. A third ate nothing unless he stole it, so that his food was put in odd places so that he thought it was not meant for him.

When I have a new pup or a rescued dog I know won't bite me, for the first few days I mix the food with my hands, which is messy but gets my smell associated with feeding, which is the most important part of his life.

I put most of the food in my cupped hands and he feeds from them. This bonds them quickly as you are associated at once with the most important function in their lives.

When I meet new dogs that have come for training, I take care to have liver cake in my pocket and rub it over my hands so that when he first catches my scent, he associates it with food, which means that he trusts me. People who smell of dogs are usually very readily accepted by other dogs. They are suspicious of those who don't smell of any other animal.

Often a very nervous dog can be re-assured by sitting quite still with the food in your hand, and allowing it to come to you, to sniff you, and then to take the food. This may take days before the dog relaxes enough to even make an approach. It is necessary to be as still as statue and avoid looking directly at the dog.

Many people add raw carrots or raw cabbage or both to their dogs' food, but if this is introduced, it too needs to be introduced slowly.

The underweight dog looks very thin and you can see his ribs. An overweight dog has too much flesh over the ribs. With the ideal weight, you can feel the ribs, but not see them.

The best guide to the way they are digesting is the stools. If they are small and hard and difficult to pass the dog is either underfed or has too many bones given him. If they are loose and he is otherwise well, he is very probably being overfed.

A farmer friend said that the stools should be so firm that you could pick them up without leaving a stain on your hand and throw them next door. I don't recommend trying!

BONES AND CHEWS

Dogs need to chew, to keep the teeth and gums healthy.They love bones, but all bones are not good for dogs. Chicken and lamb bones splinter, and if the dog swallows a splinter then it can injure its inside. One of my dogs once stole a chop bone and swallowed it, and it jammed in the entrance to his stomach.

He was actually at the vet, waiting for his operation, when he vomited it up. He had been unable to eat for about five days, as there was a blockage and food couldn't pass it. All kinds of purgatives were tried first to avoid operating.

The same dog when a pup dug under the garden fence that separated his area from the bin, and stole the carcass of the Christmas turkey. It took a fortnight to get him well again. Those bones caused terrible problems. I now never leave a dog outside unsupervised.

I prefer to use hollow sterilised bones, from the pet shop, as these do not go off and smell horrible, or attract flies. They can be kept in the toy box for the dog and given when he wants to chew.

They can also be filled with little treats which will keep a dog quiet for a long period, as he tries to get them out.

Bones aren't digested and even if they don't splinter they can cause problems if they don't pass through, which may mean a blockage and surgery.

There are all kinds of chews, but it is best to look for good quality as some may be treated in ways that are not desirable. Really good rawhide chews are digestible. Many dogs love pigs' ears.

Some of the chews are coloured and these Troy can't take...she has an upset tummy if I give them to her. When we visit our pet shop they know she has to have the flat almost transparent chews, and not any of those that look more fancy.

There are chew ropes, but some dogs have had problems with the fibres which weren't digested, so I use these for a tug toy, but they are put away so that she does not spend her time destroying them.

There are also special plaque remover chews on the market, in the shape of big pineapples. A large one can last a big dog for several months. There are smaller ones for the little dogs, and most dogs enjoy them enormously.

EXERCISE

The young pup does not need long walks. In fact they are bad for him. It is best to let him frolic in the garden; he will crash out occasionally as pups play until they are almost too tired to move and then sleep to recover.

Puppy bones are soft, and if they are walked for considerable distances the muscles firm up and become hard and can bend the bones, so that you end up with a crippled dog. Many owners of the giant breeds walk the pups to far in their early days, being misled by the fact that they are so big. I have known several develop problems due to this.

The bones don't harden until fourteen months which is why the Kennel Club does not allow young dogs to take part in agility and working trials. Jumping should not be started until at least fifteen months old though they can jump over six inch hurdles.

If your dog class teaches jumping to four month old pups, leave it. That should never happen. The instructors are very ignorant.

Many pups have mad half hours during which they have a burst of energy, and behave like greyhounds. It is best to take them outside to race round the garden as using the house as a speed track can cause problems and broken ornaments. A lively puppy at this stage may well leap over chairs, along the settee and even over small occasional tables if he is born to jump as some seem to be.

Pups ought not to be allowed to jump in and out of the car, or to go up long flights of stairs or steps when very young as this too can affect their bones. Even if they

177

come from parents with good hips, the extra strain may distort their own hips and you end up with a damaged puppy.

It is better not to allow unrestricted play with the children, who may over excite the puppy and get nipped. Also those games set the pattern for future games, and what is funny in a tiny pup may not be at all funny in a full grown mastiff.

The puppy should be taught to lead walk in the garden before taking him out anywhere, so that he is happy at your side. He should never be taken on a long walk without getting his muscles used to short ones. His first walks should not be of more than half a mile, twice a day, when he is six months old. Then it can be extended to a mile twice a day.

At a year old he should, if he has been conditioned properly, be able to come for much longer walks. Young pups should not jog with their owners until they are about a year old as most joggers go for miles. Nor should they be exercised beside a horse or a bicycle.

A dog with bad hips can be kept fit by several short walks a day. They should never go on very long walks and certainly never run beside a horse or a bike.

If time is short and long walks are difficult there is plenty of scope to get a dog well exercised by a training period with games in between the teaching. Running after a ball or a kong or a frisbee several times daily for some twenty minutes will give a dog much stronger muscles than a quiet amble at a slow pace every day.

Swimming is good, but care needs to be taken. I keep my dogs on a long line if they go in the sea as there is always the danger of currents. One Golden Retriever in the summer of 1996 was picked up by a boat four miles out at sea, as he had been unable to swim back on the turning tide. Others may not be so lucky.

I prefer my dogs to exercise in fields. They are not nearly so likely to be polluted as the sea. My Golden Retriever cured me of beaches as some of the trophies he brought back to me were revolting. He could never resist picking up things that were lying around.

Beaches are also likely to have tarry matter lying around and after a bank holiday there is often broken glass as boys take bottles on to the beach and throw stones at them. Thrown away half eaten sandwiches rot and a dog or bird eating them can suffer from botulism, which is a very unpleasant complaint indeed. Many seabirds with this come into the sanctuaries during the summer. Few are saved.

HEALTH

Few dogs go through life without some health problem. Even those that are trouble free in most ways will have an upset tummy, or a cut or other injury at some period in their lives.

It is always difficult to know whether we ought to call on the vet, or whether this is some trivial problem that will right itself in a day or so.

There are a number of symptoms that do require a vet immediately. Obviously if the dog is in pain, a vet is needed. Deep cuts may need stitching and also an injection to prevent infection.

Sudden lameness can be due to a thorn or a holly leaf, but if there is no sign of either and the lameness persists then the dog may have strained or sprained itself. Injections and tablets will ease the pain and the dog will have to be rested, which is not easy. This is another reason why I like a crate.

Any puppy suffering from vomiting or diarrhoea needs to be seen at once, as they dehydrate very quickly, and you can end up with a dead pup if not treated. Today an animal that has become dehydrated can often be saved by being put on a drip.

Older dogs may eat grass and vomit, which does not usually matter, but if they vomit several times on one day, and it is food, not just bile and grass, or have persistent very loose stools, then they too need a vet. They may have an infection, they may have picked up poison.

If the vet says the dog must be starved for twenty four hours, it is wise to do so as this speeds recovery. It is immensely hard to do, especially if there is more than one dog in the house and only one is ill, but it can make all the difference between a prolonged bout of sickness and one that is over within a couple of days.

Dogs which never put on weight, have ravenous appetites and produce large quantities of very loose porridge coloured stools may have pancreas deficiency. If you do come across this, tell the vet the colour of the stools when you report the symptoms as that is part of the diagnosis. They are very pale, and often almost explode out of the dog.

It is not a common complaint but I have met over twenty dogs in the past thirty years which show some or all the symptoms mine had. Radar, the dog in the TV programme, Softly Softly, in the 1960s, was a sufferer, but he lived to twelve, and it did not stop him having a very successful acting career. Mine lived to thirteen.

This can be controlled by diet, which is an important part of the management, and by additions to the diet either of a supplement that replaces the enzyme he does not make (trypsin) or of raw pigs' pancreas if it can be obtained.

It is not easy to diagnose. My dog suffered from it for two years before it was identified, though that was over twenty five years ago and it may be easier now, as more is known about it.

He had tryplase powder added to his food, but I found that it was necessary to work out a diet for him, and to weigh it, as if it varied by so much as an ounce either way, he was in trouble again. Tryplase is very expensive.

He was very underweight for those two years, so much so that I was frequently reported to the RSPCA, but once my vet had intervened, they ignored the reports, as they knew we were trying to deal with an unusual condition.

Once his diet was sorted, I added commercial baby foods to his meals for about three months and within that time he gained weight. There are lamb and beef dinners for babies, which are, I am told, pre-digested, so that they are easily absorbed.

He did succumb very easily to any digestive bugs that were around, which always meant a long careful period of special feeding, but the baby dinners always brought the weight back on.

One problem with a dog with this condition is that he is very hungry all the time and great care has to be taken to see that he doesn't steal unsuitable food or eat anything he can manage to chew. Friends have to be warned never to give him titbits, as I could say 'who fed my dog yesterday? What did you give him?"

A morsel of cake, part of a sandwich, a piece of meat, could all cause trouble.

Obviously a dog that has a fit must have attention; epilepsy can occur in many breeds, but usually it can be controlled by drugs. Friends who have had epileptic dogs tell me that talking to the dog and re-assuring it during and after the attack does help them.

Ears and eyes can cause problems. If there is a black or dark brown deposit in a dog's ear it is due to some form of infection or a parasite. Dogs that live with cats seem especially prone to earmites which the cat harbours.

It needs treatment or he may develop an ulcer or an abscess. Ears should be examined daily when the dog is groomed, and the external part can be gently washed with a damp tissue. Dogs like spaniels and retrievers which have long drooping ears that are shielded from fresh air can be more prone to trouble than those like the German Shepherds with erect ears open to the air.

Drops are usually prescribed for treatment.

The dog often has a little hard black deposit round his eyes when he wakes which is quite normal but needs to be washed away daily. A gummy deposit may mean a problem but some dogs develop this when it is windy, and all that is needed is a wash with clean boiled water.

If the discharge is coloured or the eyes are reddened then they do need treatment. Sometimes in summer a dog running in long grass will get a seed in its eye. These seeds are sharp and very irritating and the dog may paw its eyes. I don't like trying to get anything out of my dog's eyes and always ask the vet to do this. It is so easy to cause more damage.

Dogs that are well exercised on hard ground rarely need their claws clipping, but those exercised on grass often have them grow too long, which is uncomfortable and if not checked they can curve over and cause pain.

There are special clippers and it is possible to clip the dog's claws at home, but those with black claws are difficult as the inside has blood vessels and nerves and if you cut too much off you end up with a badly bleeding claw. With white claws you can see where the blood vessels begin.

Blood from the mouth, in the urine, or in the stools needs investigation.

Coughing may be due to kennel cough, which, if not treated, can have complications and is dangerous for young pups and for whelping bitches as well as for older dogs.

Instant treatment as soon as you hear that cough and a good cough medicine usually clear it up.The dog is very infectious and ought not to mix with other dogs until given the all clear by the vet. Those who knowingly take coughing dogs, or vomiting dogs, to shows or to classes are not fit to have dogs, and it should be made plain to them that this behaviour is far from desirable.

Dogs that suddenly lose weight may have a problem, and need to be seen by their veterinary surgeon.

Old dogs can have a variety of symptoms; they may seem to lose their balance; they may salivate a lot; they may become mildly incontinent. They can suffer from heart or kidney problems, or even develop diabetes. All these today can be treated. Many of them respond well to homeopathic remedies, as did my old dog when she had a stroke.

SKIN IRRITATION

I am often rung up these days by people whose dogs spent their time scratching frantically. This can be due to any number of reasons. They may have fleas or harvest mites. If so, the correct insecticide will stop that.

They may be moulting and not groomed often enough. The loose dead hair must be irritating to them, and when they are moulting, they need grooming at least twice a day.

They may have mange, which not only means they lose their hair but they also have sores. This can't be dealt with without a vet. Special shampoos will be provided if necessary.

Ringworm causes circular patches and is highly infectious to us as well, so that if that does occur, it needs clearing up as fast as possible and great care taken not to infect other animals and people.

Eczema is another cause of scratching. This can be due to allergy, and dogs can be allergic to very odd things, such as carpet shampoos, or the dyes in certain carpets, red in particular. One dog suffered considerably until his owner discovered her new red carpet was the cause of his problems.

Once he had his own rug and was encouraged to lie on it, and not on the carpet, the eczema cleared up, with help from the vet. Grass can cause problems for some dogs, especially at haytime.

Again, if no other cause can be found, a change of food may prove all that is needed, but it is always advisable to seek for help from your vet, as it may not be so simple.

OLDER DOGS

These, like us, can suffer from various problems due to aging. Often they go deaf, so that a dog that has been well trained by hand signals as well as by voice, is going to be far happier than the dog that suddenly finds itself in limbo with no guidance.

A first sign often is that the dog doesn't come when called, and doesn't respond at feeding time to the rattle of the bowl. It can happen very suddenly, almost overnight, in some older dogs. Mine could hear until she was eleven. Then one day she could and the next day she couldn't.

At this stage they can't be let off lead when out, as they won't hear any call to come back. Few have problems at home. They are also in more danger from vehicles than before.

They may startle easily if woken suddenly. I always made a point of stroking mine very gently, and of rapping on the floor by the bed, which caused a vibration and enabled the dog to wake without being alarmed.

There is a very useful booklet titled HEAR HEAR by Barry Eaton, which gives advice for the owners of deaf dogs. It can be obtained directly from him from Pine Cottage, Station Road, Chilbolton, Hampshire SO20 6AL.

Older dogs may develop cataracts; or may go blind. Provided the furniture is not moved around at home, they can manage very well in a known environment.

Another dog in the home may act as guide, as they seem to understand that their companion is now lacking a major sense.

Keeping something in your pocket that rattles, like a number of coins, enables them to keep track of you around the house and not feel deserted. It is necessary always to speak to them when you approach as if startled and afraid, they may bite.

GIVING PILLS

It is always useful if your dog regards pill taking as a normal part of life,so that I teach my pups to take a vitamin pill as if it were a medicine.

The dog is encouraged to open its mouth, so that it's useful to practice washing around the mouth, and gently opening the lips, so that it isn't alarmed, but considers this a daily function.

Teaching the dog to fetch toys or a dumbbell and taking it out of his mouth also gets him used to hands round his mouth and helps cure the compulsive nibbler.

The pill is placed right at the back of the dog's throat, as far inside the mouth as possible. Then, holding his lips closed, with a hand round his muzzle, his throat is stroked gently to make him swallow.

If this is done as a matter of daily care when he is groomed, with a vitamin pill or a liver treat, giving him medication is no problem whatever.

Liquids can be given by a syringe, which the vet will provide, or using a teaspoon; the syringe is easier as the dog may knock the spoon and spill the medicine. The syringe can be inserted at the back of the lips and the liquid dripped into the mouth. The medicines have to be given at set times and it is easy to get confused or to forget, so it is well worth making a point of having the bottle in a place where it will catch your eye.

If pills have to be given every twelve hours then it is easy to give them at 9 a.m and 9 p.m which does not disrupt the day at all. Every eight hours can be worked out at 7 a.m, 3 p.m, and 11 p.m, which again is not disrupting.

It is easy when busy to forget and wonder if you actually gave the dog a pill at all. I find it easiest to have a small polythene bag in which I put each day's pills, with the time of giving, and then can cross it off.

If I find that there are two pills left at 4 p.m, when the second should have been given at 3 p.m. I know I haven't given the second and can give it then, knowing I haven't given two instead of one within that hour.

Any course of pills needs to be completed otherwise the complaint may return because the bugs weren't knocked right out. Some dogs are allergic to certain types of medicine, so it is worth making a note of what you have and of any adverse reaction so that you can tell the vet. I have had dogs allergic to some pills; others allergic to certain creams. I myself am allergic to penicillin.

SURGERY

This may be necessary for medical reasons, or to neuter dogs.

It is very important not to feed the dog the night before or the morning of the operation, as if it is fed, then surgery has to be delayed as that causes real problems. Usually the dog is collected when it is almost recovered from the anaesthetic, but it may be a bit dizzy and disorientated when it first comes home. The other dogs will be wary of it as it will smell extremely odd, so keep them away.

Complications are very rare, but they can occur. One of my many cats had violent shivering fits all night after she was spayed. I always sleep downstairs with any animal that has just had surgery so that I am there if anything does happen to go wrong and can take instant action. I have only once in over fifty years of animal keeping had to visit the vet in the middle of the night, but it can happen.

On that occasion my dog had picked up poison from eating grass in the country park where someone had thrown away paraffin from a stove. She did survive, but would not have done had I waited until morning to contact the vet.

Some dogs can be an immense nuisance with a wound. When Troy had a lump removed from her leg she managed to take off the bandages and remove the stitches twice.

After the second effort she wore a large bucket like collar which my vet provided until the injury was healed. This is a nuisance as the dog is unsighted and blunders into furniture but it does save what could become a very serious problem.

Exercise has to be restricted and only on the lead as running could cause the wound to open, and in any case if it is stitched the stitches will pull as it moves.

If the dog has been out of action for some weeks then once it is better and exercise is resumed this needs to be built up again. A long walk the first day after a long period of restriction will result in very sore muscles. Remember the first day back at PT at school? Or the day after a long bicycle ride after a lay off. Or the first long horse ride. All kinds of muscles complain painfully.

A book I consider a must for all dog owners is First Aid and Health Care for Dogs by Charles T.P. Bell, M.A.VET, M.B, MRCVS. which is published by the Lutterworth Press. It is a paperback, very reasonably priced and is quite the most useful I have found.

It covers almost every eventuality in the life of any dog, and gives both symptoms and immediate first aid treatment, and is a life saver.

CONVALESCENT DIETS

I feed my dogs, as they are recovering, with about four small meals a day. At first they only get a teaspoonful and if that stays down, then the next feed contains more. They need a special diet and it is possible to get a convalescent diet from the vet.

If I have a very sick dog, I get a cow syringe from the vet, and make a glucose solution of about a tablespoonful in a pint of water. I drip this into the dog's mouth every hour. I also use Bach's Rescue Remedy, which is a life saver. Five drops in the drinking water works wonders, and again if the dog is very ill it can be given with a syringe.

I feed chopped chicken and rice; or white fish and rice, taking care to sieve out all the bones. I moisten it with baby food as these are very easy to digest.

As the dog improves and its insides recover, I gradually return to the normal diet, taking about a week to do so.

This sort of diet is good for any dog recovering from any kind of illness. Often their appetites need tempting, especially if their sense of smell has been affected. Then something like tinned salmon juice, or a taste of sardines may stimulate them.

Any dog that changes its habits suddenly needs to see the vet; the dog that ceases to drink or eat; or the dog that, having only drunk a reasonable quantity of water previously, suddenly starts to drink copious amounts, as this can be a sign of a kidney problem.

11
LOST, STOLEN, OR STRAYED

There comes a time when we have to say goodbye to our dogs. Usually they are very old and life has become a trial. That is when we need the support of a very good veterinary surgeon, who will tell us that our faithful companion has reached the end of the road. To keep him alive now would be for our own sakes, as he no longer has any pleasure left in life.

It is always very hard. Only those who have been through the experience understand how we feel. Those with first time dogs who have not yet followed that path can begin to comprehend; but even they will not appreciate the feelings we undergo.

I like to be there at the end, to hold my dog in my arms, unaware that anything more is happening to him than a routine injection from his vet. It is over very fast, without any pain, the dog falling asleep, only this time he won't wake again.

My vet has a poem on the notice board in his surgery, about a dog asking his master to let him go when the time comes, and not to keep him alive for selfish reasons. It is the last thing we can do for him.

What happens next depends on us. Some have them buried in the garden at home, where they used to play. Others have them cremated and it is possible to have the ashes buried with the owner when he too dies. There are special pet cemeteries where each dog has its own plot and its own headstone. There have also been crooks in this area too, so it is wise to make enquiries before committing oneself.

There are worse ends than death. It is devastating when we lose the dog, not through illness, but because he simply vanishes, either through straying and not being able to find his way home, or through theft.

Pups can get lost if they escape and are chased by older dogs, running miles in terror and not yet old enough to know the territory.

A dog may be in a car accident. If a door opens, or a window is smashed or the hatchback springs open, the dog may run from the noise in panic, and keep on running, again being lost.

Thieves target pups, brood bitches and stud dogs, or maybe even the domestic pet like that belonging to the owner who left her little dog in her car at the petrol station while she went to pay. A man took the dog out of the car and drove off with him, so now all of us lock the car even when leaving it for a very brief interval.

Dogs have been stolen out of gardens and outdoor kennel runs. They have disappeared after burglaries, either escaping in fright when a door is opened to let the thieves out with their booty, or stolen too.

They can have micro chips inserted under the skin, which can be scanned and reveal the dog's real owner, but a dog stolen to be re-sold can't be identified. The buyer won't realise he is actually not the property of the seller, so won't report the dog as missing, and won't have him scanned to see if he is away from his own home.

Dogs can also be tattooed and I think it is more likely that someone honest, finding they have just bought a dog with a number in its ear will want to check and find out why it is so marked and then can be given the address of the original owner.

A collar and tag alone is not a protection against a thief who will simply remove the collar.

It is so easy for a thief to steal a dog in London, drive down to the South Coast and sell it there, with the story that they have become redundant or had the house re possessed and are having to move into a place where dogs aren't allowed. Conmen can put on wonderful sob stories that wring one's heart.

Dogs are stolen to sell abroad as guard dogs; to use as bait by the dog fighting people; or to sell to vivisection laboratories. They can be stolen so easily. One group that went missing over a period were exercised on a common with a wood at the end of it. Dogs ran into the wood and were never seen again. The police thought a van was waiting, and the dogs were enticed, either by a whistle or by a bitch in season.

I was told of someone in one area who targeted dogs at stud, and lined up a number of bitches for them. The dogs were then taken, and when they had done what was required, at a very good fee for each mating, though not as high as his breeder would have charged, they were dumped.

The pups would then be sold with false papers.

It is not pleasant to contemplate but we live in a very unpleasant world, and dogs are as much as risk as children from unsavoury characters. It is as well to be aware of what can happen and make as sure as we can that our companions are safe. Thieves will know who lets the dog play alone in the garden all day, or which kennel is easily accessible, as nobody is at home during working hours.

Whole litters of puppies have been taken, just before they were ready to sell. Again they would be sold cheap. When dogs can cost up to £500, there is a ready market for puppies costing only £200, and eight of those will bring in £1600.

Dogs can be recovered if the owner is persistent.

The first obvious move is to ring all the veterinary surgeries in the area. One stolen dog was sold not far from its home.The new owner, thinking it a simple case of re-homing, took it to the vet to have it checked and given its injections as there was no guarantee that it had them. The dog belonged to a client and the vet knew it was missing, and recognised it. That had a happy ending, apart from the person who bought the dog in all innocence and had lost his money.

Vets are also useful to contact if a dog or cat is found lost and injured, as often one of them will recognise it and can alert its owner.

Contact all the local police stations within an area of at least twenty miles. If you report at Station A, they may not contact Station B, which might actually have the dog.

Next are the various rescue organisations and boarding kennels, any one of whom might have a wandering dog brought to them if they have room. One friend found what happened to her cat after a long period when she visited a rescue home some two years after the cat went missing.

She saw a photograph of the cat on the board which showed successful resettlements. Purdey had been brought in as a stray, having wandered for some unknown reason some distance from her home.

She now had a new home, as the owner had not thought to contact the rescue places, and she has been left with her new owner who is very caring. At least my friend knows that her pet is alive and well and in a very good home. She had been missing for well over two years before that photograph of her was seen.

Another cat that disappeared was found to be living over a mile away. He had been chased by a dog and arrived very upset and miserable in the new owner's garden. He was recognised by his previous owner when he went to do a job at the house. The rescuer was very old, and adored puss, who had now been living with her for four years. He was left with her, as his first owners hadn't the heart to take him away.

The old lady died a few months later and left instructions for Smokey to come back to his original owners. There was a wonderful reunion, with the dogs recognising their old friend, who now is in his original home. I see him nearly every week.

It is well worth carrying on with the campaign to find the pet.

Make fliers; details of the dog, its size, its colouring, any special markings, any tattoo number, the fact that it is microchipped if that is so, and a photograph. It is easy these days to photocopy these in quantity and put them in shop windows, in veterinary and doctors' and dentists' waiting rooms.

Give details of any illness the dog may have or if it requires medication. Make a point of saying if a bitch is spayed as she may have been taken with a view to breeding from her and will then be useless.

Alert all the neighbours and ask them to search any outbuildings. One of our cats, together with a neighbours' cat, was missing for three days. We both thought they had been picked up by cat thieves. Another neighbour came home after a weekend away and opened up the garden shed. The two cats had gone inside, and fallen asleep on a pile of sacking. They were safe and very hungry indeed.

I missed another of my cats many years ago and noticed that neighbours were moving. I asked the removal men if he was inside the van. Of course not, they said, but I had a feeling he was, and insisted on looking. He was fast asleep on a settee and had I not found him he would have been transported over two hundred miles with our neighbours' furniture. He would probably have run out of the van in a totally strange place and been terrified, and maybe never found again.

Local radio will give out the details of missing animals and they don't charge.

Advertise in the local papers. It is better to put in a box advertisement rather than just a line or two, and include a picture of the dog. It is far more noticeable. This produced results with a dog that had been missing for twelve days. Someone rang to say a dog very like the one in the advertisement was living down the road with people who had only brought him home a few days before.

It is as well to write to the national dog papers, Dog World and Our Dogs, and to Dog Training Weekly. Dog people know their local animals and one that has been shifted across the country and suddenly appeared will have been noticed. If this is tied in with a dog that has made a recent appearance and looks like the one that was lost, they will notice and report.

Offer a good reward either for returning the animal, or for information leading to his return.

Dogs and puppies have suddenly re-appeared in their own gardens or kennels after a campaign like this, as the thieves have become worried, and sure that the dogs will 11 be seen, and they will then be punished for their crime.

Dogs have escaped and come home of their own accord, but they are in a minority. The secret is not to give up. To ask everyone, and ask them to tell other people.

Hopefully it won't happen, but it is as well to know how to proceed if it does. Even if the campaign does not produce results, some of the misery is alleviated by knowing that everything possible has been done to try and find our missing companion.

Advice from Pet Watch which seems to have vanished ends " Never give up on your pet. He never gives up on you."

12
USEFUL INFORMATION

LIVER CAKE

One pound of liver. I mix pig's and lamb's.

One egg.

Blend these together to a liquid, and then add enough flour to make a very stiff doughy mixture. Wholemeal is best but for dogs allergic to wheat, you can use potato flour, rice flour, gluten free flour or rye flour instead.

Spread the mixture thinly in a swiss roll tin and bake at one hundred and eighty degrees for about half an hour. The result should be brown and cakelike, not crisp and biscuity.

I cut mine into one inch strips and deep freeze, taking out what I need as I need it. It does not keep very well; I find it lasts about four days in an ordinary refrigerator.

BOOKS.

There are numerous dog books on the market, some of them excellent, but I do not think there is any substitute for a good dog club, with instructors able to teach owners how to train their own dogs.

It is necessary to see the dog to give advice on how to handle it. There are dogs so sensitive they go to pieces if you raise your voice. There are dogs so insensitive they need a very firm strong voice. Nervous dogs require very different handling and teaching to those that are overbold.

There are dogs that are ticklish and can't bear to be touched. There are other dogs that seem to need constant physical contact to re-assure them. Those of us who are always with dogs have usually seen some odd behaviour pattern before and can point out why it is happening.

A book can't tell you that your dog is excessively dominant or over submissive: or that its inability to sit fast may be due to some physical problem such as a tumour on the prostate, rather than disobedience.

A good instructor will see a dog walk round the room shaking its head and at once suggest there may be an ear problem.

Dogs that live in very isolated places need different teaching to those that live on a crowded housing estate. It is no use trying to treat a German Shepherd as if it were a collie. A pup cannot be taught in the same way as an adult. A dog that is brought up correctly from the start does not need remedial treatment which may be required on a rescued dog that has been abused.

I have not yet found a book that points out that though a dog may appear to understand and obey a command, it may only do so because the handler has moved in the right way and given clear understandable signals. The dog has not yet learned the behaviour, and cannot repeat it on command only without guidance. This takes weeks, not hours.

I have never seen advice on any of these specific problems in any book I have yet read. I have over one hundred on my shelves, many of them dealing with training, but when it comes to my own dogs and those I teach I find I often have to work out my own methods to gain success. None of the books seem to help with the particular dog I am now working with. There is no stereotype. They are all so very different.

However, below is a short list of books which I would not part with as they really are excellent.

WHICH BREED?

The MacDonald Encyclopaedia of Dogs.

This describes over three hundred and twenty breeds, devoting a page to each, describing their characters, their temperaments, and classifying them as guard dogs, herding dogs, etc.

It also specifies which breeds need special attention. e.g. The poodle needs periodic clipping, is highly intelligent, good with children but not good with those who try to use heavy handed methods of training.

The Boxer is good natured and loyal, needing long walks, and easily trained. There is a warning that it is not a long lived breed.

There are breeds in here from all over the world, and it makes fascinating reading.

ADVICE

Dogwise   by *John Fisher* (Souvenir.)

This is a thought provoking book and if you take on board the ideas put forward they can be adapted to any dog with success. John Fisher has long experience in dogs and is a founder member of the Association of Pet behaviour Consultants.

The Family Dog   by *John Holmes* (Popular Dogs)

This is another must for any family thinking of buying a dog or owning one. It is not only interesting but is very easy to read. Many dog books are written by experts using language only understandable by those who work with dogs. John Holmes has vast experience over many years and trains dogs for displays, for film and advertising work.

The Perfect Puppy   by *Gwen Bailey*. (Hamlyn)

This is quite the most comprehensive book I have read on this subject. It tells you all you need to know in a very easily understandable and readable way. The author is the Blue Cross Society's Animal Behaviourist.

Don't Shoot The Dog by *Karen Prior.* (Bantam New Age Books).

Karen Prior trains dolphins which can't be put on a lead and yanked around, so that other methods have to be used. They are very highly intelligent animals and the training ideas used for them are ideal for other types of animal when teaching. They are particularly successful with dogs.

It is a book that repays frequent studying.

A Dog And A Dolphin by *Karen Prior*
An introduction to 'Click and Treat' Training
Dog Training   by *David Weston* (Gazelle Books.)
Many dog training books are out of date. Many of those written in the past few years are a re-hash of methods of training no longer used by the knowledgeable. This author is aware of modern research and the book is very useful.

FOR ALL PUPPY BREEDERS

Nursing and Hand Rearing Newborn Puppies by *Betty Bloomfield.*
(Able publishing Knebworth.)

The author has for many years run a clinic for newborns, and a rescue service, taking in orphans, ailing pups, and bitches who have lost their litters and can foster other puppies. She has immense experience and the book deals with everything from hypothermia to heat stroke, to premature pups, infections, transport to and from the vet, or to the clinic as well as other problems most breeders will never have heard of, let alone encountered.

There is always a first time and this could well be a life saver. I recommend it as a necessary piece of equipment. For those about to start breeding.

OTHER USEFUL ADDRESSES

The Cinnamon Trust...for dogs whose owners may die or need to go into care. Also for lists of sheltered homes where pets may live with their owners. Poldarves Farm, Trescarve Common, Penzance, Cornwall TR20 9RX

CRATES

1) Oakenshow Grange, Doncaster Road, Crofton, W.Yorks WF 1SD
2) Barjo folding kennels for house and car.
      Ruth Caldwell (DW11) 55 Lyon Road, Crowthorne, Berks. RG11 6RX
3) MMG (Guards)—made to measure for all vehicles. Supply police vans.
      Dept 00, Alfriston House, North Road, Gedney Hill, Lincs. PE12 0NX
      Telephone: *Office* - 01406 330160, *Mobile* - 0860 722074
4) Collapsible Dog Cages.
      Ralph Allen Eng Co., Forncett Road, Norwich, NR16 1HT
5) Guardsman (Athag Ltd.) Supply police, security & dog rescue homes.
      Carlyon Road, Atherstone Ind. Est., Atherstone. CV9 1LQ
6) Croft Engineering Dept. DW,
      2. Swan Meadow Mill, Swan Meadow Road, Wigan, Lincs. WH3 5BD
      Telephone 01942 497677
      This is the one I have; they are well made, and very reliable on delivery. I had mine very fast. Thje first was too small; so they changed it without a problem.

DOG PAPERS

Those listed below are informative with all the up to date news in the dog world,. The first two as well as breed notes, and news stories relating to dogs, also report cases of dog abuse, or of dogs wrongly arrested under the Dangerous Dogs Act. There are articles on genetics and on breeding, veterinary articles, and some light hearted looks at dogdom.

Our Dogs.
Oxford Road Station Approach, Manchester. M60 lSX

Dog World.
9. Tufton Street, Ashford, Kent. TN23 lQN

Dog Training Weekly
4/5 Feidr Castell Business Park, Fishguard, Pembrokeshire, SA65 9BB
The last is a subscription magazine with the latest Obedience show reports, as well as reports on Working Trials and agility, together with articles on training.

The Kennel Club,
1-5 Clarges Street, Piccadilly, London WIY 8AB

National Dog Tattoo Register,
Trenarren, Mersea Rd, Langenhoe, Colchester C05 7LL

Association of Pet Dog Trainers,
Greengarth, Maddox Lane, Bookham, Surrey, KT23 3HT
This is an association which has a code of conduct for trainers. There is a useful directory of instructors who are affiliated, with their addresses and the areas where they teach.

It applies to individuals, not to clubs.

Among its rules is one that states that the welfare of clients and their dogs shall be paramount and shall not be made subordinate to any commercial consideration. Another, that the use of force or of punitive techniques has to be avoided. Also instructors may not use check chains or electric collars or any other suspect training aid. They are assessed before becoming members.